Five Evangelical Leaders

Five Evangelical Leaders

Christopher Catherwood

HODDER AND STOUGHTON
LONDON   SYDNEY   AUCKLAND   TORONTO

British Library Cataloguing in Publication Data

Catherwood, Christopher
    Five Evangelical leaders. – (Hodder
    Christian paperbacks)
    1. Evangelicalism – History – 20th century
    I. Title
    270′.8′2   BR1640

    ISBN 0 340 36142 5

Contents

Acknowledgements

I should first of all like to give my very warmest thanks and encouragement to my parents and to my agent, Edward England. Without the support, warmth, help and encouragement of these three people, the book would never have been possible. They can take credit for the strong points, but any faults are mine. I should add that the views in the book are my own. I also wish warmly to thank my two successive editors at Hodder and Stoughton, Rob Warner and David Wavre, for all their advice, patience and encouragement.

Many people spoke to me and helped during the course of my research. Several of them wish to remain anonymous; some of those who spoke to me on record deserve special mention. I was greatly assisted in the Schaeffer chapter by Ranald and Susan Schaeffer Macaulay – staying with them was one of the most enjoyable experiences of the year I spent researching this book. I should also like to thank the staff of L'Abri in Switzerland, and of Greatham in Hampshire. Deidre Ducker, Os Guinness, Joe Martin, Steve Turner, the Diamonds and several others all gave me their precious time. In the Graham chapter Russ Busby and Roger Palms both helped me well beyond the call of duty – my debt to them is immense. Maurice Rowlandson, Cliff Barrows, Stirling Huston, Lewis Drummond, the Wilson brothers, Howard Jones, Stanislav Svek and Don Bailey all gave me cheerful assistance in the USA, as did the staff of Mission England in the UK. (I must also thank Chris and Sue Berkeley and Nick Perham.) Chua Wee-hian of IFES and Dr Oliver Barclay helped with several of the chapters. Lastly, the four subjects of the book still alive during my research all proved willing to co-operate and my gratitude to Jim Packer, John Stott, Billy Graham and the late Francis

Schaeffer is enormous. To spend time with such men was a privilege, and I only hope that the sense of God alive and at work through the five men in my book comes over as vividly to the reader as it did to me.

Introduction

Evangelicalism in Britain and North America has come alive in a new power since the Second World War – Evangelicals have come out of the ghetto in which they had incarcerated themselves since the turn of the nineteenth century. The growth of Biblical, Evangelical Christianity has been a work of God, as is always the case. But, as we know from Scripture, and from Christian biography, God often chooses to bring his purposes about by raising up faithful, God-honouring men and women to do His will on earth. The Pauline picture of the Christian life is that of a battle. In an army, each type of soldier has a different and very vital task to perform – some are infantrymen, some the heavy artillery, others the cavalry. Each division fights a different part of the battle, but all share a common purpose, a common motive and, above all, each soldier has been enlisted through the same Captain, Christ Himself. This book aims to look at five of the men whom God has raised up in this century to be His lieutenants in the battle.

Each man is different in many ways from the others, yet all five have preached the same Gospel, and served the same living Saviour.

To Martyn Lloyd-Jones, preaching was logic on fire, eloquent reason, theology coming through a man who is on fire. He revolutionised the place of preaching in Evangelicalism, restoring its power and relevance to the ordinary Christian. He resurrected much solid, Biblically based theology, but also gave the thoughts of an earlier generation a new life and vigour. In helping to establish the International Fellowship of Evangelical Students, he founded a Christian movement of international zeal and vision perhaps unique in the world.

Billy Graham has transformed the face of evangelism, and

shown that the Gospel is both alive and relevant in every country on earth. His stand on the truth of Jesus Christ has been a witness from the cities of America to the jungles of Asia, and the way in which he has cleaned up evangelism and used it as a means of racial reconciliation has been a potent factor in the spread of the Gospel.

Francis Schaeffer has demonstrated that in an age of scepticism and doubt, the message of Jesus Christ is still absolutely true. He has translated the eternal Gospel into a language that can be understood by those whose minds have been twisted by humanistic, relativistic thinking. He showed at L'Abri that Christians have nothing to fear from the twentieth century, and that it is they alone who, in Christ, have the answers to today's questions. Jim Packer has done much the same in theology – he has demonstrated the bankruptcy of liberal thinking, and shown that theology is not only a live subject but also a vitally important one for Christians of all abilities.

Last, John Stott has not just made clear the importance of Biblical, expository preaching, but also illustrated that it is possible for Christians to be conservative in their theology – guardians of the Gospel – and radical in their application, people who care about the world in which God put them and creators of His new society.

Why these five? Each one has influenced me in many ways. Martyn Lloyd-Jones was my maternal grandfather, someone with whom I enjoyed the warmest and most formative of relationships all my conscious life. Francis Schaeffer, too, has greatly helped the way in which I think and view the world – both Schaeffer and my grandfather moulded me in many ways. My student career was enhanced by hearing Stott and Packer speak on many occasions, and their books provided discussion till the early hours of many mornings. In 1979 I was part of the Overseas Student Outreach Team at Cambridge, and took many students from all over the world to hear Billy Graham's sermons in the CICCU Mission. So each of these men fascinated me before I came to write their stories.

But it can also be said that the growth of Evangelical

Christianity in Britain and North America cannot in human terms be understood without these five men. They have, in their very different ways, been at the heart of the movement, and have profoundly influenced its direction. Their zeal for the Gospel, their resolute reliance on Scripture as God's true and living Word has set the course. In an age in which men and women have ceased to have hope, they have demonstrated without apology the certainty and hope that is only to be found in Jesus Christ the Risen Saviour. Scientific and materialistic humanism has failed, and each of these five has been able to preach the Good News with a renewed power and confidence. Each has done so in a very different way, and often to a totally dissimilar audience, but the basic message has been consistently the same.

The five have not always agreed with each other on methods, or particular emphases, however, and it would have been impossible to write this book in a way which suggested that all of them were right in every detail. I have given my own interpretation of their respective roles and impact, and of their contributions to the battle. For example, four are Calvinists in theory and practice, one in theory only. Two are Anglicans, two separated Free Churchmen, and one indifferent to such labels. Three have been active with Third World Christians, two less so. Inevitably, great men attract disciples, who often argue their master's case more vigorously than the master himself. Not everyone reading this book will therefore agree with everything expressed in it.

But all five have been unashamedly Evangelical, and proof of the power of God at work today. My grandfather Lloyd-Jones always used to say that he could forgive a preacher almost anything if he gave him a sense of the presence of God. It is my hope with this book that it will convey just such a sense, one of the acts of almighty God, through the lives of these His five children.

Balsham,
Cambridgeshire,
June 1984.

JOHN STOTT

John Stott was born on April 27th, 1921, the only son of a leading Harley Street physician, Sir Arnold Stott, and his wife Emily. His father, like Martyn Lloyd-Jones who knew him, trained at Bart's and went on to become a consultant at the Westminster Hospital and then into the Army. He was not, a childhood friend of John Stott's recalls, always a very sympathetic man, but the warmth and kindness of his wife, who had German blood, made up for this. They were, nevertheless, a very united family. Sir Arnold was an agnostic and very much part of the secularist, scientific world, while Lady Stott was a Lutheran. Young John's first words, he once joked to his Californian study assistant Mark Labberton, were 'coronary thrombosis', and this was indicative of the kind of atmosphere in which he was raised.

He was, however, brought up in the parish of All Souls, Langham Place, which was strategically placed near Harley Street, the BBC headquarters and all the major department stores of Oxford Street and Regent Street. Little John would sometimes sit up in the gallery and, as he told me with a mischievous twinkle in his eye, would occasionally throw paper pellets on to the congregation below (contrary to popular rumour, they were not ink-tipped).

Even as a small boy he developed a deeply-felt awareness of the underprivileged and of social justice that has been one of his main characteristics. One year he spent his summer holidays near Tenby in South Wales, the same region where he now has his country cottage. On near-by Caldy Island was a monastery, whose monks had their mail delivered by local fishermen. Little John saw one of the boatmen open and read a monk's letter. This outraged him, he recalls, and made him upset for two to three days afterwards.

He felt he had, even then, a 'God-given sense of fair play'.

At 13 he went to his father's old school, Rugby, made famous by its portrayal in the novel *Tom Brown's Schooldays*. Under its distinguished headmaster, Dr Arnold, it became known for founding not only the sport named after it, but also the public school tradition of the 'stiff upper lip', with the scorning of emotion, and the cultivation of the gentlemanly image that so long marked the English middle and upper classes. Needless to say, as one old boy has recalled, such a school was not at all sympathetic to Evangelical Christianity.

Stott, despite having a 'scientific secularist' for a father, had been taught the Christian faith by his mother. He and his sisters had gone to church, read their Bibles and said their prayers. But, he has written, he did this 'more out of affectionate loyalty to her and out of routine, than as a personally meaningful discipline'.

He was, however, as he remembered many years later, 'high-idealed as an adolescent'. At the age of 15 he founded the ABC Society – to give tramps a good bath. (Whether ABC stood for 'Always be a Christian' or 'Association for the Benefit of the Community' he cannot now remember.) He was, however, 'high-idealed but weak-willed'. It was then that he realised his own alienation and defeat.

He became convinced, he has since written, 'that there was more to religion than I had so far discovered. I used on half holiday afternoons to creep into the Memorial Chapel by myself, in order to read religious books, absorb the atmosphere of mystery, and seek for God. But He continued to elude me.' He went to the Christian Union which, a contemporary told me, was a rather secretive affair because of the disapproving attitude that the school authorities had towards it. (Needless to say, this added to its appeal for quite a few boys, including Stott himself.)

Then, after he had been attending for several months, it was visited by the Revd Eric Nash, commonly known to generations of schoolboys as 'Bash'. Nash had founded a camp at Iwerene called Varsity and Public Schools (or 'Bash Camp'), geared exclusively for the evangelism of public schoolboys which, in effect, meant for the sons of the social elite. Many outsiders, especially in the Free Churches, disliked the emphasis on sport and distrust of the intellect, and the fact that they were socially so narrow. But scores of boys had been converted through them over the years (and are still today). For all his faults, Nash was an effective evangelist, and one with great spiritual concern for the lost.

At a meeting organised in February 1938 by the CU leader, John Bridger, he spoke on the subject of Pilate's question: 'What then shall I do with Jesus, who is called the Christ?' Rugby was the school at which 'muscular Christianity' had begun – an unthinking, nominal and very English kind of belief more to do with 'being a good chap' than having a personal relationship with Jesus Christ as Saviour. When young Stott saw Nash, he recalled, 'He was nothing much to look at, and certainly no ambassador for muscular Christianity. Yet as he spoke I was riveted.

'That I needed to *do* anything with Jesus,' Stott has recorded of the meeting, 'was an entirely novel idea to me, for I had imagined that somehow he had done whatever needed to be done, and that my part was only to acquiesce.' Nash, however, made clear to them that neutrality was impossible – either they must copy Pilate, and weakly reject Him, or 'accept Him personally and follow Him'.

As Stott later told me, Nash wisely did not press for decisions there and then – there was no altar call. But he saw that the young 17-year-old was a 'seeking soul', and clearly one who had never had such a personal challenge before. So he took him for a drive in his car and, in response to John Stott's questions, explained to him the Way of salvation. 'To my astonishment,' Stott has written, 'his presentation of Christ crucified and risen exactly corresponded with the needs of which I was aware.'

Significantly, however, Nash did not even now press for a decision. 'He had the sensitivity and wisdom,' Stott remembers, 'to let me go, so that I could "open the door" to Christ by myself, which I did that very night by my bedside in the dormitory, while the other boys were in bed and asleep.'

John Stott thereupon became very active in evangelism – a 'mirror image of Bash', a contemporary has told me, carefully leading several of his fellow pupils to faith in Christ. When Bridger left for Cambridge, he took over the leadership of the CU. He was also, coincidentally, made head boy of the school. This was despite his Christian activities and – this was 1939 – despite the fact that he had become a pacifist.

When war broke out in September 1939, those pacifists wishing to register as conscientious objectors had to register before a tribunal, to decide whether their pacifism was genuine or not. Clergy were exempt from military service, and those conscientious objectors who could prove that their wish to be ordained predated the outbreak of war were excused appearance before the tribunal. Fortunately for Stott, he had told his headmaster as early as 1938 of his pacifist convictions and of his wish to enter the ministry. He felt at the time that to take part in war was against the teaching of the Sermon on the Mount. (He told me, years later in his study in London, that he had not thought out his position as thoroughly then as he has now. While, as will be seen, he would call himself a 'nuclear pacifist', he no longer holds the total pacifist position.)

He went up to Trinity College, Cambridge, in 1939 and initially studied modern languages. This subject required considerable self-discipline and rigorous logic, two characteristics that many people feel have been hallmarks of his subsequent preaching style. As with medicine and Martyn Lloyd-Jones, his early secular studies were far from wasted. Translation involves close study of the text, and a former colleague recalls that the close attention Stott pays today to what the Biblical text actually says, and the effect this has had on his preaching, can be traced back to those days.

Although he was very active in evangelism among his fellow students, Stott was not officially active in the Cambridge Inter-Collegiate Christian Union. This was partly because, on top of his academic studies, he acted as Nash's camp secretary, helping to run the camps. Nash wrote to him once a week after his conversion, for over five years. Those letters were a mix of theology, in neat paragraphs and section headings, and pastoral advice – how to pray, read the Bible, and 'how to practise the presence of Christ each day' in the real world. Nash's expectations, Stott has written,

> for all those whom he led to Christ were extremely high. He could be easily disappointed. His letters to me often contained rebuke, for I was a wayward young Christian and needed to be disciplined. In fact, so frequent were his admonitions at one period that, whenever I saw his familiar writing on an envelope, I needed to pray and prepare myself for half an hour before I felt ready to open it.

For all Nash's single-mindedness and concern for the young Christian, he remained deeply suspicious of theology and of the intellect. Many of his old boys would enter the Anglican ministry. But, Nash's approach often meant that they were thus totally unable to cope with the liberal theology with which they were confronted. They would go to lectures, put their feet up, and read copies of *The Times*. Derek Kidner, now well known as a Bible commentator, helped change this at Cambridge. He became President of the CICCU – and also obtained a First Class degree. Another Cambridge student was the scientist Oliver Barclay, later to become General Secretary of the Inter Varsity Fellowship, and chairman of IFES. He was, during the war, the exact contemporary at Trinity of John Stott.

The two undergraduates, Stott recalls, were soon close friends, and would go for long walks discussing Christian matters. It was a significant friendship. For, if Stott was Nash's 'right-hand man', Barclay was that of Douglas Johnson, general secretary of IVF. As seen elsewhere Martyn Lloyd-Jones was in the process of turning the IVF into a much more vigorous organisation in which Christians would be unafraid to use their minds and show their emotions – the exact opposite in many ways of the very simple, stiff-upper-lip Christianity that Nash represented.

'God had given me,' Stott has said, 'an enquiring mind'.

This was shown in the First Class he obtained in the Language Tripos at Cambridge. He now transferred to reading theology and, as Oliver Barclay told me, decided to take it seriously. (Nash, apparently, never tried to stop him.) There was, he told me, 'practically no help' for Evangelical theology students at the time. He was, however, determined to bridge the gap between Evangelicals and the intellectual world, while at the same time retaining his Christian commitment and evangelistic zeal.

Ridley Hall, Cambridge, where he and the other ordinands studied, was, he pointed out in an interview, at its nadir. Stott's arrival, Oliver Barclay remembers, altered the situation. The principal was a liberal theologian of vague beliefs. Once, at a lecture, he told students that there was no evidence in the New Testament for a particular major doctrine. Stott therefore asked him to explain a set of verses that spelled the doctrine out very clearly. The principal replied, 'You probably know the New Testament better than I do.' Many of the Evangelical students at Ridley beavered quietly away with their work, never raising the issues, whereas others created mayhem. Stott mixed the two – by organising a quiet revolution. Others saw what could be done, and one of the effects this had was a substantial increase in the number of CICCU men who obtained Firsts.

'Bash,' John Stott once said, 'had given me a great love for the Bible,' but he had now gone a considerable way beyond the non-intellectual kind of Christianity represented by Nash (which, the more doctrinal Evangelicals felt, was rather too pietistic in approach and divorced from reality) while fully retaining his Evangelical faith. He was much more in the vigorous, thoughtful IVF mould which, under Martyn Lloyd-Jones's influence, enabled one to have one's intellectual integrity and be a fully committed Evangelical Christian at the same time.

But Nash had planted firm foundations, all of which were to stand Stott in good stead in later years. This has been well summarised by his American former study assistant, Mark Labberton. 'Single-minded commitment to Christ, passionate concern for sharing the Gospel, disciplined devo-

tion to the Word, simple and direct preaching were all,'
Labberton has written, 'hallmarks of Bash's influence on
Stott and on many other leading Evangelicals . . . in the
Church of England.'

Nash concentrated only on the few, those from privileged
backgrounds. But, as Stott has written, what 'motivated him
was not snobbery but strategy. He believed that God had
called him to work in these schools, and that the reason for
his Divine call was that the future leadership of Church and
state was to be found there.' This was certainly very true of
Stott's own generation. Many leading Anglicans, such as
Stott himself, Michael Green of Oxford, Mark Ruston of
Cambridge and Dick Lucas of London are former Bash
campers, as are several non-Anglican influential Christian
laymen, such as two successive chairmen of the IVF (now
UCCF): Fred Catherwood, the industrialist and politician,
and John Marsh, the surgeon, both of whom were also
Cambridge contemporaries of John Stott.

Several former Bash campers, like Nash himself, remained
bachelors. John Stott has never married, and many have
attributed this partly to the influence of Nash, whose ideal
of the celibate clergyman, giving his whole life to Christian
service without the distraction of family, caused several of
his followers deliberately to remain single. Needless to say,
many women deeply resented these eligible bachelors who
refused to become available, and at Oxford Martyn Lloyd-
Jones's daughter led the fight against the kind of influence
that Nash was felt to have at Cambridge. (By one of the
many ironies of life, she married one of the few Bash camp
leaders who decided neither to enter the Church of England
nor to stay single – Fred Catherwood. Had he, like others
of Stott's generation, followed Nash's advice, you would not
now be reading this book!)

Not everyone who remained unmarried for this reason
was able to cope. One clergyman eventually had to resign
his job, and subsequently became an artist, living in the
USA. Christ, in Matthew 19, refers to those who do not
marry for the Kingdom of Heaven's sake. But Stott himself,
as he once told Martyn Lloyd-Jones (who strongly favoured

marriage), felt that it was God who had called him to be single, and had given him a gift for it.

There is little doubt that he would not have been able to do many of the things that he has done had he been married, with a dependent wife and family. He has been able to devote himself in a special way to study and to pastoral ministry. In particular, he has been able to travel extensively, often to the Third World, without any of the usual problems of family separation suffered by married men. While some (mainly women) feel that he would have seen some issues either more clearly or sooner had he had a wife to advise him, his life has, in human terms, been strongly affected by his singleness.

Certainly, as Mark Labberton has written in a paper for Fuller Seminary in the USA, the 'pains of loneliness, the feelings of being in the battle alone, the emotional constrictions of a background that teaches one always to keep "a stiff upper lip" and the many other circumstances he has experienced have all had their impact' in helping Stott develop pastorally and as a preacher.

Sir Arnold Stott had always hoped that his son would join the Diplomatic Service, and there are many today who think that John Stott has played the role of diplomat in many Evangelical gatherings, such as the Lausanne Congress of 1974 (of which more later). But young Stott was ordained into the Church of England instead, to the parish of All Souls, Langham Place – where he has remained ever since. The rector at the time of his ordination, the Revd Harold Earnshaw-Smith, was a sick man, and his curate found himself with a considerable number of responsibilities straight away.

All Souls is very strategically placed. Many of the congregation are students and professional people – London University, some of the major hospitals, Harley Street and the BBC, are all a short walk away. Some have commented that All Souls has a rather rarefied, artificial atmosphere, which makes it a poor cross-section of society. But the same critics are usually the most enthusiastic supporters of the local church principle, and the main point about the students and professional people in the congregation of All Souls is that they were, and still are, very varied.

There were, however, in Stott's early days, some working-class areas (which still exist), whose inhabitants were reached through the All Souls school, and subsequent club house. Dick Lucas remembers how John Stott and several of the local children went charging off to Kent in the car for a picnic on several occasions. The other particular feature of the parish, one which still continues, is the presence of most of London's top department stores. At one period one of the curates was specially delegated to look after this vital area of witness.

Stott used many of the methods he had learned in Bash Camp and at Cambridge when he arrived at All Souls. As he reminded me in his book-lined study, he had been giving Bible readings from the age of 19, warmly encouraged by Nash. The love for the Bible that the camps had instilled in him naturally led him to give preaching the highest priority. As Oliver Barclay pointed out, it was the preaching ministry of All Souls that brought the church to people's attention. The Doctor, over at Westminster Chapel, was then at the height of his preaching powers, and the Chapel was to remain London's main preaching centre for some time to come. But in Anglican circles, such expository sermons as were being given at All Souls were a new phenomenon, because of the sad decline of preaching in the Church of England that had continued since the end of the nineteenth century.

Earnshaw-Smith had a major heart attack in 1946, six months after Stott's arrival, and a second not long after. As a result, his curate was, in Stott's own words to me, 'thrown in at the deep end'. Any thought of transferring to another parish, as was quite usual for a young curate after two or three years, was thus impossible. Stott was offered chaplaincies at Eton and, by contrast, at the Mayflower, the Christian family centre in the heart of London's East End. Earnshaw-Smith's frail health had led him to refuse both.

Had Stott accepted either of the above posts, he would not have been in place when Earnshaw-Smith suffered his final – and fatal – third coronary. The congregation took the unprecedented step of petitioning King George VI, who was technically responsible for the new appointment, for the curate to be given the post of rector.

The appeal succeeded, and John Stott became rector of All Souls (and also of the associated church of St Peter's, Vere Street), at the unusually early age of 29.

A new man meant new methods. As well as the concentration on regular, Biblically-based expository preaching (which will be examined in more detail later), he made some innovations. Evangelism, especially at the new monthly guest services, was increased, with a regular flow of conversions. (Stott gained the idea from the weekly evangelistic addresses run by CICCU in his Cambridge days.) Follow-up, by members of the laity, also became increasingly vital, especially after the lay Training School was set up in 1961. Above all, the church had confidence in God. 'Ultimately,' Stott wrote, 'evangelism is not a technique. It is the Lord of the Church who reserves to Himself His sovereign right to add to His Church. We need to humble ourselves before God and seek His face. Then, if we are expectant in faith He will add to His Church, not from mission to mission or even month to month but daily, such as are being saved.'

Stott did not limit himself to church activities, even in those early days. He was soon recruited as a missioner at the first post-war university missions, along with Martyn Lloyd-Jones. Between them they altered the nature of missions. Hitherto these had often been rather simplistic affairs, completely lacking in appeal for the more intellectual type of student. The new style was, however, according to Oliver Barclay, 'thoughtful, expository preaching', and to one university professor at Oxford, Stott was a 'new phenomenon' in Anglican Evangelicalism, bringing in a 'scholarly evangelism'.

This gave new heart to many in the University Christian Unions – they realised for the first time that a Christian did not have to be suspicious of the intellect to survive, as had often been the case hitherto. It meant that outsiders had to respect the Christian Gospel in a way that increased Christian morale and which helped their own evangelism. A student could be a committed Christian and an intellectual, someone who did not have to unscrew his or her head in order to prove a zeal for the Lord.

Many young men, especially new converts, were deeply influenced by hearing expository preaching – the careful working through the Biblical text that was the characteristic of both Stott and Lloyd-Jones. As a result, many of these men went into the ministry themselves, deliberately adopting the same style of doctrinal yet moving preaching through which they had become Christians, or had their Christian lives changed. An example of this is St Helen's, Bishopsgate, London, where, through the expository preaching ministry there of Dick Lucas, a formerly down-at-heel church now has over 1,200 at its Tuesday lunchtime evangelistic meetings, through which scores of people have been converted over the years.

Dick Lucas is one of the many who has been influenced by another group in which John Stott was active in the 1950s – the Eclectic Society. This was initiated by Stott with other members of staff at All Souls. It was a group, Stott recalls, based on common acceptance of Biblical authority – it was for conservative Evangelicals only – but one in which there was mutual acceptance and openness to radical applications of Biblical principles, as well as complete freedom of speech. Many of the members were curates (the age limit was 40) and some served under very liberal vicars who were either unsympathetic to, or even against, the Evangelical faith of their young assistants. This created numerous problems for the curates and questions of faith and intellect, and doubts as to whether a truly Evangelical Church was possible frequently confronted members of the Eclectic Society.

The existence of All Souls showed to many of these men what could be done, and how to do it. It showed that one could be an Evangelical, and have an 'outstanding mind', as Dick Lucas has put it. It was, another said, 'a very great thing when it started', an organisation whose meetings were a 'liberation' to its often hard-pressed members. The clergy at other churches also saw in All Souls a church that was both intellectual and evangelistic, Anglican and Evangelical, a place which adhered to the Prayer Book and was also thoroughly contemporary. At a time when liberals in the Church of England often gave the impression that to be Evangelical was to be a suspect Anglican, All Souls showed that to be an Evangelical was to be truly Anglican, loyal to the principles on which the Church of England was founded.

John Stott once told me that he was 'by temperament an activist', and the list of organisations in which he has been involved, or which he has established, is a very long one. (Often he sets the organisation up then, after a while, hands it over to others.) Some of these have been purely Anglican in scope – such as NEFAC, whose group member, the Church of England Evangelical Council, has been instrumental in helping the growing influence of Evangelicals within the Church of England in recent years; or the Evangelical Fellowship of the Anglican Communion bursary scheme, which has helped many Anglicans from the Third World to receive the kind of thorough Evangelical training in the West that would not otherwise have been possible.

Some specialist groups, which have not always been specifically Anglican, have also been brought together by John Stott. These have either been subject orientated – for Christian doctors or educationists, for example – or ad hoc gatherings of specialists in many fields to think through the issues in an interdisciplinary, but thoroughly Biblical, way. Such groups have often given John Stott valuable advice, enabled him to see all sides to an argument and to be accurate when speaking on that particular topic in a sermon or public debate. These specialists have included people from Stott's Cambridge days, such as Fred Catherwood, or younger men, such as the writer Os Guinness.

But two of his involvements are worth mentioning in more detail – the first because it is part of his life on a wider front, the second because it is his current main activity. These are the international work at All Souls, and his directorship of the London Institute for Contemporary Christianity, which meets in St Peter's, Vere Street.

The idea for the All Souls International Fellowship (ASIF) began in 1961. Like Nash, Stott was able to spot areas from which future national leaders would come – and in the case of the Third World, this was often from the ranks of those who had been educated in the West. By the early sixties, there were nearly 50,000 overseas students in Britain, about 35,000 in London (constituting a quarter of the entire London student population), of whom 5,000 were attached to the British Council Overseas Student Centre in Portland Place, next to All Souls itself. But, as John Stott wrote to Lorne Sanny, the director of the Navigators in the USA, 'There is still no one working full-time in this field so far as I know.'

In 1963 Stott went on a mission to Royal College, Nairobi (now Nairobi University). Ever since Cambridge days his main hobby has been ornithology and, on a bird-watching safari in Kenya, he asked an ex-All Souls student, Robert Howarth, now working in Africa for the Navigators, to establish an overseas student organisation. Howarth and his wife began work in London with ASIF in August 1963.

As Stott wrote at the time, students from other countries should be the concern of local Christians for two main reasons. First, they were strangers in a strange land – Christians should be people 'given to hospitality'. Second, it was an opportunity to reach out with the Gospel. Some students, already Christians, were under the illusion that Britain was a Christian country, and it was important to nurture them in the faith so that, instead of becoming despondent, they returned to their home countries stronger in their faith. Others were from lands where Christianity was difficult to preach, and many would naturally become interested in the Gospel while in Britain.

'Here,' Stott wrote, 'is a mission field on our doorstep, with potential leaders of the future brought to our shores without our needing to cross the seas to find them.' He was emphatic that it was an international not an overseas fellowship. It was not to be 'English Christians entertaining overseas visitors. It is a fellowship of all nations, with several nationalities represented on the committee.' During his first ten years as rector, the number of overseas visitors had been steadily increasing. He wrote,

Come to All Souls on any Sunday and you will see, in nave, side aisles and galleries, men and women of every race and colour. It is to us a joy and privilege to welcome them. After the service, on the portico steps, members of many nations linger to greet one another, and join in animated and happy conversation. There can be no racial barriers in Christian fellowship.

By the end of the first year, Howarth has remembered, there were four hundred on the register, representing fifty countries. Thirty-seven professed faith in the first ten months. Stott himself was very active, always attending the monthly Visitors Buffet Lunch, the International Carol Service and the ASIF Christmas Party. He would preach so that those with limited English could understand and, indeed, was so involved that one British former member of staff remembers English people in the congregation muttering that the rector 'concentrated too much on overseas members!' However, many British and American students in London were deeply challenged by meeting fellow students from the Third World on equal terms.

Several international students lived in the rectory in Weymouth Street. (It was known by the irreverent as 'The Wreckage' or 'The Monastery' because of its bachelor inhabitants. The current rector of All Souls is married and now, to get to John Stott's 'pad', one has to risk bumping into bicycles in the hall.) One of the former residents is Professor George Kinoti, now chairman of the Department of Zoology at Nairobi University in Kenya, who shared some of his memories with me. He had known Stott since 1959, when he showed Stott around Makerere University during one of his early visits to Africa. Several future prominent African Christian leaders were befriended by Stott, including Bishop Gitari of Kenya, Bishop Misaeri Kauma of Uganda, and he also knew the late, martyred, Archbishop of Uganda, Janani Luwum, who was brutally put to death under Idi Amin.

Stott often visited Africa and, as Professor Kinoti recalls, took part in several University missions there. East Africa has seen considerable revival over the years. Recently some of this has been connected with the charismatic movement, and John Stott's emphasis on the 'vital importance of a balanced, Biblical Christianity' has influenced ministers there in keeping away from the excesses that misguided zeal in revival can sadly often bring, especially in areas where knowledge, particularly of Scripture, is weak and in need of strengthening.

John Stott's missionary addresses, in Britain and abroad, are now to be found in large measure in his book *Basic Christianity*, his best-known work. It is perhaps through his writing that he is familiar to most people. He has always been a very private individual, perhaps all the more so because he has never married. His friendships extend far and wide and he is a keen correspondent. Bishop Gitari of Mount Kenya East wrote to me that his 'frequent letters . . . remain a great encouragement'. In many Third World countries, the fact that he is uncompromisingly Evangelical and also deeply concerned over social issues is, in Bishop Gitari's view, one of the reasons why he has been accepted as a teacher in so many different countries. In America, John Alexander of Inter Varsity Christian Fellowship has recalled that his expository ministry has influenced many young US and Canadian students, especially through his frequent appearances at the great triennial missionary conferences at Urbana, Illinois, often before 17,000 students or more.

Yet the first to disclaim any special merit for himself would be John Stott himself. Apart from his innate desire for privacy, he has felt that it should be God who ought to be the focus, and not human individuals. Like Martyn Lloyd-Jones he has not wanted any biography written in his own lifetime. He therefore agreed to co-operate with this chapter on the basis that it would contain only the biographical information necessary for an understanding of his thought.

The germ of the London Institute for Contemporary Christianity began ten years ago when he was asked by his friend Jim Houston to preach at Regent College, in Vancouver, Canada, on contemporary issues and the Christian response. Stott became a frequent visitor, and became enthused with what Regent was trying to do in formulating a Christian point of view on secular issues. He then read Blamires's famous book, *The Christian Mind*, which, as he pointed out to me, proved a 'seminal book for a lot of Evangelicals'.

He began in 1974 a series of annual lectures by Christian specialists on selected topics, which have over the years covered a wide range of subjects. From this arose a more permanent structure – the London Institute for Contemporary Christianity, which began in 1982/3, with John Stott himself as the director. Lectures are given to stimulate the students to think Biblically about the World in which they live, to challenge their preconceptions, and to help them better to fulfil their Scriptural role as salt of the earth and light of the World in the societies in which they find themselves. Lecturers are from a wide variety of background and opinion, but are all Biblically-based Evangelicals.

There have been two characteristics of John Stott's career, and thus of his thought. The first – the high place he has given to sound, doctrinal, expository preaching – has been with him since the beginning, and the love of Scripture instilled in him from early on. The second – the demonstration of the fact that one can be both conservative Biblically and actively involved in social issues – is one that has come more recently and has caused controversy in some Evangelical circles.

As a leading, and internationally well-known, African Christian told me, these two strands of Stott's life are interwoven, with preaching (and his high view of Scripture) coming first. It is because he is known to be theologically conservative that his sometimes radical social views command attention. By showing that it is possible to hold two such sets of views in tandem, and without compromise to either, he has stirred many Christians to think through their own position – and always on a Biblical basis.

John Stott is above all a preacher – it is impossible to understand the man, and the impact under God that he has had, without grasping this. Fortunately he has written on the subject, in *I Believe in Preaching*. Significantly, it is also the nearest to an autobiography that he has put in print. It is his high view of preaching that has led him, in the eyes of many, to become the leader that he is today.

'Preaching,' he states, 'is indispensable to Christianity. Without preaching, a necessary part of its authenticity has been lost. For Christianity is, in its very essence, a religion of the Word of God.' Jesus Christ himself was the 'Word . . . made flesh', and his disciples continued to preach. When the Reformation came, it 'gave centrality to the Sermon', and great Christian leaders have continued to preach ever since. 'God himself,' Stott writes, 'speaks to us by the preacher'. Tragically, in the twentieth century, preaching has reached a low ebb. 'In the Western world, the decline of preaching is a symptom of the decline of the Church.' Christ made preaching so important, so why has it now declined?

Stott has outlined some causes. There is an 'anti-authority mood', a sense of relativism in a revolutionary age. So he feels that Christians should, while recognising the modern trend, stick by the historic truth. Christianity is a revealed faith, preachers are the 'stewards of the mystery of God', whose authority is God Himself. It is supremely His Word that the preacher expounds, not views of his own. The Gospel is relevant, relating as it does to the World as it really is. Then there is the technological revolution – the TV age, which has lowered people's ability to absorb and concentrate. The preacher should, Stott thinks, 'fight for people's attention'. His consistency of life and practice should assist in holding it. But preaching is still 'unique and irreplaceable', God 'speaking through His Minister to His people' in the power of the Holy Spirit, feeding the flock. 'Nothing,' he writes, 'could ever replace this'.

Indeed, in an age in which the joy of worship has been rediscovered by many Christians, Stott reminds us that 'acceptable worship is impossible without preaching'. Knowledge following exposition brings forth true worship. The basis of the Gospel has been forgotten, basic truths denied, and there is 'dialogue rather than proclamation'. There needs to be a recovery of Christian morale, a 'certainty and full assurance', both in prayer and in preaching the

Good News of Jesus Christ. Doubt is a symptom of 'spiritual sickness in our spiritually sick age'. There should be persistent and expectant prayer 'for grace from the Holy Spirit of truth'. Stott believes that this is God's time 'to push back the forces of unbelief and to set the pendulum swinging in the direction of faith again', and that the Church should therefore 'resume the bold proclamation of her unchanging message'. In such a time, it is vital to assert the 'indispensable and paramount place of preaching in the purpose of God for His Church'. As Stott says, it is 'a stirring summons'.

What is preaching – and how can it be made truly effective? Stott points out that it is a not a matter of 'mastering certain techniques but being mastered by certain convictions'. The first of these is about God Himself, that He is Light, that he has acted and revealed Himself, above all in Jesus Christ, and that He has spoken. This is the preacher's authority, and leads on to the next conviction – about Scripture, 'God's Word written'. The responsibility of the preacher is not to give a twentieth-century testimony to Christ, but to relay to the twentieth century 'the only authoritative witness there is', the Word of God.

To Stott, it is shameful that Evangelicals are often not the preachers that they ought to be. The preacher should be the fervent herald of God's message, 'a living word to a living people from the Living God'. God's Word, in the power of the Holy Spirit, speaks to every generation and changes their lives.

The third conviction is that the 'Church is the creation of God by His Word', His sceptre to rule the Church and His food to nourish it. 'For whenever the Bible is truly and systematically expounded, God uses it to give His people the vision without which they perish.' Fourth, the Minister is not a priest but a pastor, administering the Word to the flock – he is 'essentially the teacher'.

Therefore, fifth, 'all true Christian preaching is expository', a conviction that firmly echoes the views of Martyn Lloyd-Jones. The Bible should not be a peg for the preacher, but his master. Exposition establishes the limits, and also demands integrity – the clear, evident and original meaning, without manipulation. It is surely no coincidence that Stott and the Doctor, two of the most effective preachers this century, have been expositors. It is, of course, the sovereign power of God that has made them what they are. But it is arguably their certain belief in the primacy not just of preaching, but also in unfolding faithfully the Scriptures as the best means of accomplishing the task that has, in human terms, given their proclamation its power.

The preacher, as seen already, is many things – herald, steward and ambassador. But he is also, Stott feels, a bridge-builder. This conviction came later in his career through the influence of a young New Zealand curate at All Souls named Ted Schroder. He was a 'brash colonial who was quite willing to speak his mind'. (The English curates, it seems, tended to be more reserved, and in awe of their rector.) Some felt that Stott's preaching, as he himself has put it, was 'Biblical but not contemporary', whereas Schroder was often 'contemporary but not Biblical' enough. What was needed was to be both Biblical and contemporary, at the same time. Christ becoming Man showed that He identified with the human race, without ever losing His Divine nature. Similarly, Christian preaching should be something to which the World could relate, without losing its clear Christian identity.

The tragedy of much preaching today, Stott feels, is that Evangelicals are often conservative and Biblical, but not contemporary, whereas liberals are radical and modern but not Biblical. The real aim should be to 'relate God's unchanging Word to our ever changing world', since the 'earthing of the Word in the World is not something optional'. A sermon must be understandable – Stott agrees with Martyn Lloyd-Jones in saying, 'the business of preaching is to relate the teaching of the Scriptures to what is happening in our own day'.

'Above all else,' Stott has written, 'we must preach Christ . . . and not Christ in a vacuum . . . but rather a contemporary Christ who once lived and died, and now lives to meet human need in all its variety'.

This means that the Bible has profound relevance to the

society in which God has placed us. It lays down His principles for justice, human dignity, and other ethics. While the Kingdom of God is not a political unit, but is comprised of His people on earth, it is, Stott points out, 'really absurd to say that social amelioration by Christian influence is impossible'. John Stott has himself been actively involved with those who seek both to defend the Gospel and to proclaim the need for Christians to play their part as salt and light in God's world. But he has shown that for Christians to relate the preaching of ethics to personal ethics only would be wrong. The preacher should not play politics from the pulpit, but he should enunciate those clear Biblical principles upon which Christians in secular life should base their actions.

The preacher has a duty, he feels, to help 'Christians develop a Christian mind'. The 'systematic exposition of the Bible over the years' should give Christians a 'framework of truth' – the 'whole counsel of God'. The preacher should not be partisan, but expound Biblical principles, look at the conclusions that other Biblical Christians have made, state his own position, and then allow the congregation to make up its own mind.

Some have questioned whether a minister should preach sermons on unemployment, or on nuclear weapons, as John Stott has done in All Souls and elsewhere. They feel that a minister should stick to preaching the great truths and provide a doctrinal framework within which lay Christians can work out the details. It was asserted that Stott used to preach within these constraints until Ted Schroder challenged him. They worry that he has now become controversial for the wrong reasons. They feel that for a minister to be controversial because he unashamedly proclaims the Gospel is one thing, and quite acceptable; but for him to arouse ire because he espouses a particular secular cause, such as full employment or the halting of the nuclear arms race, is quite another.

To Stott, a minister who deliberately avoids controversial topics is 'irresponsible'. The 'absurd polarisations' between conservative and radical Evangelicals, he told me, were quite wrong. He now feels that his earlier sermons lacked relevance, as he used to omit the application, since he thought that the Holy Spirit would somehow do it for him. He would divide principles from politics. In the nuclear warfare debate, for example, it seems clear to him that weapons that cause the indiscriminate mass annihilation of innocent non-combatants are immoral and incompatible with Biblical principles. He has therefore become a 'nuclear pacifist'. But he would not call himself a unilateralist. To him the mechanism of disarmament is a specialist topic beyond the competence of the Church. It is a consequential policy to be worked out in detail by those Christians and others able to judge the best technical and political means. The principle is clear, the policy is to be left open to debate.

Furthermore, as all systematic preachers have discovered, if one goes through a book of the Bible in an expository way, there are certain verses that cannot be avoided. It is sometimes impossible to escape a subject if it appears in the text, as John Stott found on several occasions. It would be wrong to omit a topic simply because it was one on which Christians disagreed.

This is surely right. Christians cannot live in a cocooned world, and pretend that the society in which they have been placed does not exist. Christians may not be of this world, but they are to be the salt and light within it with all the responsibilities that confers upon them. The Bible does indeed lay down principles, which cover everything that God created – there is nothing to which God's Word, the Bible, is irrelevant, even if Christians differ as to exactly how various verses apply to specific situations.

The question still exists, though, as to whether a minister of the Gospel is the best person to become enmeshed in such debate. All Christians agree that Jesus Christ is the Way, the truth and the life, and that it is only through His death that we are saved. This is indisputable, and any non-Christian hearing this message and rejecting it would be wrong. The problem arises when contentious issues of a lesser order are proclaimed from the same pulpit, with the confusion that is thereby created. It probably does not worry a non-Christian unduly that a minister believes in inerrancy or has particular views on baptism or the gift of tongues. But suppose a Christian, in All Souls, has a friend for whom he is burdened spiritually and wishes to bring him to an evangelistic service at the church. The friend is a US Air Force colonel at the American nuclear missile base at Greenham Common. Now it may be that the use of such weapons is unbiblical, but the prime need of the colonel is to be converted to faith in Christ. All he knows about the preacher is that he is a 'nuclear pacifist', whereas he himself is not. Would it not be better, some say, if such a man had no idea of the views of the preacher before entering the church? Not all Christians agree with the nuclear pacifist position – some are total pacifists (which Stott is not) and others, such as Francis Schaeffer, feel that the use of nuclear weapons in certain circumstances is entirely compatible with Biblical principle.

The result is that a non-Christian is put off hearing the Gospel for a reason quite extraneous to the Gospel itself, and on which Biblical Christians disagree. This is surely not right either. It is not quite so simple though. Suppose a slave plantation owner had been taken to Wilberforce's church – that of the man who gave his whole life to freeing the slaves. Slavery was an issue which divided Christians, since the great nineteenth-century Bible commentator, Dabney, defended the institution in the Southern States of America. No one today would agree that slavery was right and many would hold that nuclear weapons are just as wrong.

The answer was surely given by the Apostle Paul, especially in Philemon. Paul never explicitly denounced slavery, and the Gospel, when he preached it, could be listened to by owner and slave alike, without any previous prejudices on other grounds. Yet the logic of Paul's ethical teaching is abundantly clear, and although it was only implicit on the question of slavery it created such a climate that Christians soon saw that the ownership of one human being by another was incompatible with Christian principles. As Paul was, so can Christian ministers of the Gospel be in our own day.

The lesson could be drawn that Christian lay people should

be far more active than they are at present – then there would be no need for clergy to become embroiled in secular controversy. Furthermore, what are many ministers who claim only to preach the 'simple Gospel' doing to see that their congregations are fulfilling their God-appointed role as salt and light in the World which God has created? While Stott's own involvement in the debate between evangelism and social action will be considered farther on, there is no doubt that the division between these two parts of Christian responsibility has been unbiblical, and that while it may not be right for ministers of the Gospel to pronounce directly on nuclear weapons or unemployment, lay Christians have a very clear Biblical command to act responsibly on God's earth. Only those who do so have any right to criticise.

The essence of preaching

The best teachers, Stott has written, are 'those who remain students all their lives'. The study of Scripture is thus a foremost responsibility for the preacher. A minister's study of the Bible should always be comprehensive – Stott reads the whole of the Bible every year, following the Murray McCheyne calendar recommended to him by Martyn Lloyd-Jones. Study should be open-minded – one's own prejudices should be dropped before what the Bible is really saying. It should also be expectant – the Bible can freshen the reader and get rid of spiritual staleness.

A preacher should also be well-earthed in the real world – as Stott has said, the best preachers are always diligent pastors. (Some feel that he made a mistake when he left the full-time pastorate of All Souls in 1970.) They should listen to their congregations and ensure that they keep up a good amount of contemporary secular reading, to see what people around are thinking without in any way compromising themselves with the spirit of the age.

To help him along these lines, John Stott set up in 1974 a reading and study group to examine important current topics. He often consults with specialists before preaching on major contemporary issues to ensure that his facts are correct and he is aware of the different sides in the debate. He has a filing system that is legendary in its thoroughness and which can be seen by those who visit his study.

He sets aside special time for study (while recognising that this might not always be so possible for hard-pressed ministers with no pastoral assistance). At All Souls he saw to it that the talents of all his congregation were used to free him from administrative chores that distracted from his more important duties. Thirty years ago he bought a cottage in Wales where he goes to read and write, as well as to relax with his favourite hobbies of ornithology and photography.

To Stott, in Spurgeon's words, 'to be unprepared is unpardonable presumption'. In *I Believe in Preaching* Stott gives details of how a good preacher should prepare himself for the sermon. Personal preparation is essential – he has, he writes, 'always found it helpful to do as much of my sermon preparation as possible on my knees, with the Bible open before me, in prayerful study'. Then the preacher must meditate on what the text meant then and how it applies today. What is the passage's 'dominant thought'? A sermon, as opposed to a lecture, 'aims to convey only one major message'. Structure is also essential, so long as it arises from the text; as are words that are 'simple and clear as possible'.

Above all, 'he who preaches Christ must know Christ'. What a man does is as important as what he says – 'the practice of preaching cannot be divorced from the person of the preacher', and consistent Christian living, loyal to Christ, is the preacher's 'prior responsibility'. Sincerity is important and Stott, especially in his early days, had lay friends in the congregation whom he urged to be as honest as possible with him as to how his preaching was progressing.

Christians should, he believes, 'feel what we say'. Preaching should be both mind and heart, and Stott agrees with Martyn Lloyd-Jones that it should be 'logic on fire'. True 'preaching is never a superficial activity, it wells up out of the depths'. It should, in Newton's words, 'break a hard heart and . . . heal a broken heart'. The preacher is a humble man, dependent on the 'power of the Holy Spirit . . . Only Jesus Christ by His Holy Spirit can open blind eyes . . . give life to the dead and rescue slaves from Satanic bondage.' Stott himself discovered this 'power through weakness' to be very true when in Sydney, Australia, in 1958. He himself was ill, and felt that he had not been up to par. But he found out later that many had been converted despite his lacklustre delivery.

'Nothing,' he concludes, 'is better calculated to restore health and vitality to the Church or to lead its members into maturity in Christ than a recovery of true, Biblical, contemporary preaching.' He is surely right. The goal of the preacher should be to convey a sense of the glory of God, and Stott has described his own feelings when such an event occurs.

> The most privileged and moving experience a preacher can have is when, in the middle of a sermon, a strange hush descends upon the congregation. The sleepers have woken up, the coughers have stopped coughing and the fidgeters are sitting still. No eyes or minds are wandering. Everybody is attending, though not to the preacher. For the preacher is forgotten and the people are face to face with the Living God, listening to His still, small voice.

Christ was a preacher, the Apostles were preachers, as were the Reformers, and whenever revival has come the place of preaching has been at its very centre. Yet today it is a sadly neglected art, especially by those who claim to enjoy the fullness of the Holy Spirit's presence among them. The preaching ministry of John Stott and the case from Scripture that he makes out for the need for Biblical, Christ-centred preaching surely show that they are as much needed in our own day as they have been throughout the history of the Christian Church.

As Stott has written, the 'Christian preacher is to be neither a speculator who invents new doctrines which please him, nor an editor who excises old doctrines which displease him, but a steward, God's steward, dispensing faithfully to God's household the truths committed to him in the Scriptures, nothing more, nothing less and nothing else'.

What could be more urgent today than the faithful, expository preaching of the Word of God in Scripture to a Church that has lost its sense of direction, and to a world that cries out for a Saviour?

Evangelism and social concern

One of the most significant developments of recent years has been the fact that it is again possible to show social concern for the poor and underprivileged and still be a fully committed Evangelical Christian. The evil days when compassion for the needy was left to liberals while Evangelicals lived in a pietistic ghetto are now past. Faith and action are no longer seen as contradictory.

The reasons for the change have been twofold. First, Christians in the West rediscovered the Biblical teaching on the subject, and their own heritage of Scripturally-based social concern. Second, Evangelicals in the Third World started to play their full and equal role in God's family, a growth that became apparent in the Congress held at Lausanne in 1974. (The details of how this gathering came to be are given in detail in the chapter on Billy Graham.) John Stott took part in the earlier congresses in Berlin and in Amsterdam and was on the drafting committee for the Lausanne Covenant.

While it is not possible to mention the contribution that all those present felt he made, it can be said that the final Covenant bears his hallmark and can be taken as representing his own views, as well as those of the Congress. Lausanne has been seen by Christians from all over the world as a major turning point in the history of the Evangelical Church, both for its reaffirmation of the need to combine social concern with the primary task of proclaiming the Gospel, and for the way in which it marked the coming-of-age of the Church in the Third World.

The preamble started with thanks to God for the way in which He was working throughout the world, with repentance that the Church had not done all that it should, but with a resolute desire to affirm the Congress' faith and resolve to make disciples of every nation. The Covenant itself began with a declaration of continued Evangelical belief in the being and purpose of God, and in the authority and power of the Bible, which was infallible and without error. 'The message of the Bible is addressed to all mankind', for 'God's revelation in Christ and Scripture is unchangeable'.

In an age of ecumenism and compromise, the 2,700 participants, from over 150 countries, emphatically affirmed their faith in the Gospel. There 'is only one Saviour and only one Gospel'. They rejected as 'derogatory to Christ and to the Gospel every kind of syncretism and dialogue which implies that Christ speaks equally through all religions and ideologies. Jesus Christ being Himself the only God-man, who gave Himself as the only ransom for sinners, is the only mediator between God and man'.

This meant that evangelism – the 'proclamation of the historical, Biblical Christ as Saviour and Lord' – is as vital as ever, especially as over '2,700 million people . . . more than two-thirds of mankind, have yet to be evangelised'. However, some Christians, in seeing this, regrettably neglected social concern, regarding it as incompatible with evangelism.

Although reconciliation with man is not reconciliation with God, the Covenant states, nor is social action evangelism, nor is political liberation salvation, nevertheless we affirm that evangelism and socio-political involvement are both part of our Christian duty. For both are necessary expressions of our doctrines of God and man, our love for our neighbour and our obedience to Jesus Christ.

Furthermore, the

message of salvation implies also a message of judgement upon every form of alienation, oppression and discrimination, and we should not be afraid to denounce evil and injustice wherever they exist. When people receive Christ they are born again into his kingdom and must seek not only to exhibit but also to spread its righteousness in the

midst of an unrighteous world. The salvation we claim
should be transforming us in the totality of our personal
and social responsibilities. Faith without works is dead.

As the Covenant continues, Christians 'need to break out
of our ecclesiastical ghettos and permeate non-Christian
society'. It makes quite clear that 'evangelism is primary',
but, by way of balance, makes it equally plain that the
Church must maintain its integrity – 'a church which
preaches the Cross must itself be marked by the Cross'.
The Church must be scrupulously honest and loving, and
not in any way linked with 'any particular culture, social or
political system or human ideology'. For it is, as Stott has
pointed out in his commentary, 'the community of God's
people. It bears God's name and so puts God's name at risk'.

Much of the Covenant dealt with the fact that the age
of Western domination of the Christian Church was now
over – that we live an in age of a genuinely multiracial,
cross-cultural, international body of Christ. Churches now
worked in equal partnership – Lausanne was the recognition
that the Third World Church had come of age. Too often
the Church had fallen prey to secular mentalities and adopted
worldly methods, and this, like the old cultural imperialism
of the past, was quite wrong.

But, above all, it set two vital priorities. People at Lausanne were forcefully reminded of the 2,700 million unevangelised people mentioned earlier. But there was now 'in
many parts of the world', many of which Stott had himself
visited, 'an unprecedented receptivity to the Lord Jesus
Christ'. National churches could take the opportunity, and
the Congress noted (in a way which vindicated the stand
made twenty-five years earlier by Martyn Lloyd-Jones in
IFES) that sometimes for a local church really to grow in
self-reliance, it might be necessary for the number of foreign
missionaries to be reduced, so as also to release resources for
other fields.

Controversially, the Covenant also stated that the Church
could not hope to attain the goal of bringing the Good News
to every land without sacrifice. 'All of us are shocked', it

stated, 'by the poverty of millions and disturbed by the injustices that cause it. Those of us who live in affluent circumstances accept our duty to develop a simple life style in order to contribute more generously to both relief and evangelism.'

This created some division. Some felt that the call to a simple life style was in itself simplistic – the idea that restraint among Western Christians could in any significant way alleviate the ocean of poverty in the Third World was to fail to understand the basic problem of the causes of poverty. The radicals, whose name was derived from the Latin word, *radix*, or 'root', had failed, in their view, to go to the root of the issue, which was that the cultures of the Third World were, at base, fundamentally pagan in structure. As a leading Indian Christian told me, the problem with India was not that it lacked resources, of which it had plenty, but that the prevailing culture was thoroughly Hindu, and that this created a basic spiritual malaise that permeated throughout society, which he felt caused the mass of poverty for which India was famous. Christians he knew had set up a community designed to rid their area of poverty, only to be persecuted and beaten by local Hindus, determined to destroy their efforts.

Others, especially in North America and other parts of the developed world, were innately suspicious of anything to do with radical action at all. To them, for Christians to become involved in social action was to compromise the Gospel itself – even though Lausanne had not ceased to stress the primacy of evangelism.

For the radicals, many of whom came from South America, the Covenant had not gone anything like far enough. For them, the simple life style was an article of faith. God, they felt, was emphatically on the side of the poor, the underprivileged and oppressed. Christians therefore had the duty to engage in the struggle for justice, and to aid attempts to alter the social structure of the societies in which they lived. Sin was not just an individual matter, but also corporate – what they called 'structural sin'.

So Lausanne, far from ending the matter, stirred up the

debate even more. There was, however, common ground between all the protagonists, and this was their loyalty to Scripture and willingness to submit to its authority. It was on this basis that an international gathering representing all viewpoints and many different nationalities was held in Grand Rapids, USA, in June 1982, to discuss the whole issue of 'evangelism and social responsibility'. The chairman of the Drafting Committee (who drafted the report according to one person closely involved) was John Stott. Because of the disagreements, the conference needed a leader who was trusted by the traditionalists for loyalty to evangelism and known devotion to the exposition of the Word of God on the one hand, and who had an evident concern for the poor and oppressed on the other.

The relationship between these two areas of Christian activity was, the report noted, 'Lausanne's unfinished business'. All were united on the fact that Biblical Christians, 'who seek to live under the Lordship of Jesus Christ and the authority of Scripture, and who pray to be guided by the Holy Spirit, should not be divided on an issue of such importance'. Thanks to this desire to come together and, in human terms, to the exercise of considerable diplomatic skill, the conference was able to produce a united report – although, as the Drafting Committee observed, 'we have found it a struggle'. All races and nations had their blindspots, each of which was part of the Fall experienced by all humanity.

The facts were that there were both 3,000 million unevangelised in the world, and 800 million people who were destitute or in some way oppressed. 'Only the Gospel can change human hearts', the report noted, but Christians could not 'stop with verbal proclamation'. God was both Creator and Judge, and the basis of all social action was surely 'the character of God himself', shown in Jesus Christ. The first fruit of the Spirit was love.

Historically, the report proved, Evangelicalism and social action have been closely linked. (John Stott made this clear in a talk in his own name to mark the Wilberforce anniversary in 1983.) Wilberforce, who helped free the slaves, and

Shaftesbury, who put a stop to the cruel exploitation of children, showed that in the nineteenth century one could be a committed Evangelical and care in an active way for the poor and oppressed.

Unfortunately, at the end of that century, some people 'confused the Kingdom of God . . . and they went on to imagine that by their social programmes they could build God's Kingdom on earth' – what is called the 'social gospel'. As a result, there was 'an over-reaction to this grave distortion of the Gospel', so that 'many Evangelicals became suspicious of social involvement'. This dichotomy was unhealthy – and unbiblical, since Acts 6 clearly shows that the early Church practised both social action and evangelism, without contradiction.

As Stott has pointed out on many occasions, social action can both lead to evangelism and stems from it. James shows that good works are 'an indispensable evidence of salvation', and, as Stott himself reminded me one day, 2 Corinthians chapters 8 and 9 demonstrate that those who have abundance should help those who do not. Those who have been evangelised – and born again – will thus naturally have a compassion for the poor and wish to do something about their plight.

In addition, 'social action can be a bridge to evangelism', opening otherwise closed doors. Evangelism is, of course, the 'logical' priority – people cannot have Christian compassion for the underprivileged unless they become Christians in the first place. Furthermore, 'evangelism relates to people's eternal destiny . . . Christians are doing what no one else can do'. So Christians can act in two ways – in the unique work of spreading the Gospel and in the shared task of social action, carried out by them from a different base than the non-Christian one.

Christians are the 'new community' – a theme which also runs through John Stott's book on Ephesians, *God's New Society*, and his commentary on the Sermon on the Mount, *Christian Counter-culture*. The Church is the salt of the earth in a fallen world, and should act as a 'challenge to the old' community. It is the Biblical duty of Christian people 'simultaneously to permeate the World and to retain their Kingdom distinctives'.

Many of the participants at Grand Rapids agreed on the principles. The problem remained as to how Christians acted in practice in the social sphere. All united on the fact that the 'Bible lays great emphasis on both justice (or righteousness) and peace'. But there was disagreement on how far to go. Social service was one thing, but some interpretations of social action included a degree of radical political involvement that some found difficult to swallow. Some felt that the Christian attitude to the State should be one of outright opposition and rejection, others that Christians should be separate but parallel, while others thought that the Church should permeate and transform the secular society in which it found itself. There was also a major difference observed as to the scope of action for Christians in open, democratic states, and those who lived in closed, authoritarian regimes.

John Stott once told me that he stood between the two extremes – he is neither a materialist nor an ascetic. He believes that Christians should be able to enjoy the good things of creation, and that the New Community of Jesus Christ should be one in which poverty is abolished. Christians, he feels, should stick to principles, and avoid getting bogged down in the technicalities of macro-economics. (Those who disagree with him feel that this is one of the severest defects in Ronald Sider's works, quite apart from one's reactions to his Biblical exegesis.)

As Stott reminded me, Dives went to hell not because he was rich, but because he was scandalously indifferent to the poor around him. It was not a case of cause and effect – Dives was rich, therefore Lazarus was poor – but an indictment of indifference to the suffering of fellow humans. Those who have should, as Paul states, help those who have not. This is surely right – one should help not out of guilt, but out of love, out of a Christ-centred compassion for one's fellow (and equal) human beings, and not out of a man-centred hairshirt asceticism. If more Christians saw this, then many more Evangelicals would be active in social concern than are at present. In rightly rejecting a liberal-social Gospel and a hyper-spiritual radical asceticism they have neglected their clear Biblical duty to be God's salt and light in society. The answer to any extreme is not to be extremist, but to be Biblical, a message urgently needed today.

John Stott, as the title of his book *Balanced Christianity* implies, believes deeply in maintaining what he holds to be the Biblical balance. In some areas this has meant that he has been attacked by both sides. An example of this is his nuclear pacifist position, one that he has developed in recent years.

On the one hand, there are those – notably Francis Schaeffer in the US debate and Jerram Barrs in Britain – who hold that the traditional Christian view of the Just War can embrace within it the use of nuclear weapons. They point out that a Christian has a duty to resist evil, if needs be by the use of force as in the Old Testament, and as implied by Paul in Romans 13. A country that is attacked has the right to defend its citizens, especially if the opponent is a regime as evil in structure as the Soviet Union. Justice must be defended and there are, in the real world, 'totalitarian states which must be resisted'. Nuclear weapons, through their deterrent value, they feel, have kept the peace, prevented global war, and contained unjust regimes.

On the other hand, there is the total pacifist view, one formerly held at Cambridge by Stott himself, and often espoused today in Britain and the USA by Mennonites. To them, the fact that Jesus did not himself use force means that Christians should renounce it altogether today, so that not only are nuclear weapons wrong, but the whole concept of armed defence. They advocate 'transarmament' which involves the use of discussion with invading armies. To them, 'nonviolence was a part of conversion'.

Stott, however, takes a line between these two views. He has shifted his position in recent years, rejecting the pacifist option in the 1950s. He has been careful to stick to the idea of outlining the moral principles, while leaving the details to more expert hands, in order to avoid the problems of those mentioned earlier who got bogged down in macro-economic detail over the world hunger issue.

He would, he told me, now believe in the Just War doctrine long espoused by the Christian Church. However, as he has written, 'our Evangelical concern is with Scripture, rather than tradition'. The nuclear pacifist position is compatible, he feels, with both.

The Just War theory states that resistance to evil must be both proportionate to the amount of suffering caused, and discriminate in its effects – which in practice means that armed defence can lawfully destroy military targets, but not civilian, since innocent civilians are not part of the conflict. A nuclear war, however, according to Stott, would be both disproportionate and indiscriminate, since millions of civilians would be killed or injured – 'a nuclear war could never be a just war'.

This view, he feels, has two Biblical bases – firstly, that the shedding of innocent blood is forbidden in the Old Testament; and secondly that the state, whose powers are laid down in Romans 13, is, in the light of Romans 12, entitled 'to promote good and to restrain and punish evil' but with 'the minimum necessary force'. Both these doctrines are, to him, incompatible with what would occur in the event of a nuclear war.

Although he is a nuclear pacifist, he is emphatically not a unilateralist. As he has written, he finds himself as a result in a 'moral dilemma . . . Morality leads me to declare use [of nuclear weapons] evil; Christian realism to warn that unilateralism might make nuclear war more likely. Therefore, the urgent search for balanced, multilateral and verifiable disarmament . . . is more prudent than unilateralism.' He conceded that his view, 'immoral to use, prudent to keep', of nuclear missiles, is 'a paradoxical position', and certainly both Jerram Barrs and Mennonites such as Alan Kreider have gently accused him from both sides of being inconsistent. But perhaps the most important thing is that in the debate the proponents of all three positions agree that the supreme arbiter is Scripture, 'God's Word written' as Stott has described it, to whose authority they must all as

Evangelical Christians submit.

John Stott has written on many more issues, and in all of them he has sought resolutely to base himself on Scripture – to try to discern what God is saying to us through His Word. That is why Stott has such a high view of preaching – what could be more important than the proclamation of the revealed truth of God? This is also why he has the ear of both sides in many disputes – they both know that he will base his view on the Bible, and that even though they may differ on interpreting what the Bible is actually saying, they none the less believe in its authority.

The truth of this is vital today – perhaps all the more so in our present climate. Os Guinness, a writer close to both Francis Schaeffer and to John Stott, has shown clearly in his book *The Gravedigger File* that present-day Western Evangelicals have been infiltrated to a very large degree by existential thought. It is subjective experience rather than objective, Scriptural truth that is the base of too much of today's Christian faith and practice. Perhaps one of the reasons that John Stott has been so well received in the growing churches of the Third World is that they, like he, are determined to resist this trend.

Others also feel that John Stott's career has been too sheltered, and that he has been overinclined to concentrate on the more intellectual in society. There is some measure of truth in this – as noted earlier, All Souls, where he has been all his adult life, is not exactly a typical parish, and he has been heavily involved both in student work and with thinking people generally. Many also feel that his approach has been based on theory, and not from hard-bitten experience.

Two things can be said. Firstly, as with Francis Schaeffer and the work of L'Abri, intellectuals need the Gospel too. All depends on the people to whom God has called a particular individual. Some He sends to the slums of Calcutta, others to a central London church with many students and other intellectuals. The main point is that we each do our duty before God as He has called us.

Second, we live in an age where many Christians have thrown their God-given minds out of the window. Too many today live in pietistic Evangelical ghettos, neglecting their duty to be Christian salt and light in the World in which God placed them. Their Christianity is both mindless and irresponsible. John Stott, the author of *Your Mind Matters*, has fought for a Christianity that is both firmly based on Scripture, and one which cares for the World around us. He believes, as his book on Timothy, *Guard the Gospel* (IVP), clearly shows, that as Evangelicals, there is a sense in which we must be profoundly conservative. We are to keep to the faithful deposit that God has given us in Scripture.

Another important aspect of John Stott's thought is that he believes a Christian can be fully Christ-centred and radical at the same time. Many, especially the younger, Evangelicals in the USA have reacted against the dead, formal, civic religious Evangelicalism of their parents, where to be a born-again believer was all part of being a patriotic American. This pseudo-Christianity lacked any kind of love to the poor and oppressed, unthinkingly backed the status quo and discredited Evangelical belief in the eyes of many of the children raised under its wing.

Unfortunately, a larger number of the 'New Evangelicals', in their desire to rediscover Biblical teaching on social justice, peace and other issues, went too far in their rejection of the tradition from which they had come. They rightly laid stress on Christ's teaching of the Kingdom, and the fact that it had profound economic, social and even political implications. The incarnation was re-emphasised – Christ on earth, the friend of the poor and oppressed.

Sadly, however, this often led to a failure to realise the primacy of Calvary. The older generation, with its constant desire to win 'decisions' had emphasised the fact that to be born again meant taking a very personal step of repentance. In a vital sense, Christianity is a very personal and private faith, resting as it does on the individual's relationship with God the Father through Christ the Son. But the traditionalists had privatised Christianity altogether – they had utterly neglected the fact that such a personal step as conversion has the most momentous public consequences. Christians are not just people who have good private morals, but members of God's New Society, the salt of the earth, redeemed humans who share their Saviour's love and concern not just for the souls of those around them, but their bodies too. The radicals, in rejecting the extreme from which they had come, went all too often to the other, and reduced the centrality that Calvary should have in the Christian's life.

John Stott's writings could be said to show that he is a Calvary-centred radical. His book *Basic Christianity* makes it clear that it is through Christ on the Cross we are saved – this is what matters. But, equally, his works such as *Christian Counter-culture* on the Sermon on the Mount, and *God's New Society* on Ephesians, demonstrate the life-changing consequences that conversion has. Christianity is both personal and corporate – we are individually born, but into an international, multi-ethnic family where there are rich and poor, young and old, clever and dim. Christians have a duty to evangelise, but they also have an obligation to ensure that God's standards prevail on God's Earth, in fighting poverty as much as pornography, and in standing for social justice as well as for school prayers.

Above all, for Christians to know these things, they need to have Scripture at the centre of their lives, so that Christ can be at the head. They need to have the Word of God faithfully proclaimed to them in all its richness, and for this to happen they have to have it preached Biblically in their churches. This has been at the very heart of John Stott's life and message. This is why he has been involved so much in the Third World, in social and peace issues, and why he has now set up the London Institute to help Christians think through secular issues in a Scriptural way. His actions have stemmed from his deepest convictions, about Jesus Christ, and about God's Word proclaimed to God's people – convictions to which we need to pay urgent heed today.

MARTYN LLOYD-JONES

Early life

Martyn Lloyd-Jones, the great expository preacher and pastor, was born on December 20th, 1899, the second son of Henry and Magdalen Lloyd-Jones. Although he began life in Cardiff, it was in the beautiful countryside of Welsh-speaking Wales that his roots really lay: in the hills, farms and villages of Cardiganshire that were little touched by outside, English, influence. Despite the fact that most of his life was spent in England, especially in London, he always regarded himself first and foremost as a Welshman.

In 1905 he moved with his family – his parents and brothers Vincent and Harold – to Llangeitho, the small town where the great Daniel Rowlands preached in the eighteenth century. Henry Lloyd-Jones ran the general store. With his culture and learning, he would nowadays have been to university, but higher education in those days needed money. Nevertheless, he raised his three sons in a lively, stimulating atmosphere, filled with talk and debate. He himself was a keen Liberal, but, unlike his son Martyn, who supported the fiery Welsh radical David Lloyd George, he followed the more moderate H. H. Asquith. He also advocated the 'new theology', which mixed social action with Nonconformist churchmanship. His wife, Magdalen, came from a successful farming and horse-breeding family at near-by Llwyncadfor, none of whom were Christians.

Martyn's early childhood was happy. At first he was more interested in playing football with the boys than in schoolwork. As his home was also a shop, he met all kinds of people, and later in life maintained that small country communites like Llangeitho produced more 'characters' than the big, anonymous cities of today. He particularly enjoyed watching the local blacksmith who, it was said, could spit farther than anyone else! He had great fun visiting his grandfather on the big farm, and riding the ponies, a pleasure he never lost. In 1908 he had a special treat – a ride to London and back in a car. On the way home, the car had a puncture in Oxford and so they had to buy a new tyre from a small bicycle shop owned by a Mr Morris, later Lord Nuffield, founder of Morris cars.

But sadly the happy days came to an end. Early in 1909 a fire destroyed the family store and Martyn survived only by escaping from an upstairs window. His grandfather foolishly let slip to him that the accident meant hard times ahead for the family, and little 10-year-old Martyn became more serious and studious from then on. In 1911 he won the second scholarship to the County Intermediate School at the near-by town of Tregaron. Unfortunately the daily journey there was too long for Martyn to be able to continue living at home and so he joined his older brother Harold as a weekly boarder in the town from Monday to Friday. He became desperately homesick, and always regarded his three years in Tregaron as miserably unhappy.

At the school itself, however, his talents blossomed and, thanks to the teaching there, he began to realise for the first time that he had an above average ability. His favourite teacher was the history master, S. M. Powell, and throughout his ministry Dr Lloyd-Jones was to urge Christians again and again to know their history, especially that of the Church. It not only explained the present, and showed what mistakes to avoid, but also revealed the great Divine interventions – the Reformation, for example, the Puritans and the eighteenth-century revival – which could teach Christians so much. In 1913 he visited the Summer Association of Calvinistic Methodists, held that year at Llangeitho. Many people were later to call him the last of the great Calvinistic Methodist preachers, combining as he did the love of truth and sound doctrine of Calvin with the fire and enthusiasm of the eighteenth-century Methodist revival.

In 1914 Henry Lloyd-Jones went bankrupt. For a while it looked as if the family would emigrate to Canada, but in God's providence they moved instead to London, where Henry set up a new business. The early days were extremely discouraging, and Martyn almost had to become a bank clerk in order to help out. But, fortunately, trade at No 7 Regency Street picked up sufficiently for him to go on to the famous St Marylebone Grammar School, where he quickly shone, and prepared himself for the medical career upon which he had already decided.

The family decided not to attend the near-by Westminster Chapel (of which Martyn was later to become minister for over 30 years), but went instead to that great meeting place of exiles, the Welsh Chapel in the Charing Cross Road. On their first Sunday they sat in the row in front of the family of the eminent Harley Street eye surgeon, Tom Phillips. Bethan Phillips, the daughter, remembers noticing the three Lloyd-Jones brothers, little realising at the time how one of them would change her life.

The minister of the Welsh Chapel, the Revd Peter Hughes-Griffiths, was a strong character and individualist, and like Martyn, he had a passion for politics. Martyn would often be home late, having spent the evening in the gallery of the House of Commons, watching his hero and the other great orators perform. But the grand hopes of the Liberals faded, instilling in him a lifelong distrust of the attempts of Acts of Parliament to change the world. It was the Gospel, he was later to argue, that was the only hope for a fallen world.

The Bart's man
In any case, nothing deflected him from his desire to study medicine. 'I was never an adolescent,' he used to say, and at the age of only 16 he entered the medical school of St Bartholomew's Hospital (commonly known as Bart's), near the centre of the old City of London. Bart's was undoubtedly one of the best of the famous London teaching hospitals – and all its students knew it. It was said that you

could always tell a Bart's man, but you couldn't tell him much. Martyn's teacher was the leading physician of the day, Sir Thomas (later Lord) Horder, the Royal Physician, who his admiring pupil later described as 'the most acute thinker that I ever knew'.

Above all, Horder was a 'thorough diagnostician' – he taught his pupils to collect the facts and then reason through them until they had reached the correct diagnosis. They were always to work from first principles, and never to jump to conclusions. Horder ingrained into them the Socratic method – asking the right questions and precise, logical thinking, were essential to the effective practice of clinical medicine. Young Lloyd-Jones became a star pupil and Horder rewarded him with his own copy of Jevon's book, the *Principles of Science: A Treatise on Logical and Scientific Method*.

If preaching is 'logic on fire', Martyn Lloyd-Jones un-doubtedly inherited the 'fire', in human terms, from his Welsh background. The Welsh are a very emotional race, and he was no exception. But sheer emotion by itself often lacks depth – a failing that was very true of the Welsh preachers of his day. What was to give his preaching such power was the 'logic' – the way in which, in evangelistic sermons, for example, he would examine the facts of the plight of man, reject all the false remedies, and then show the true Biblical diagnosis and the only cure, in Jesus Christ. He would maintain to the end that his rigorous medical training under Horder was God's preparation for his later preaching ministry.

His time at Bart's also helped him as a pastor. He often discovered that people who came to him with what they thought were spiritual problems were medically ill in some way or another, or even, simply, just overtired. When minis-ters visited or telephoned him about difficulties in their church, he would not give them direct advice, but would ask them questions about their situation. Many soon found that he had guided them to a solution to their problem by making them think logically through the issue. Such help proved even better than advice, because it enabled ministers to learn how to think for themselves and to face difficulties in future, especially when they had to deal with them on their own.

Martyn Lloyd-Jones kept up his medical interest till the end of his life. He continued to read the learned journals – and, indeed, often knew more about the latest cure for an illness than many practising doctors or even specialists. (He acted as an unofficial doctor to his family and close friends till his late seventies.) But it was as a physician for the spiritually sick that he was to become best known. It was with good reason that he was universally nicknamed 'The Doctor'.

The call to Wales

In 1921 he obtained his MB, BS with distinction, and his MD and MRCP not long after. (In later life he was consistently to refuse all honorary degrees and other distinctions on the basis that his London doctorate was honour enough.) The same year he was, as the result of an especially brilliant piece of diagnosis, appointed Horder's junior house physician and two years later, aged only 23, made his chief clinical assistant. In 1924 he received a major scholarship to study bacterial endocarditis (though he never became a heart specialist).

But despite his meteoric progress in the medical world, his mind began to turn to other things. He had been struck by the ungodliness and moral emptiness of many of Horder's aristocratic patients, and this in turn had made him painfully aware of his own sinfulness. The death of his father and the tragic early death of his older brother Harold gave him an acute sense of the fleeting nature of life, and made him realise that he was spiritually dead to God. He had been trying to escape God, and needed to turn to Him for forgiveness.

His changing attitude can be seen in the three talks he delivered to the literary and debating society of the Welsh Chapel. In 1921 he spoke on 'Modern Education', followed in 1924 by an address on 'Signs of the Times', an attack on contemporary fashions. (One of the most fashionably dressed people in the church was the girl he most admired – fellow medical student Bethan Phillips, for whom his ardour was at that time unreturned.) But by 1925 his subject was 'The Tragedy of Modern Wales', a sermon on his country's loss of true spirituality. Christianity, he now felt, was the only answer to Wales's problems – and the real Christian Gospel, not the social Gospel preached from the pulpits. Such views were highly controversial, and the public uproar against him, when his talk became more widely known, was immense. But it convinced him more than ever that he was called to Wales to preach the truth.

His first sermon was in Pontypridd in April 1925. Once again, he preached a message very distinct from those normally heard in Welsh pulpits of the time. Social action was all very proper, he proclaimed, but what Wales really needed was a 'great spiritual awakening'. However, after much deep thinking, he decided that he should continue with his medical career for the time being. He still felt unworthy to be called to the ministry and struggled with himself throughout that year. By 1926 his turmoil was over – as he said, it was 'God's hand that laid hold of me, and drew me out, and separated me to do this work.' At the end of 1926, he was called to be minister of the Bethlehem Forward Movement Mission Church in Sandfields, Aberavon, and accepted their offer.

Many years later in his book *Preaching and Preachers*, he argued that men should never enter the ministry as a profession, but should only do so if they felt they had no other choice and were being compelled to enter it by God. Ministers certainly ought to have the natural talents necessary for a preaching career – a clear public speaking manner, a good mind (though not necessarily an academic one) and a fine character. But they should also be men filled with the Spirit, with a concern for the spiritually lost, and with a thorough knowledge of Scripture. Such men did not call themselves, but were recognised by the Church as called by God. Preachers, he believed, were born and not made.

He never had any formal theological training. To him, a minister was not a Bible scholar skilled in expert knowledge of New Testament Greek – though ministers ought to have learned it – but primarily a preacher and pastor with a Divine commission. To be a preacher was to possess a gift from God and too much academic learning could even be harmful. So when, fifty years after becoming a minister himself, he and a group of friends set up the London Theological Seminary, they took immense pains to emphasise the essentially practical nature of the course. There were to be no degrees awarded. All students were to be men recognised by their local churches to have the gift of preaching, and all the lecturers were to be pastors of churches skilled in particular areas – Church history, Greek, etc.

He always maintained that his medical training under Horder had been, in human terms, as crucial a part of his training for the pastorate as anything else, and many have felt over the years that it was his diagnostic approach, both in his sermons and as a pastor, that made him the great preacher and Christian leader that he became, skills that no amount of seminary training could ever have given him. In an age in which book learning is often rated above practical experience, where a business will often employ a fine arts graduate, rather than a man who left school at 16 and worked in industry, because the artist possesses a degree, this is something that we need to remember.

Another equally important event happened in 1926. Bethan Phillips, whom he had loved from afar for over nine years, now finally returned his affection. He proposed to her (for the second time) in June, and she accepted. The wedding took place on January 8th, 1927 – and attracted far more attention than either of them had imagined. By now the fact that he was abandoning one of the most promising careers in Harley Street to go off to South Wales to preach was becoming widely known. The fact that the beautiful daughter of an eminent surgeon was marrying such a man amazed people even more. But it was a real love match – and one that was to be totally happy for the rest of his life. The couple complemented each other and were able to strengthen each other in the difficult task that now lay ahead.

Early days in Sandfields

The young pair were off to Wales almost immediately. The doctor had been strongly influenced by his father's radical views and felt called to preach among working-class people. The Forward Movement Mission Church in Sandfields, Aberavon, in South Wales, was in an extremely poor area, centred round the rather rough Port Talbot docks and the great steel mills, then privately owned. The town was best known for the fact that it had Ramsay Macdonald, the then leader of the Labour Party, as its MP.

The church itself had been noted for its social activities, but was not very successful. Dr Lloyd-Jones scrapped all these on arrival – the sports club, the drama group, the temperance league. Unlike many today, he felt passionately that the 'business of preaching is not to entertain, but to lead people to salvation, to teach them how to find God'. It was preaching that would get people into church not activities or attractions designed to try to win their interest.

He also believed, unlike many middle-class ministers then and since, that working-class people were just as capable of listening to preaching as anyone else. His style reflected his medical training. He would argue not only that Christianity was reasonable, but that nothing else was. The Gospel was open to all: the 'most respectable sinner', he preached, had 'no more claim on it than the worst'. The offer of salvation was open to the 'very worst man in Aberavon' – and the town had many contenders for that position.

He refused to model himself on any of the famous local preachers – he was markedly distinct from the start. He was neither emotional, nor liberal theologically. He adopted a 'medical approach', with the listeners as his patients. It was the mind, he felt, that needed to be struck first – a Welshman could easily be moved, but to change him, and the way in which he thought, was much more difficult. So the Doctor's message was that Christianity was 'very relevant and urgently important'. He never used jokes, anecdotes or personal stories, as he felt both too aware of the glory of God to do so and also that such things deflected from the seriousness of his message. He therefore based himself firmly on the Bible instead. The Gospel was Truth – 'not based on experience', as were many false faiths, but 'on great external facts'.

Such preaching was to form the basis of his style for the rest of his ministry, and was to be his hallmark. It was Biblically based – or expository – yet also relevant to the modern age. It was reasonable, appealing to the minds of the listeners, yet the effect it produced in them was also highly emotional. He would refer to current events, yet show that it was the Biblical text from which he was preaching that had the true – and only – answer. It was no coincidence that his first-ever sermon in Aberavon, in November 1926, was on the text: 'I determined not to know anything among you save Jesus Christ and Him crucified', the words which now appear on his gravestone in Wales.

The ministry grows

The whole church in Aberavon would meet regularly on Wednesdays to discuss practical living while the men's 'Brotherhood Meeting' gathered for a more theological Bible class on Saturdays. The Doctor took the view that working-class men were just as capable of logical, Biblical debate as those better educated than themselves. Indeed he often felt that his people had a finer grasp of the great doctrinal truths than many a professor. His method of leading them was the same, Socratic, diagnostic, one he had learned under Horder, and which he was later to use both at the Friday night discussions at Westminster Chapel and, above all, in his thirty-eight years as chairman of the Westminster Ministers' Fraternal.

He felt that the best way for someone to learn something was by working the issue out for themselves. So he would ask them to find reference to the issue in Scripture (no other sources allowed), see what the passage said about it, how it fitted into the context of other passages, and then go on to work out what the Bible's teaching on the subject must therefore be. He would make people pursue the logic of their conclusions and point out to them if necessary where they had gone wrong. He was always on top of the discussion, and his own wide knowledge of Scripture enabled him to keep it on the right path. As with the ministers who came to him for advice, ordinary Christians learned through his diagnostic approach how to think and reason for themselves through what Scripture taught. Many who knew him throughout his ministry would say that when crises arose in their own lives, they were able to survive them because they had learned from him how to deal with them *Biblically*.

. . . and widens

His distinctive preaching soon marked him out in a Wales dominated by liberal theology, and also bore a remarkable fruit in his own church. Where social activities had failed, the proclamation of the Gospel in the Spirit's power worked. The Doctor was convinced that it was the action of God which saved, and not human effort, though it was through the words of Christ-centred preaching that people heard it. He felt deeply that sinners needed not to be entertained but to be humbled and convicted. The result of this radical approach was that many were converted, including many nominal Christians in his own congregation, the church secretary among them.

As a secular journalist wrote at the time, there was 'no drama except the great drama of salvation . . . Public emotion leaves him cold, yet his passion for human salvation sets his people on fire.' There were 70 converts in 1929, 128 in 1930, often from among the deprived and unemployed – the very categories which the Church in the West is so singularly failing to reach today – and without any of the gimmicks usually thought so necessary to win them now. The corporate life of the church changed and made a massive impact on the locality. Faithful, regular, expository preaching of the Gospel, and the day-to-day witness of ordinary Christians whose lives had been transformed, brought about a remarkable growth. One of the converts, 'Staffordshire Bill', had been a notorious drunk, yet he died a radiant Christian. Such things had a far greater effect on the locality than any amount of publicity could ever have hoped to achieve.

Dr Lloyd-Jones also found himself called upon medically. He was far better qualified than most of the local doctors and solved many cases which had baffled them completely. Initially he was resented by them, but when they saw that he had no intention of setting up in competition with them, a close relationship soon developed, and his part-time medical practice became a help in spreading the Gospel, the greatest cure.

Canada

Inevitably his fame spread far, first of all in Wales, where he would pack the meeting places with people flocking to hear his message. He always spoke in a language which everyone could understand and with a logic that convicted them.

Then in 1932, he was asked to preach in Canada. His first sermon was in Toronto, at the church of a Dr Richard Roberts, a Calvinistic Methodist who had become a liberal. But the main minister in the city was the Revd Dr T. T. Shields. He had much in common with the Doctor – both were keen Calvinists, believing in God's sovereignty in salvation. But Dr Lloyd-Jones soon disagreed with Shields, because he strongly disliked the Canadian's polemical approach, always disagreeing with others. This, he felt, was far too negative.

'You can make mincemeat out of the liberals,' he told Shields, 'but still be in trouble in your own soul.' Rather than adopt an antagonistic, surgical approach, the Doctor preferred that of the physician. 'Preach the Gospel to people positively', he suggested, 'and win them.' Dr Lloyd-Jones never believed in being aggressive and always stressed the positive aspect of the truth. He never hesitated to enter enemy territory – he held strong views on many subjects – but he would do so in a Christian spirit, not one of worldly spite.

It is important to remember this, because there have been

those who have, after his death, given him a negative image, stressing more what they felt he was against, rather than, as he would have preferred, emphasising what he was for. He believed in reasoning with people whose opinions on various issues differed from his own – whether in the context of debate with fellow Evangelicals, or that of explaining the truth to those who did not know it. Even in his evangelistic sermons, he would not so much denounce error, as demonstrate its futility in a reasoned manner. As will be seen, for the majority of his ministry, he worked with fellow Evangelicals of all groupings, seeking to persuade them by discussion and by example to his own point of view.

After Toronto he went on to a conference in the USA organised by the Chautauqua Institute, near Buffalo, New York State. This gathering was no longer remotely Evangelical, with speakers such as Eleanor Roosevelt and the humanist Sir Julian Huxley. But the Doctor felt that God had guided him there, and the unknown preacher from Wales was such a success that the small meeting place allotted to him had to be changed to the biggest auditorium of all, where he was listened to by an audience of over 6,000. As he said, Paul did not hector Peter in Jerusalem, but won him round.

Beginnings with student work

In 1935 he began his lifelong involvement with the Inter Varsity Fellowship (IVF, now the UCCF), which had been set up in 1927 by Christians from all denominations in order to bring together the student Christian unions in all the different universities and medical schools. He was asked by its General Secretary, Douglas Johnson, himself a former medical man, to speak at its annual conference, as his 'Pauline' preaching manner had impressed them. The Doctor was hesitant at first, as he was unhappy about the rather English, hearty, anti-intellectual style then prevalent in IVF. But he finally agreed, and soon made such an impact that in 1939 he was chosen to be its president.

In those days truly Evangelical students were in a minority, and often frightened by the bigger, respectable, but extremely liberal Student Christian Movement. As a result, they had retreated into a shell, emphasising experience and sporty, non-intellectual, Christianity, with a doctrinally rather feeble kind of evangelism. The Doctor, with his robust Welsh background and his emphasis on the mind, totally rejected this kind of approach. But instead of denouncing it from the outside he joined it and, by so doing, completely transformed it. He breathed a new air of confidence into the IVF that led to its becoming the main Christian group in every university.

He did so by giving it the solid doctrinal base in Scripture that it had hitherto lacked. He taught students not only how to think, but to be unafraid to do so in public. He removed the rather other-worldly ghetto atmosphere by telling students how to relate their Christian faith to the subjects they studied. Although a medical graduate himself, he enabled arts and literature students to feel that what they were studying was perfectly proper so long as their faith did not suffer as a result.

The idea that Christians should be only doctors, ministers, missionaries or prep school games teachers was to him ridiculous. He strongly disliked the influence in England of the public school ethos – that of the sports-mad, unthinking chump, who repressed his emotions in the stiff upper lip, distrusted the intellect and cultivated the tradition of the gentleman amateur. Partly this was because the Doctor himself had been miserable living away from home and because he had a Welshman's innate suspicion of the English ruling classes, who had suppressed the Welsh and their language for so long.

But it was also a matter of emphasis. To him, the rather pietistic climate of English Evangelicalism was caused by the malign influence of the public school tradition and therefore did great harm. The Welsh, by contrast, were able to express true emotion and, at the same time, loved doctrine and revered the mind. By introducing the Welsh outlook into English Christianity, the Doctor made a major contribution to Evangelicalism as a whole.

He therefore encouraged those Christians entering the

mainstream professions, such as industry and law, just as much as those going into the traditional callings, such as medicine or paid Christian work. At the same time, he enthusiastically supported missions overseas and served for many years on the Candidates Board of the China Inland Mission (now OMF) and spoke at several missionary conferences. He was also a strong supporter of the Christian Medical Fellowship, frequently lecturing at their meetings, and always interested in their problems and ready to give advice.

Decisions

Revival and the need for it remained a passion in Dr Lloyd-Jones all his life. The secular press called him the greatest preacher since the Welsh revival of 1904 (in which his wife's grandfather, Evan Phillips, had played a leading part). But, as he told the 7,000 who came to hear him at the Daniel Rowlands Centenary meeting in 1935, Wales had forgotten the truths upon which revivals were based. Nor, as he said to a packed Albert Hall the same year, could revival be artificially induced. Evangelism had become too obsessed with 'results', and 'decisionism' was no substitute for the chief need: the preaching of the truth, simply and boldly. The Doctor always preached the Gospel on Sunday evenings, and a regular flow of conversions took place. But he never made a special appeal, or altar call. Those who wished to see him could visit him in his vestry after the service. If the Word was faithfully proclaimed, God could be trusted to work in the sinner's heart.

His own preaching had become highly successful and this has been attributed, in human terms, to three causes. First he preached to everybody, regardless of age, class or sex – he never preached to special categories. Second, the language he used was the sort that everyone could understand, regardless of ability. Third, and most important, he possessed a clarity, seriousness and note of authority that compelled people to listen and take notice of what he said – 'logic on fire'.

In 1937 he went again to the USA, and preached in Philadelphia. Sitting in the congregation was Campbell Morgan, minister of Westminster Chapel. He was deeply impressed and felt that he must ask the Doctor to join him at the Chapel. For the time being, Dr Lloyd-Jones decided to remain in Aberavon, but by the end of the year he felt that God was calling him to leave the church there and he did so in 1938, to the sorrow both of his congregation and himself. Then the most remarkable series of coincidences took place, demonstrating clearly to him what God wanted him to do.

Earlier in 1938 he had been called to be minister of St Marylebone Presbyterian Church, in London. He refused because there was the possibility of his being chosen to be the principal of the Calvinistic Methodist College in Bala in North Wales. While he was waiting for the College's decision, he was persuaded by Campbell Morgan to fill in the time by helping temporarily at Westminster Chapel. In September 1938 he preached his first sermon there – on the importance of doctrine in the Christian life.

Then, in December the Chapel asked him to stay on permanently, but he refused as he was still uncertain as to his future. Soon after, the College rejected him – his main supporter having missed the train and failed to appear at the selection meeting. They had disliked his strong and uncompromising stand on the Gospel and his attacks on liberal theology.

There was now no hesitation in his mind – he accepted Westminster Chapel's call, and was to remain there for the next twenty-nine years, until his retirement in 1968. As a preacher he was different from Campbell Morgan, whose joint minister he now was. Morgan was an Arminian, and mainly exegetical or scholarly, whereas the Doctor was expository, taking the wider meaning, and believed staunchly in the sovereign power of God in salvation. (Although he was very much of a Calvinist, he disliked labels and would say that he only supported Calvin in that Calvin agreed with what he felt was clearly taught in Scripture.) But in spite of these differences, a warm relationship existed between the two men, and they were able to work happily together. Both were Evangelicals who loved the Gospel, and that was what mattered.

Some have felt that he had made a mistake in leaving Wales. But this is probably a mistaken view. First, it could be said, as with his influence on the IVF, that he brought Wales to England, to the benefit of English Evangelicalism generally. He was able to exercise considerably more influence in England than he could ever have done had he remained in Wales. This was all the more true because Westminster Chapel, being in London, was at the centre of the British Empire. As will be seen, people came not just from all over Britain, but also from all over the world.

It is very difficult to imagine thousands of such people going regularly, over a period of many months, or even years, all the way to Wales on Sundays, however good the preacher was: it would have been physically impossible. As it was, the Doctor was able to exercise an enormous influence over an exceptionally large number of people in a key place at a crucial time. In addition, he frequently went back to Wales, either on holiday or to preach, and retained a very close interest in the spiritual health of his native land. His influence in Wales was undiminished despite his having left it for London.

The start of international student work

In 1939 the Doctor's presidency of the IVF led him to take part in what later turned out to be one of the most influential Christian gatherings of this century: the international conference at Cambridge that was ultimately to lead to the setting up of the International Fellowship of Evangelical Students – the IFES. This organisation was to be an umbrella to all the national movements like IVF and IVCF(USA), and is now one of the biggest international student organisations in the world.

Many of those closest to the Doctor feel that his role in establishing the IFES, and especially the doctrinal stand on which it rests, was undoubtedly one of his greatest achievements. When asked the question, 'What did the

Doctor stand for?' they would unhesitatingly answer, 'the Christ-centred, international vision of IFES'.

The 1939 conference, held under the shadow of approaching war, was attended by 800 students and staff from 33 different nations (including countries soon to be fighting each other, such as Britain and Germany), and represented committed Evangelicals from many denominations, state churches and Free Churches alike. In sharp contrast to the events around them, the delegates were united. The doctor preached on 'The One Essential' – the need to have Christ both as Saviour and Lord.

Dr Lloyd-Jones felt an especially deep commitment to this particular movement among the students of all nations. As a Welshman he had a strong empathy with those Christians from colonial nations, such as Indians and Africans. He also very much supported the firm doctrinal stand taken by many of the Christian Unions, especially by the Norwegians, under the influence of their great leader, O. Hallesby.

The outbreak of war in September 1939 stopped their plans from being put into immediate effect. But the vision of a united, international, uncompromisingly Evangelical body that arose out of the Cambridge conference was not forgotten, nor were the words spoken by the Doctor.

'The Chapel'

Martyn Lloyd-Jones remained joint minister of Westminster Chapel until Campbell Morgan's retirement in 1943, and then remained as sole minister for a quarter of a century until 1968. Unlike many provincial preachers who lost their reputation on coming to London, his increased dramatically. By 1947 the Chapel averaged 1,500 in the congregation in the morning service, and 2,000 every Sunday night. What drew them was the quality and power of his preaching. To him, preaching was 'theology coming through a man who is on fire', filled with the power of the Holy Spirit and called by God to proclaim it.

For him, Scripture showed that preaching was 'God's own method'. The object of the preacher was not to give his own ideas but to make known the message of God, based on God's Word, the Bible. The preacher was Christ's ambassador, and it was this that gave him his authority. Preaching, and lecturing, or 'sharing', were simply not the same – preaching was on an altogether spiritual plane. All preaching had to be based on Scripture. As all the Bible fitted together as a single whole, all preaching 'must be expository', i.e. based firmly on systematic study of the Biblical text, yet never taken out of context. Ministers, he felt, should always know the whole of Scripture, and read it at least once a year.

So he would preach through a book, verse by verse, showing clearly what it taught, how it fitted in with what the Bible taught elsewhere, why it was important, and how it applied to the problems of the day. As Chua Wee-hian, a former Westminster Chapel regular and now general secretary of the IFES, has said, the Doctor, unlike so many preachers, always gave one the *whole* message. Graham Harrison, a colleague and fellow Welshman, has written of the 'power of argument and logical progression as he unfolded his message in such a way that the simplest could follow him and the deepest could but marvel at his profundity'. The Doctor felt that everyone was a sinner, whether intellectual or not, and could be convicted by the Holy Spirit.

The idea that, because of TV, people could not follow logical argument, was to him simply not true. Furthermore, he believed that it was wrong to preach a different Gospel depending on one's audience – which was why he preached in a language that could be understood by all. All were sinners in need of the same message. The minister did not need to know the needs of individuals in his congregation when preaching because it was sin itself that was the problem, and not specific sins.

He always pointed, Harrison has written, to the glory of God, the living God who intervened in human affairs. He would confront his listeners with this – not often a 'comfortable experience' for those in the pew. When he proclaimed the Gospel of salvation, it was with the firm and sure belief that it was the only solution. He 'reasoned with men as he preached', making them think hard as he argued in 'big, bold, logical steps that were so compelling in their presentation of the truth'. He was always diagnostic – as John Stott has said, he 'combined the analytical prowess of a scientifically trained mind with the passion of a Welshman', which is yet another way of saying that his preaching was 'logic on fire'.

He was pastoral on Sunday mornings and evangelistic in the evenings. He had a ministry that was prophetic in its breadth, and authoritative in its presentation. In his sombre Geneva gown, he would amaze visiting Americans by his seriousness and lack of gimmicks. He never made jokes in the pulpit (although privately he had an enormous sense of humour) and one of his first acts on becoming sole minister was to scrap the choir. Yet when his long prayer began, everyone felt the whole atmosphere change. As one American visitor, Eric Fife, later wrote, the Doctor was simply the 'greatest preacher this century'.

To Martyn Lloyd-Jones, preachers were born and not made. To that extent, the main secret of his success is that it was from God, in whose sovereignty he believed very deeply. But in human terms it could partly be said to be the unique degree of authority that his preaching possessed, not just in its presentation, or because of any particular physical characteristics, but because he was able, in what he said, and the serious way in which he said it, to convey a sense of the majesty of God that made people sit up and listen. He himself often said that he could forgive poor sermons if the preacher gave him a sense of the presence of God.

He really believed what he preached, and in its urgency. He was relevant and up-to-date, but never trendy. He disliked the fashion of preaching from topics, preferring to stick to systematic exposition instead. But he knew about, and was able to refer to, all the important current trends, not in order to show off his learning (he always disliked ministers who did so) but in order to show the folly of contemporary thought so that the need of his listeners for the Gospel would become plainer to them.

His reading, both spiritual and secular, was enormous.

His daughter Elizabeth often remembers her father, fully clothed (including waistcoat, socks and hat), sitting on the beach, reading what seemed to be a library of books. Ministers, he felt, should be fully aware of what was going on around them, yet without being influenced by the spirit of the age.

He was opposed to pressure, emotional or otherwise, being put on his hearers. This was why he never made 'altar calls' at the end of his evangelistic sermons. To him, it was wrong to put pressure on the will. Conviction, brought about not by human manipulation (he had an especial dislike of certain kinds of emotive music) but by the convicting power of the Holy Spirit, came first to the mind, and never to the emotions, and then to the will. As he said, in preaching, a minister was 'to present the truth, and, clearly, this is something first and foremost for the mind'.

On the other hand, although he always used reason and logic in his sermons, he felt that no one could ever be reasoned into the Kingdom. All had first to be humbled, and to come to see that they were sinners in urgent need of salvation. He never sought to make the Gospel attractive, but many were converted through his preaching of it week after week. Nor did he ever 'go for decisions'; rather he urged people to repent and turn to Christ as their only hope. In human terms he did none of the things thought so necessary to win people today. There was no excitement, no rock music, no trendy language – only the preaching of the Word by a serious man in a sombre Geneva gown. Yet above all he believed in the power of the Holy Spirit. Freedom in the Spirit when preaching was to him the key. It could be described as the secret of his success.

The Congregation
All these different factors – logic and emotion, relevance and Biblical-centredness, reason and urgency – drew to him one of the most varied congregations that London has probably ever seen. There was not only a cross-section of ability and social class, but also of country and race. The fact that

people from such a wide background came to hear him, Sunday after Sunday, year after year, shows that his preaching could be understood by everybody.

Many of the congregation were from abroad. The Chinese Church in London, for example, used to come en masse every Sunday morning. Many former international students went on to hold key positions in their own countries and elsewhere, and include an African head of state and Gottfried Osei-Mensah, now general secretary of the Commission for World Evangelisation. What these students especially valued was the fact that the Doctor, unlike many of his contemporaries, treated them on a level of complete equality with everyone else. As a patriotic Welshman (who always spoke in Welsh to his wife and daughters at home), he fully understood – and shared – the feelings of those who felt dominated by Anglo-Saxon culture. They, in return, had a deep reverence and affection for him that lasted all his life.

He rejected the paternalist approach so often shown by whites to those of different skin colours, and while this utter lack of racial consciousness partly showed itself in his pioneering work in IFES, it was also a mark of his internationally-reaching ministry in Westminster Chapel, and in the preaching success he had in other countries. (His family, in their travels, have often met Christians in other countries who recalled the Doctor's exact words many years after the visit.) His appeal to Christians of so many different places is especially interesting as, consistent with his policy of treating everyone the same, he made no special effort to attract them to the Chapel. As with all the wide variety of groups that came, they attended because he had a message that they wanted to hear.

In the rest of the congregation there were civil servants and tramps, professors and the simple-minded, students and labourers, young and old. He would see anyone who needed to speak to him in his vestry after the service. As Ray Gaydon, a former East End 'rocker' who under the Doctor's ministry became first a schoolteacher, then a minister himself, has said, the Doctor could be a 'lion in the pulpit and a lamb in the vestry'. (In this side of his work, Dr Lloyd-Jones found his medical training to be especially useful because, in talking to people who thought they were suffering from spiritual ills, he was often able to diagnose that they had physical caused illnesses.) He was also probably the only preacher in London who had more men in his congregation than women.

For many years in the Church Hall every Friday night he held discussions on practical Christian living, in which he would use the same Socratic method he had employed in Aberavon. But in 1953 so many people came that he decided to move into the main church building and to preach instead. He began with a series on Christian doctrine. But increasingly he felt that doctrine should arise out of an exposition of a whole book and that if he preached on one from start to finish his congregation would learn all that was important to know. So he began his famous series on Romans, to go alongside the series on Ephesians that he was preaching on Sunday mornings. Both these series were turned into books after his retirement and have reached a new congregation of hundreds of thousands all over the world, who could never have hoped to have heard them at Westminster Chapel.

He was able to sustain a sermon, or indeed whole group of sermons, on just one verse. He could do so because he always stuck to the main point and refrained from using Scripture as a hobby horse for pet theories of his own. Sadly, as a good Free Church colleague has said, few have been able to avoid such a temptation in trying to emulate his method. Many of his wiser followers today, knowing their own limitations, have preferred instead to preach on passages or chapters, and thus have kept away from the tendency to meander far from the text.

The Student world – at home

A large part of the Chapel's congregation were students and recent graduates, among them the past and present general secretaries of the UCCF (the old IVF), Oliver Barclay and Robin Wells, both of whom enjoyed a good relationship with the Doctor. While he would never preach specially for students, he had a lasting impact on the thinking and general spiritual outlook of many generations of them over the years.

First, as Oliver Barclay has written, he taught them to 'value and love doctrine', by making it powerful and alive. Next he showed them, especially the theological students, how to be unafraid to stand on Biblical truth by ridding them of their inferiority complexes. He gave them a boldness in the face of attack that was not worldly but was firmly rooted in Scripture. Lastly he taught them to bring everything under Scriptural authority, and to 'see human knowledge in its place under the revelation of God'. People (and not just students) were encouraged to reason, and to do so from a Scriptural base.

Dr Lloyd-Jones also applied these principles to the student world at large. He served for many years as the chairman of the IVF's advisory committee on doctrine and policy. He was a regular conference speaker, moulding the way in which the movement thought and acted. Many of the students who attended such conferences went on to hold important positions in British Evangelical life, or to lead secular careers where they were able to put into practice the Biblical principles they had learned from him. Often, it was not so much a particular talk that helped, but the fact that they could now reason Scripturally for themselves.

The Doctor also conducted several university missions, but never felt at home on these. He preferred instead to preach the Gospel Sunday by Sunday in the Chapel and although he never made allowances for them, he knew that many students were converted as a result of the sermons they heard preached there. He did, however, enjoy the pastoral side of student conferences at which the young people would gather around him to listen to his advice.

. . . and abroad – the vision of IFES

When war ended in 1945, those who had met in Cambridge in 1939 were able to get together again and start the International Fellowship of Evangelical Students – the IFES.

Stacey Woods, its general secretary for the first twenty-five years (and also general director of IVCF USA for many years) wrote:

> No history of the IFES would be complete without some account of its first chairman, Dr Martyn Lloyd-Jones . . . He did more to lay a solid Biblical foundation than anyone else . . . His influence and leadership in the growing international movement was great. From his busy life, not only was he always available as an occasional speaker to students, but always for counsel to the General Secretary. He freely gave several days each year to the Executive Committee and longer periods to the General Committee

which student delegates attended every three to four years. He also went to several of the IFES Conferences. He had, Woods recalled,

> great skill as a chairman, patience so long as the speaker dealt with the matter in hand, but insistent that time was not wasted with irrelevant gabble. He loved keen debate, liked to be challenged, but woe betide the opponent who entered into the lists of debate with him unprepared but full of self-confidence . . . In spite of that keen, incisive mind, our chairman was a leader in Committee, not director or dictator.

One of the main features of his chairmanship, which he held from 1947 to 1959, was the way that he would insist that the evening before the executive meeting, all the members would get together not to discuss business, but to pray and to talk over important theological issues in order to put themselves in the right spiritual frame of mind for the next day. As Stacey Woods wrote, 'decisions and questions on the following day seemed clearer, answers more obvious, as a result of the stimulus and enlightened conversation of the previous evening' under the Doctor's guidance.

Dr Lloyd-Jones was asked by the IFES to draw up their

basis of faith and action. The executive committee thanked him for the 'able, patient and very clear manner' in which he did so – another example of his medical mind at work. He made the aims of IFES plain from the start. These were first to foster 'Christian fellowship and helpful association between existing' National Evangelical unions (NEUs). Second, that 'there was a great missionary evangelistic work to be done in the many countries where there are as yet no NEUs and in other countries were NEUs are weak and need help'. Then came the statement which for those days was quite revolutionary and shows how deep a vision for the future of Evangelicalism that he had. 'The task of IFES is to initiate and to help establish National Evangelical Unions that are to be autonomous, and, once they are established, withdraw from any direct action except at the request of the said National Committee when some aid or co-operation in some new activity were asked.'

This was still the age in which Western missionaries dominated the Christian lives of Third World countries, many of which were still under colonial rule. But the Doctor had powerful memories of how the English had oppressed his people in the recent past – his own father's generation included. He had a strong sense of how the African and Asian Christians felt. He therefore insisted that national Christians in each country should take over the leadership of their national movements as soon as possible.

This has been a firm IFES rule ever since and is one of the features that makes it unique among the major Christian organisations in the world today. It is now largely led by Christians from the Third World. It was thanks to the Doctor's deeply held beliefs that IFES was thus distinctive from the beginning and has been highly successful in the developing world in a post-colonial era, where European and American dominated missionary movements have often failed.

One of the other distinguishing features of IFES is that it represented a coming together of conservative Evangelicals from many different denominational backgrounds. Some, like the Scandinavian Lutherans and British Anglicans, were

from state churches, others, such as the Doctor himself,
from Free Church backgrounds. But what separated them
was nothing like as important as what bound them together –
a common love for the Lord Jesus Christ in their shared new
birth in him, and a desire that the spiritually lost would hear
his Gospel, the only hope of salvation. While denominational
differences were never minimised, they were subordinated
to the greater purpose of true, Biblical unity among all
Evangelicals despite disagreements on lesser matters.

One of the reasons for this unity between Evangelicals in
different kinds of denomination was the solid doctrinal stand
of IFES itself. This position was in no small way due to Dr
Lloyd-Jones himself, and was why he remained totally loyal
to it and all it represented for the rest of his life. The basis
of faith, which he wrote, and a separate statement on IFES
clear doctrinal distinctiveness, are, along with his address to
the IVF in 1952 (published as *Maintaining the Evangelical
Faith Today*), the best guides to his personal doctrinal position.

He was, he told the IVF, 'by nature a pacific person', but
one who felt obliged to be controversial because of the
growing challenge of the Ecumenical movement, especially
that of the World Council of Churches. Evangelicals now
had to defend their position more than ever before, not out
of party spirit (he always opposed such a mentality) but
because the Bible gave them no alternative. Christians had
to be quite clear as to who Christ was and why He had come.
They had no need to fear being called intolerant, since so
had men like Martin Luther been before them.

God demanded faith in Himself, and obedience, and such
a stand made compromise impossible. Biblical unity, as
plainly shown in Acts and in the Epistles, was always on
the basis of 'doctrine and fellowship', centred on Christ.
Evangelicals should therefore separate themselves from those
who 'preach another Gospel'. But they should only split on
matters 'absolutely essential' to the truth, not on issues
such as baptism or the millennium. They should also watch
carefully what men did not say, as all real Christians were
bound to preach certain things sooner or later. The Evangeli-

cal faith was not a new one but the historical Biblical position, one on which all Evangelicals ought to be abundantly clear themselves.

The IFES statement added a paragraph on the Evangelical view of the true Church. The last fifteen years of the Doctor's life were to be taken up with this issue, and it was one which caused immense controversy among fellow Evangelical believers. His views on the subject went back considerably beyond 1966, however, and they appear strongly in the IFES statement. As will be seen, it was not so much his views that were later to change, but the method of putting them into practice and their relative importance in relation to other issues. The memorandum read:

> The Church of Christ consists of all those who in all ages have been or are in vital relationship with our Lord Jesus Christ as a result of the 'new birth'. The New Testament itself recognises only two aspects of the Church: (i) the whole company of believers in heaven and on earth; and (ii) the local manifestation which is the gathering in fellowship of all who are in Christ and, in the midst of whom, according to his promises, Christ is present, who is the only Lord and Head of the Church.

This meant that the Church consisted of all true Christians regardless of denomination – the only two categories recognised were individual believers and local churches consisting of those same individual believers in that particular area. The unity that mattered was the unity of the Gospel, which brought together those whose lives the Holy Spirit had changed on their hearing it, and who now wished to proclaim it in His strength to others. Such unity knew no human barriers. IFES was therefore composed of state and Free Church Christians alike, but who came together as Evangelicals first and last.

However, the logic of the position held by those in denominations that contained non-Evangelicals, such as the Lutheran and Anglican Churches, soon became, by implication, quite untenable. If, as the IFES paper made clear, the true

Church was the fellowship of all those who were born again, what then were the Anglicans, Lutherans and others doing in denominations with people who denied the very tenets of the faith?

The immense strength of the Doctor's position at this time was that although he made his views abundantly clear, he did so in a very positive way. This was the principle he had enunciated to T. T. Shields in Canada all those years before. 'Preach the Gospel to people positively and win them' – the physician's not the surgeon's approach. So throughout his chairmanship of IFES he worked with those of his fellow Evangelicals whose Gospel he shared but whose decision to remain within doctrinally-mixed denominations he felt was clearly inconsistent with their Evangelical faith. True unity mattered more. Further, by being positive rather than negative, he was able to exercise a far wider and deeper influence than he would have been able to had he adopted a more negative, antagonistic attitude. As it was, he stayed in fellowship and active partnership with them, and was able to steer IFES firmly on to the doctrinal path in which he felt it ought to go.

Another of his beliefs that made a major impression on IFES during his long chairmanship of it was his resolute conviction that it was essential to trust totally in the power of the Holy Spirit. The role of IFES, he taught them, was to be both faithful and prophetic in their own generation. God was sovereign, and it was only by trusting on His Spirit and His Word, the Bible, that the IFES would bear fruit.

He therefore rejected all five and ten-year plans and all the long-term planning goals that were put forward, especially those by certain Western nations. If, he argued, the IFES was walking in the Spirit, and remained true to Scripture, God could spring surprises on them for which they would be ready, but not if they had committed themselves to a plan that bound them for years ahead. (It was the same principle that always made him reluctant to announce sermon titles for the week ahead, in case the Spirit led him to preach on something else from the text instead.)

In 1959 he retired as chairman and was elected to serve

as president, which he did until 1967, then becoming vice-president, a post he was pleased to hold for the rest of his life. The executive committee in 1959, 'conscious of its privilege of association with Dr Lloyd-Jones during the last 12 years' and of the 'leadership, counsel and inspiration he had given to IFES', unanimously passed a motion stating that it wished to 'express its thanks and appreciation to him and to his wife for the unstinting giving of themselves to this work', and to him for 'his leadership not only in the Committee as chairman but more particularly for his spiritual leadership and direction in the work as a whole'.

Not only was he to be president, but he was asked by the executive to find time to 'be with us and address us at each General Committee meeting and whenever possible to be present at future meetings of the Executive Committee. We would also assure him', the committee continued, 'that we feel the need of his continued leadership and counsel in the work and therefore in no sense do we regard him as having retired from IFES'. This turned out to be true. He never lost his deep love for and enormous interest in all that IFES did and stood for until his death.

In 1971 he attended and spoke at the twenty-fifth anniversary meeting (and general committee) of IFES, and retained close personal links with many of the staff, including Stacey Woods, and Chua Wee-hian, Woods' successor as general secretary. His establishment of the organisation on firm doctrinal grounds kept it loyal to the faith in stormy theological times.

IFES – the positive unity of Evangelicals across the denominational barriers on the basis of the Gospel of salvation in Jesus Christ – was what the Doctor represented. It was a Biblical emphasis that brought people together on the one essential, and sought, within the Evangelical family, to win people of differing viewpoints to a Scriptural outlook, not by hectoring or denouncing them, but by showing them the Way by example and reasoned debate among brothers and sisters in the Lord. It was this attitude that explains the immense and beneficial influence for the truth that the Doctor was able to have, and which had such an effect in countries throughout the world. The IFES was his vision under God as to what could be done to reach the lost across the nations in his generation and it will serve as a fitting memorial to all that he fought for and believed in.

The 'Fraternal'

Dr Lloyd-Jones was also involved in groups at home in Britain. The first, and the one for which he would most want to be remembered (even more, he said, than for being minister of Westminster Chapel) was the Westminster Ministers' Fraternal, which he chaired for forty years. As his closest collaborator and right-hand man in this work for thirty-eight of those years, John Caiger, has said, the Doctor was the pastor's pastor. Dr Lloyd-Jones himself described his membership of the Fraternal as 'one of the greatest privileges of my life'.

It was set up in 1941, originally just as a study group, at the request of Douglas Johnson of IVF. But by 1943 it had become a much wider body of ministers who met monthly on Tuesdays in Westminster Chapel for lunch. By 1954 it had expanded to meeting for the whole of one Monday a month, averaging 200 ministers a meeting in the 1950s and climbing to 400 in the 1960s. It was essentially a pastors' fellowship and, for its first twenty-five years, was open to Evangelicals of all denominations, doctrinally mixed and pure alike. Any minister could raise an urgent matter, always in the strictest confidence. The Doctor, with his incisive, diagnostic mind, would help them sort out their problems, and clarify any unclear matters of doctrine.

He regarded these men very much as his flock, and several of them became like the sons he never had. Many of their families were also to become close to him, especially after his retirement from Westminster Chapel in 1968, when he was free to go and preach in their churches. (In one family he was the only visiting minister for whom the little girl never made an apple pie bed. The Doctor, with two daughters, and then six grandchildren, of his own, was always natural and at ease with children and they with him.)

The Puritan Conference

He was also involved at an early age with what has been called the Puritan Conference (since 1966 the Westminster Conference). It enabled him to bring out his conviction of two things: the importance and relevance of history to present-day Evangelicals, and that of Reformed, Puritan thought in particular. He would deliver the final paper, based on solid historical research, every year. He felt that Christians should never forget their Protestant doctrinal foundations and the Puritan era, in which the theological implications of the Reformation had been fully worked out, above all.

What was especially important, he felt, about the Puritans was the way in which they combined sound doctrine with a sense of the reality of life. To them, truth was not just something grasped with the head, but experienced in everyday life – 'experimentally' as they described it. This combination, truth on fire, naturally attracted the doctor, who aimed at producing such a synthesis himself.

But his main reason for supporting the Puritans (as with his great love of the eighteenth-century revival) was not because he felt they were right in and of themselves, but because he considered their teaching to be true to Scripture. It was the Bible, and what *it* taught that really mattered. Even if someone could prove that Calvin or the Puritans had taken a particular line on an issue, his reply would be: What did Scripture teach? What made the Puritans so important was the way in which they made the eternal truths of Scripture come alive in their own generation, as he tried to make those same, unchanging, truths live in his.

His great strength was that he made Puritan, Reformed, doctrine relevant to the twentieth century, and in a thoroughly straightforward, contemporary language that everyone listening could understand. He always despaired of those of his followers who, helped by the Puritans to see the application of Scripture to everyday life, insisted on preaching these insights to their congregations in exactly the same seventeenth-century language in which the Puritans had written. It was not the language that mattered, but the message.

Many young ministers and others were influenced by the renaissance of Puritan theology fostered by Martyn Lloyd-Jones. As his son-in-law Fred Catherwood has written, he 'established a tough theological position in the face of the rise of situational ethics and the general repudiation of authority by the clerical establishment in the fifties and sixties'. To start with, the Conference was open to Evangelicals of all denominations, and one of the doctor's chief early assistants was the young Anglican theologian, J. I. Packer, who had been a contemporary of his elder daughter at Oxford.

Connected with the revival of Puritan theology was the foundation of the Banner of Truth publishing house by his personal assistant and subsequent lifelong close associate, Iain Murray. The Banner's aim was to republish many of the great Reformed texts, and solid doctrinal material generally. Dr Lloyd-Jones warmly supported the enterprise from the beginning, and gave them many of his own books to publish, notably his series on Romans and Ephesians. The Banner's publications influenced a whole generation of ministers and theologians. As Dick France, the Anglican New Testament scholar, has commented on his own contemporaries, 'We were all Banner men'. Through the Banner, the doctor's books were to reach Evangelicals across the world, from Nigeria and the USA to many other nations.

The Welsh movement

Dr Lloyd-Jones was also involved in a remarkable moving of the Spirit that took place among many young students in Wales in the late 1940s. He had kept a keen interest in his native country, and so became very active in doing all possible as a spiritual adviser and encourager to these men. Eventually an interdenominational body, the Evangelical Movement of Wales was set up, one that always had an especially warm place in his affection. Many in it saw him as a spiritual father-figure, and they stayed particularly close and loyal to him in his doctrinal thinking. One of the young

Welshmen, J. Glyn Owen, later became his successor as minister at Westminster Chapel (before moving on to Knox Presbyterian Church in Toronto, Canada).

It was no coincidence that Martyn Lloyd-Jones's funeral service in 1981 was taken in Wales by Hywel Jones, Graham Harrison, Omri Jenkins, Elwyn Davies and Vernon Higham, all men deeply involved with the Evangelical Movement of Wales. They had not been converted through him, but they had all received their solid doctrinal base through him. They felt, one has recalled, that life and doctrine went together, and in its simultaneous emphasis on both knowing the truth and experiencing it, the EMOW had the kind of doctrine that was especially close to the doctor's heart.

1966: Crossing the Rubicon

By 1966 his thinking on the doctrine of the Church, while essentially unaltered, underwent a change of emphasis. As seen earlier, he had long been of the view that true Evangelicals could not really remain loyal to their Evangelical position and at the same time be in the same denomination with those who openly denied the basic tenets of the faith. The standing of such Evangelicals was, to him, utterly illogical. But for forty out of what turned out to be a total of fifty-five years of his ministry, he had adopted a positive approach to such people, hoping to win them by argument and example, and by keeping in close fellowship with them in groups such as the IFES, IVF and so on. Many of his closest friends were in doctrinally mixed organisations, including his own brother-in-law, Ieuan Phillips, who was for a year moderator of a mixed denomination, the Presbyterian Church of Wales.

But in 1966 he decided that such was the menace to true Evangelical faith posed by movements such as the World Council of Churches that Evangelicals could not in good conscience remain in denominations affiliated to the WCC. He therefore chose to use the opportunity of a talk he had been asked to give to the National Evangelical Assembly in Westminster Central Hall on October 18th, 1966 clearly to declare his new position. He thus created a storm that has continued in Evangelical circles in England ever since.

The organisers, the Evangelical Alliance, knew that he was bound to be controversial, and asked the chairman, the leading Evangelical Anglican, John Stott, to say a few words. They had no idea how explosive the Doctor intended to be, as he made it clear from the start of his speech that Evangelicals should face up to the issues raised by the Biblical doctrine of the Church. Too often, it seemed to the Doctor, they appeared 'more concerned to maintain the integrity of their denominations than anyone else'. The growing power and influence of the Ecumenical movement made the matter more vital than ever before.

There were now two urgent issues. First, were Evangelicals prepared to be no more than a wing of their own denominations? Second, what exactly was the true Christian Church? Evangelicals, he stated, 'rightly put doctrine before fellowship'. The Church was made up of the saints, and for true Christians to insist on staying in different denominations was to be guilty of the sin of schism. The need for the 'ancient witness' as shown by the Protestant Reformers, had never been stronger. Only by standing together could Evangelicals expect the Holy Spirit to send them revival.

There would be difficulties to face for those in doctrinally mixed denominations who pulled out and joined their fellow Evangelicals outside. But Christians, the faithful remnant, had never had to fear, as the Bible clearly showed. Evangelical Christians should 'rise to the occasion and listen to the call of God'. If they had one objective only, namely the glory of God, they would be 'led by the Spirit to the true answer', which was to pull out of the denominations in which many of them still remained.

John Stott, whose views are given in an earlier chapter, became seriously alarmed that many young Evangelicals in mixed denominations, such as the Church of England, would suddenly pull out that night, on the spur of the moment. So, in his own description of the event, he thanked the Doctor for his talk, and added, 'with much nervousness and diffidence', that Dr Lloyd-Jones's view of the remnant had 'both history and Scripture against him'. The intensity of his emotion created a highly charged atmosphere in the hall for which Stott later apologised to the Doctor. Unfortunately neither this, nor the kindness he showed to Mrs Lloyd-Jones during her husband's illness two years later, became publicly known.

As John Stott has written, both he and the Doctor 'continued to have a warm personal relationship'. But the general debate caused much dissension. Many who had been close to the Doctor for a long time, such as J. I. Packer, felt that Dr Lloyd-Jones, by making the Church issue the most important one, had removed himself from being able to influence the whole of English Evangelicalism, to become the leader of a particular group within it.

Certainly, the Doctor separated himself from much of what was now going on and was, in turn, ignored by many of the younger Anglican Evangelicals. (Older ones, such as Dick Lucas, regarded him as a father-figure as affectionately as ever.) But he maintained that it was he who was following the Word of God, and that misunderstanding and misrepresentation was what the faithful remnant had always had to suffer. While some Anglican Evangelicals missed him deeply, there were others, such as Herbert Carson, who had already left the Church of England and become his assistant at the Chapel, who supported his views. He gave especial care to those who suffered as a result of their decision to follow him, as was shown by the unstinting support he gave to Vernon Higham in Cardiff who had come out of the Presbyterian Church of Wales. This particular case shows that it was not solely the Anglican Church he urged people to leave, as is often supposed, but *all* denominations that belonged to the WCC.

He also always emphasised the positive side to his position, and many felt that he was done a severe disservice by the harshness and unforgiving and unloving negative attitude shown by some of his followers. As a leading Third World Christian who worked particularly closely with him for many years has said, the 'Lloyd-Jonesites', by attributing their own hard prejudices to him did him harm, most unfairly, because not only did he frequently not believe what they thought and claimed he did, but also when they proclaimed his opinions, they did so without any of the love and concern for the glory of God that was at the centre of everything that he preached.

To him, he was asking his fellow Evangelicals to pull out in order to come in, into the Church made up of true believers. When he and a few close associates drew up a private memorandum stating their position, they made it very clear that they recognised that 'all conservative Evangelicals do not see eye to eye with us over the issues' and that it was perfectly possible to be a true Christian while remaining in a doctrinally mixed denomination. The Doctor would never accuse someone who disagreed with him on this issue of ceasing to be an Evangelical – even though he would vigorously assert that that particular Evangelical's position on the Church question was quite mistaken.

He kept several Anglicans as close personal friends. One of them, Professor Philip Edgcumbe Hughes, the theologian, was, he told his family, completely at one with his way of theological thinking. Another very dear friend was John Gwyn Thomas, Herbert Carson's successor as vicar of St Paul's in Cambridge. As John Stott has written, the Doctor 'always distinguished between principles and personalities'.

Dr Lloyd-Jones knew that his grouping would not stay pure for ever, but he felt that each man had to do what was right in his own generation. He strongly opposed any faction fighting and empire building among his followers. When he removed Westminster Chapel from the newly formed United Reformed Church, he insisted against some opposition that they join their brethren in the Fellowship of Independent Evangelical Churches (FIEC), instead of trying to form a group of their own. Passionately though he held his beliefs, it was always in a spirit of humble obedience to God, and not out of any concern for human glory.

The strength of his beliefs can be seen in the address he gave to over 3,000 people in 1967 in Westminster Chapel to commemorate the 450th anniversary of Luther's nailing of the 95 Theses, the event which marked the start of the Reformation. He had become extremely worried, he told them, by the trend of the Ecumenical movement towards reunion with Rome. He often enjoyed reading individual Catholic authors, including charismatic priests. But for the Roman Catholic Church herself, there could be 'no compromise' between her and Evangelicals.

He was concerned, too, at many of the statements made that year at the Evangelical Anglican Conference at Keele. It was, he felt, 'impossible' for an Evangelical 'to be yoked together with others in the Church who deny the very elements of Christian faith'. Evangelicals who remained in mixed denominations were, he said, 'virtually saying that though you think you are right, they may also be right', in their doctrine and interpretation of Scripture. 'That,' he asserted, 'is a denial of the Evangelical, the only true faith'. The idea put forward by Stott, Packer and other Evangelical Anglicans (whose views will be looked at in the relevant chapters) that Evangelicals could, by staying in mixed denominations, reform them and make them truly Evangelical again, was to him 'midsummer madness'.

As he said in the private memorandum quoted earlier, there was 'no hope whatsoever' of such internal reforms taking place or being successful. For him, there was only one option for Evangelicals, and that was to heed Revelation 18 verse 4: 'Come out of her my people!' He urged them to 'come into fellowship with all like-minded Christian people', to join, in the private memorandum's words, 'together on an uncompromising Gospel basis' with those whose 'first loyalty' was to the 'conservative Evangelical faith, rather than to any inherited traditional position'.

Many heeded the call and followed him in taking their churches into groups such as the FIEC. Not many Anglicans followed him, however. The Ministers' Fraternal and the Puritan Conference were also reformed to accept only those who took his position – though as he said, the reason for this, which must be underlined, was to prevent endless internal bickering on the subject, and not to impose any kind of dictatorial uniformity.

His vision of a united Evangelical Church, with the Gospel of Jesus Christ at its centre, was a great and glorious one.

To him the division of Evangelicals into different groups was tragic. While he recognised that Evangelicals would continue to disagree on less important issues such as baptism, types of church government, the gifts of the Spirit, and so on, he felt that they should all come together on the Gospel that bound them together under Christ's headship.

The trouble was that although his vision was a positive one, it came over to many Evangelicals in the mixed denominations as negative. To him it was a move towards Biblical unity, to them he was asking Christians to leave groupings to which they had formed a strong personal attachment, and to abandon what they felt to be an Evangelical voice and influence for the good in their particular denomination. As a result, because of the different ways of looking at the same problem – the existence side by side in the same group of Evangelicals and of those who disclaimed many of the very bases of Biblical faith – much misunderstanding arose between the Doctor and those who chose to stay within. He could not understand how they failed to see the Biblical logic of his appeal; they could not fathom how he, who had worked so closely with his fellow Evangelicals in the mixed denominations for over forty years, was now seemingly going back on all he had stood for during that time.

Many Evangelicals in the Free Church mixed denominations did heed his call – former Baptist Union or English Presbyterian churches pulled out and joined the Fellowship of Independent Evangelical Churches. Some of those closest to him in the last years of his life were those he helped through the terrible transition period between withdrawing from one denomination and finding renewed fellowship and support in another. (One minister used to phone him every Sunday – the Doctor's grandchildren used to fetch him to the telephone to speak to this minister before picking the receiver up to answer the call.)

One large group failed to heed his call, however – the Anglicans. Very few responded. Some Anglican Evangelicals – such as John Stott and Jim Packer, whose views are examined elsewhere – had deeply-held theological reasons for remaining within. For others, their grounds were possibly more pragmatic – people in England would be more likely to speak to the local vicar on the doorstep, or visit the parish church, than talk to the near-by Baptist minister.

As Don Carson, the Canadian theologian, has pointed out, it could be that the Doctor's strong Welshness prevented him from seeing the powerful attachment the idea of the English national church had for many English Anglican Evangelicals. In Wales, especially the rural Wales in which the Doctor had spent so much of his childhood, the Anglican vicar was a strange, alien creature. His own father had taken part in the national struggle of Welshmen against the legal imposition that compelled them to pay tithes to the Church of England's offshoot, the rather misnamed Church of Wales. (Ironically – a fact about which some of us in the family used to tease him – Martyn Lloyd-Jones's cousin by marriage was the late Glyn Simon: Archbishop of Wales for the investiture of Prince Charles!) The idea of a state church, natural to the English, was thus quite foreign to him. For the Doctor, as indeed for many Welshmen or Free Church Englishmen, the Church was built on doctrine alone – and tradition, or national affection, were unimportant.

The problem arose, as years went by, that Martyn Lloyd-Jones thereby acquired an unfortunate, negative, image in the eyes of many. He was the man who was 'against the Anglicans'. Many younger Anglican Evangelicals often did not know who he was. He preached to the Christian Union at Oxford during my time as a student there. Those students from Free Church homes all knew who he was. Those with Anglican backgrounds had either dimly heard of him or, as in one case, thought he was a famous preacher of the nineteenth century! Some of this group went up to me after his sermon and said, 'Christopher, your grandfather wasn't at all bad' – probably the one and only time that Martyn Lloyd-Jones was known for being the grandfather of Christopher Catherwood . . .

The tragedy of the split, some of those closest to him felt, was that Evangelicalism in Britain was divided over what was essentially an ecclesiastical issue at the very time when Evangelical unity became vitally important in the face of the attack on Scripture, and of the infiltration of neo-orthodox views into Evangelicalism at large. Someone who sympathised greatly with the Doctor at this time was Francis Schaeffer, who had known him since the 1940s, and who had invited him to Switzerland to conduct the marriage of his eldest daughter. (During the Lloyd-Jones's visit to L'Abri, in 1957, the Doctor found in Schaeffer a kindred spirit – someone who, like himself, thoroughly enjoyed a good, meaty, discussion till the early hours of the morning.)

Schaeffer had, as will be seen in more detail later, come out of a mixed denomination as long ago as the 1930s. The prevailing view of their churches had turned against the Gospel, so Schaeffer followed Gresham Machen and split off to form the Bible Presbyterian Church, a wholly Evangelical group of the sort that the Doctor advocated after 1966. The purity of the visible church decreed that those who truly believed the Bible could not stay in the same denomination as those who denied the very basis of the faith.

At the same time, Schaeffer noted, those who pulled out often developed a very bitter, harsh attitude towards those of their fellow Evangelicals who remained within. He regretted this – for while he could not understand their position, he felt it was not for him to dictate to them what the Holy Spirit alone should do. If those who stayed out became bitter, however, he noted that those who stayed in often had to draw the line beyond which they would not compromise ever wider and wider if they wanted to continue as members of a mixed denomination.

So the purity of the visible church decreed that Evangelicals should not unite with those who did not proclaim the Gospel. But the love that all true Christians should show one another, and the unity of the visible church, equally decreed that all Evangelicals should continue to love one another in the Lord and to enjoy fellowship together. What united them was the Gospel, and as long as unity on this remained, it would be wrong for Evangelicals to refuse to have fellowship with one another. It was no help to the cause of the Gospel if all outsiders saw of Evangelicals was a group of people endlessly bickering publicly with one another. If,

however, Schaeffer felt, an Evangelical was asked to share
a platform with a non-Evangelical on a spiritual issue –
someone with whom Gospel unity did not therefore exist –
then the Evangelical should refuse.

For what mattered above all else was the defence of the
Gospel itself. While many Evangelicals deeply sympathised
with the Doctor's position, they felt that to make ecclesiastical issues the priority – however understandable the motive
might be – was a mistake. What mattered was the continuing
defence of the Gospel against attacks from outside. The
doctrine of Scripture, vital to the whole Evangelical position,
was under assault. Some Evangelicals, they noted, were
ceasing, albeit often unwittingly, to hold fast to the stand
that Evangelicalism had taken ever since the Reformation,
and which the Bible itself took. If, however, those defending
the Evangelical faith also, at the same time, refused to have
fellowship with the erring Evangelicals who most needed
guidance, not because of their views on Scripture, but
because of the unrelated issue of their denominational
membership, then the defence of Scripture and the
struggle to maintain Evangelical unity would be all the
more difficult.

Martyn Lloyd-Jones did however recognise (unlike a minority of his followers) that many of those who stayed within
were still conservative Evangelicals – as he made clear in the
memorandum quoted earlier in this chapter. He also opposed
any harshness of spirit – the issue was principles, not
people – and continued active in the IFES. He spoke at the
twenty-fifth anniversary conference in Mittersill in 1971 and
served as a vice-president until his death, maintaining a keen
interest in all it did. This was despite the fact that it contained
many Evangelicals in mixed denominations, such as Anglicans and Lutherans. So while many Evangelicals had cause
to regret the fact that the Doctor was not with them side by
side in many of the theological struggles of the late sixties
and the seventies, because of his separatist stand, they knew
that he had not abandoned the wholly positive attitude to
Evangelical unity for which he had fought so passionately
for over forty years.

New Horizons

Despite his loss of influence in some quarters, his reputation grew in others. The first increase was through his books which, as seen earlier, now started to reach people across the world. Their simplicity and directness (they were mainly edited editions of his sermons), while often a hard task for the literary editors, appealed to the widest range of readership and not just to the more academic, for whom reading was a normal activity. The Doctor and, after his death, his widow, received countless letters from ordinary Christians in out-of-the-way places in Britain, the USA and further afield, all thanking him for the way in which his books had, under God, transformed their lives.

The second reason why his influence increased is that a change of emphasis in his thinking brought him a new audience. In his sermons on Ephesians, he had stressed the need for Christians to know the sealing or 'baptism' of the Holy Spirit in their own experience. He had himself, after the war, been responsible for the revival in Reformed, Calvinist theology, especially in Biblical systematic form. He never ceased to stress the need for sound doctrine, and kept a passionate belief in the Sovereignty of God in salvation to the end, but he became increasingly anxious lest this growth in Reformed theology turn into an 'arid doctrinaire hardness' separated from life and experience.

He felt that although Christians received the Spirit on conversion, they did not usually have it in its fullness, and needed a greater measure following and quite distinct from conversion. He never taught that any particular gift came with baptism of the Spirit – he never believed that the gift of tongues was compulsory or an automatically expected part of baptism of the Spirit – but preached, especially towards the end of his life, that what was needed above all else was a revival and a mighty outpouring of the Spirit of God: a 'baptism of fire'.

At the same time he refused to be labelled as either, as one Pentecostal minister wrote of him, a 'compromising Charismatic or a cold-eyed Calvinist'. He told a group of ministers involved in the Renewal movement that 'subjective experience should not precede objective truth'. While he opposed quenching the Spirit, he 'insisted that everything must be decided by Scripture'. As he told the Christian Medical Fellowship, although the miraculous still existed, 'phenomena must not determine belief'. The Bible 'teaches us to take our doctrine from it alone'. While Christians should never deny the present-day existence of tongues and of healing, there were 'false Christs and false prophets', who with 'great signs and wonders' would deceive God's own children.

Christians should, he felt, neither be frightened by the supernatural, nor 'become uncritically credulous' and believe that simply because something unusual had happened, the person doing it was from God. Christians needed to be filled with the Spirit, and at the same time remember that 'our doctrine must in every respect be determined by the Bible'.

The Doctor was always willing to encourage those involved in the Renewal movement. Many of the early meetings of the Fountain Trust took place in Westminster Chapel and leading charismatic Anglicans, such as Michael Harper, have paid warm tribute to all the help and encouragement he gave them in the early years. (He also gave valuable advice to Terry Virgo who, as well as being a senior figure in the House Church movement, holds the same Reformed, Calvinist views on doctrine as the Doctor himself did.)

At the same time, Dr Lloyd-Jones never believed that baptism of the Spirit could be induced, or produced either instantly or gradually by human means – it was something sent by God in His sovereign power and grace. He would never make the experience a test of church membership or a condition of church office. His deacons at the Chapel held all sorts of views on the subject, and he would have been horrified if people thought that his view of the Holy Spirit meant that he supported an interpretation of Scripture that effectively divided Christians into higher and lower forms of believer, depending on whether or not they had received a particular gift.

As in so many things, the Doctor believed passionately in

balance. Where some of his fellow Calvinists held to all the right doctrines, but lacked fire, he emphasised the importance of experiencing the truth, as well as knowing it, the need to feel with the heart as well as to assent with the head. Where some of those who shared his views on baptism of the Spirit went off into emotional excess, denigrated doctrine, preaching and the mind, he re-emphasised the importance of sound doctrine, of faith objectively based not on feelings but on what Jesus Christ accomplished on the Cross, and of the importance and centrality of preaching to true worship. It was, as always, 'logic on fire', that special combination that made him the man he was.

After the Chapel
In 1968 he became seriously ill. He decided that this was from God, who was telling him to move on to a wider ministry. The regular pastorate and preaching ministry at Westminster Chapel had become increasingly exhausting, and so he took the opportunity that the illness gave him to retire. After recuperating from an operation for the removal of an intestinal obstruction, he spent a time at Westminster Theological Seminary in Philadelphia, in the USA. There he delivered a major lecture series, now published as the book *Preaching and Preachers*. (Many of the quotations on his view of preaching cited in this chapter are from the book.) Although he had now left the full-time ministry, he wanted to inculcate into the new generation of ministers his high view of preaching and its crucial importance in the life of the Church.

His main ministry was now his books, especially the series on Romans and on Ephesians. He had had some volumes published before, such as his expository sermons on the Sermon on the Mount. But he felt that the Romans and Ephesians series contained the major Christian doctrines, and he had them published not in chronological order but in what he decided was the importance of the subject matter.

He would go to the country house of his elder daughter,

Elizabeth, and her family, in Cambridgeshire where, away from all the pressures and distractions of London, he could get on with correcting the sermons for book form. Often he would leave the spoken repetitions in, as he believed that good teaching was more important than spotless prose.

He always maintained that hardbacks were superior to paperbacks – if one bought a hardback it meant that one took the book seriously as something to be treasured and read, and re-read, again and again over many years. Yet ironically the book of his that sold the widest and probably helped more people than any other was a paperback – *Spiritual Depression – Its Causes and Cure*. (Many of his shorter works, and two of his major works originally published in hardback – *Preaching and Preachers* and *The Sermon on the Mount* – appeared subsequently in paperback. The Romans and Ephesians series were all hardbacks.)

The Spiritual Physician

Spiritual Depression shows us his spiritual insight, but also reveals two other important aspects of his life. First he was very much the pastor as well as the preacher and, as seen earlier, he was greatly helped in his pastoral work by his medical training. Often he could work out, using the Socratic method in which he had been trained by Horder, what was wrong with someone even before that person himself could. He could diagnose whether somebody had a spiritual problem or whether the real cause of the malaise was in fact physical or psychiatric.

In his sermon on Psalm 42 he stated that while 'temperament, psychology and make-up do not make the slightest difference in the matter of salvation', they do 'make a very great difference in actual experience in the Christian life'. Not all people, Christians included, were the same, and there were some who were by temperament 'particularly prone to spiritual depression'. As a doctor he knew that 'you cannot isolate the spiritual from the physical for we are body, mind and spirit'.

Often, he discovered, physical causes such as overtired-
ness, had spiritual effects. The ultimate causes of spiritual
depression, however, were the Devil and human unbelief.
Too many Christians were miserable because they had failed
to grasp the glorious doctrine of justification by faith, and
were thus unable to enjoy the knowledge that they were
saved.

To Dr Lloyd-Jones, the Christian life involved the mind,
the heart and the will, as shown by Paul in Romans 6. People
who thought that once they were converted all would be
happy, had forgotten Satan. The true life was obedience (the
will), from the heart, guided by sound doctrine (the mind).
The Doctor felt that the Bible demonstrated the 'balance of
the Christian life', revealed in the 'balanced finality' of Jesus
Christ. The 'heart', he taught, was 'always to be influenced
through the understanding – the mind, then the heart, then
the will'.

Depression came from imbalance. Indeed the 'very existence of the New Testament Epistles shows us that unhappi-
ness is a condition which does afflict Christian people'.
Christians were permanently engaged in the 'fight of faith',
and in passing through trials, and the doctor felt that those
who claimed to be Christians without ever having had any
spiritual difficulties were probably not true Christians at all.
To the countless people who had suffered spiritual torments
these words were very comforting, because they made sense
to their own experience. They had a balance that the teaching
of those who taught that Christians were always supposed
to be joyous or victorious did not.

As Dr Lloyd-Jones said in a sermon on 1 Corinthians 15,
'Christianity is common sense – and much more – but it
includes common sense'. There was no limit to God's forgiv-
ing power. It was not individual sins that were the problem,
but the whole relationship with God in itself, and for this
Christ's death was enough. Christians had within them the
'Spirit of power' and 'of love', to help them through all their
trials. To him, this was a 'superb bit of psychology'.

Christians, he preached in a sermon on 1 Timothy 1,
should not be dominated by their feelings, but what they

knew with their minds to be true. It was in this that they could rejoice. Faith was always a positive action, of reliance in an all powerful Lord Jesus. The 'great antidote to spiritual depression' was a knowledge of Biblical doctrine, not 'having the feelings worked up in meetings, but knowing the principles of the faith' – the 'Biblical way'.

The Pastor's pastor

Martyn Lloyd-Jones was not just a pastor, but the pastor's pastor. When he retired from full-time ministry in 1968, he used the freedom that this gave him to travel around preaching, and especially in the smaller chapels, where he could be of help to struggling ministers or those just finding their feet. (Peter Lewis, a minister himself and a friend of the family, has written that the Doctor was a great encourager of those whose preaching careers had recently begun.) News of his visit would invariably fill the little chapel in which he preached, and draw local Christians' attention to its existence.

Many of the ministers for whom he spoke were also members of the Westminster Fraternal which, as seen earlier, was reconstituted in 1966 in accord with his views on the separated church. It was this meeting that made him the counsellor to the whole movement, and the leader of a powerful sector of Evangelicalism after 1966. In thirty-eight years as chairman (if one includes the period 1943–66), he only missed a meeting if severely ill. To him it was a prior commitment, especially after his retirement from Westminster Chapel. As he told his friend (and successor as chairman), John Caiger, he felt 'a lunatic' for taking on so much, but he refused to be deflected from the task.

The meetings were entirely confidential, in order to encourage free speech, and the Doctor would guide the discussion, not speaking much himself, but in a careful, judicious manner. He would then summarise the proceedings, giving his considered views. In later days he would talk more, passing on his many reminiscences to the delight of the assembled ministers.

He would combine in himself, one of those closest to him has recalled, qualities that rarely went together such as believing in the importance of doctrine versus the need for freedom in the Spirit. He was both orthodox and contemporary – while despising 'topicality' for its own sake he would urge the ministers to live in the twentieth century. As a leader he was acutely aware of where people were, and would never leap ahead of them. He never demanded that people should act at once, only that they thought the particular issue through.

Different things would need emphasising at different times, and he always opposed controversy for its own sake (this included the issue of church separation). While theology was important, what mattered, he would tell ministers, was 'Life', experience, practical and personal knowledge of, and obedience to, God. Church rules had their place, but they should never imprison. He was often asked to preach at Baptist churches which would have been obliged to reject him had he applied for church membership because he had never been immersed. He would never insist on any method of baptism as being the best, and he offered Communion to all those who truly trusted and believed in the Lord Jesus Christ as their Saviour regardless of the denomination to which they belonged.

He never ceased to emphasise the need for revival and, as a Welsh colleague has said, when many ministers were distracted by all around them, 'he kept us to the main things'. He gave them the sense of perspective they needed to get on with what really mattered – the proclamation of 'empowered truth' that would change the lives of those that heard it.

He made pastors' welfare a priority, spending hours either in person or on the telephone with those who needed his help. As a result they would take from him words of advice that they never would from anyone else because they knew the spirit in which he said them. His diagnostic mind and wealth of experience, along with his prodigious knowledge of Church history (by which he set much store), all appealed to ministers in discussing their problems with him. He knew about the difficulties and heresies of the past and how they had been solved or exposed.

The State of the Nation

His diagnostic mind was seen to excellent effect in the big talks that he was asked to give after his retirement. He would often give the closing address to conferences such as those of the British Evangelical Council. One of these, 'The State of the Nation', is also evangelistic and demonstrates the careful, reasoned logic through which he would take his hearers, showing the symptoms, diagnosing the disease, and then prescribing the only cure. It was preached fifty years after he gained his MB, BS with distinction from Bart's, yet reveals that he was still as much the star pupil of Lord Horder in the seventies as he had been in 1921.

He began by quoting the book *Surviving the Future* by the eminent humanist historian and philosopher, Arnold Toynbee. ' "The morality gap" is now greater than ever before.' He then read from the book *Facing Reality* by the Australian Nobel Prizewinner for Medicine, Sir John Eccles. 'In this tragic hour', mankind must regain hope or all would be lost. Significantly, both these books were new and the Doctor had discovered them in the course of his regular reading of the literary pages of the quality newspapers.

These statements were, he argued, a perfect description of humanist despair and of Man's predicament. History showed that this was not the first time in which Britain had felt herself to be in such a state of moral decline – the Restoration and Regency eras had been the same. But it was now more serious. There was not just disobedience, but a very denial of all moral principle and law itself. In the eighteenth century people had been disobedient, but there was now a poison in the system.

This was not just seen in outward symptoms such as pornography and violence, but in a cynical, lawless attitude of mind. How should the Church respond? The state of the Church had often determined that of the nation, and she alone had the truth. What was necessary was to examine the causes of today's decline – having identified the symptoms.

The decline, he felt, had begun in a reaction against Victorian morality with its smugness and respectability that was a deformation of true Christianity. The novelists and aristocrats of Edwardian England had started a moral decline that was speeded up by the breakdown of conventional morality caused by the First World War. The popular press had trivialised the important issues, and television even more so, entertaining the people rather than informing them. Church leaders had failed to take a moral stand and the behaviour of many politicians only made people cynical.

The 'real trouble', however, was 'theological'. The Church had dethroned the Bible for philosophy and science. Darwin and Freud had reduced humanity to a machine, a helpless mechanism. So-called 'scientific thinking' had removed the supernatural, and any kind of moral restraint. Darwinism had become a religion, and science arrogant. But dehumanised man was reacting against this. Opposition to nuclear technology, a sense of futility, and a distrust of reason were all setting in. Young people were opting out, or following the revolutionary teaching of Marcuse.

But the modern world was ignoring the only cure to what it knew was wrong with itself. Man, the Bible taught, could not save himself – the Christian Gospel was the only cure. Individual Christians in key places could accomplish much, but the Church as a body, he felt, should never become either a protest movement or part of the Establishment. It existed to proclaim the Good News of Jesus Christ and the salvation He offered.

The more Christians there were, the greater the influence they could have. Romans 1 made it clear that there could be no morality without Godliness – as the Bible says, 'Where there is no vision, the people perish.' Many leading scientists were coming to believe in the soul – Schrödinger, a leading physicist, had stated that the most important issue now was: 'Who are we?'

The Bible had the answer. Man had been made in God's image, but had forgotten this because of sin. Christians, the Doctor felt, 'must proclaim the Biblical doctrine of God's

judgement upon evil and sin'. Modern man had forgotten
this, and Christians should declare that Christ had come to
save the lost. The Church's task was 'to call men to repentance, and then to offer the glorious Gospel of salvation'. It
had always been said that people would not listen to this
kind of preaching, yet a few fishermen had turned the
World upside down. 'The supreme need of this hour', he
proclaimed, was 'a spiritual revival and nothing else'.

Family life

The Doctor in his last years used to divide his time between
his two daughters. He and Mrs Lloyd-Jones lived for much
of the year in London, in a ground-floor flat in the house
of their younger daughter, Ann, and her three children,
Elizabeth (born in 1968), Rhiannon (1970) and Adam Martyn (born 1971). He and his wife, however, spent long
holidays in Balsham in Cambridgeshire with their elder
daughter, Elizabeth, her husband Frederick, and their three
children, Christopher Martyn (born in 1955) – the author
of this book – Bethan (1958) and Jonathan (1961).

At Balsham he would spend time on his books, sitting in
his favourite chairs (he had one in each room), undisturbed
by telephone callers except for the few who knew the number. He would discuss the issues that had arisen in the
sermons, or things that he had read about in the books which
he had just bought, or borrowed from his favourite library.
He loved discussion and would egg his three eldest grandchildren on, then fight back if they disagreed with him.
To all his grandchildren he was 'Dadcu' (the Welsh for
grandfather), and they would debate with him in a way that
nobody else ever dared.

For relaxation he played croquet (partnering me, against
his wife and daughter, who usually won), the word game
Lexicon (in which his granddaughter Bethan also often took
part) and billiards, which he played with his middle grandson
Jonathan. He thoroughly enjoyed the company of all his
family and was perfectly matched with his wife and close to
all his descendants, with whom he discussed everything. It

was typical of him that he showed a real interest in the lives
of all his grandchildren. He was as ready to discuss school,
TV programmes and wrestling with the younger three, as
he was to talk about Lloyd George, poetry and American
politics with the older ones. If he saw a book that he thought
one of his family would enjoy, he would either hand a review
of it over or, more often, buy it as a present.

He was also very close to his brother, Vincent, and his
family. The two of them would get together to discuss the
present (his brother had become Sir Vincent Lloyd-Jones,
a Judge of the High Court), and the past – their childhood
days in Wales and the characters they had known. They
shared a love of literature and of opera, and enjoyed cracking
puns. The Doctor often visited his relatives in Wales, many
of whom lived by farming and were very proud of their
cousin who had done so well. He was also very close to his
wife's family, the Phillips – he in his turn was proud to have
a link with the great Evan Phillips of the 1904 Revival.

Books

Books were another great love – one he inculcated into all
his family. His theological knowledge was enormous. He
not only knew the Puritans better than anyone else, and the
classics of the eighteenth-century revival, but was well read
in secular history, poetry, politics and philosophy. He also
kept his medical reading fully up to date. Once, I developed
a reaction to a series of eye operations. The hospital staff
thought somewhat dismissively that it was post-operation
nerves, but Dr Lloyd-Jones, having heard the symptoms,
was unconvinced. He consulted his reference books and,
using the old Harley Street doctors' network, got to see my
notes. I had indeed been prescribed a drug that caused the
reaction from which I had suffered – the Doctor's love of
reading and his continued diagnostic ability had saved the
situation.

At the same time, however, he felt that books should
never be a drug. They should be read for profit – and
for enjoyment, but should never dominate life. A minister

should never spend so much time reading that he failed adequately to prepare himself spiritually for preaching. Above all, there should be a balance – between sound doctrine and life, the cognitive world of books and the outer world of experience.

This was why, as Peter Lewis, the young minister from Nottingham has pointed out, the doctor so loved the eighteenth century. The Doctor, Lewis has written,

> feared a ministry which was 'all doctrine' as much as he feared a ministry which was 'all experience', and always sought to encourage the marriage of both truth and unction, doctrine and experience, in the lives and ministries of those he influenced. That was why he placed Jonathan Edwards in a category of his own among the Reformed 'Greats' and that is why he so repeatedly urged a study of the Eighteenth Century revival and its men.

'Life'

The importance of 'truth' and 'fire' led him to the conclusion that what really mattered about an individual Christian, or a church, was whether real life was present. He could forgive much about a person or a group if he felt that he or they were alive in Jesus Christ – and showed it. He utterly rejected the increasing narrowness and sectarian spirit of many of his self-professed followers. This is amply demonstrated in his address in 1968 to the British Evangelical Council (and printed as 'What is the Church?'

> A Christian is a changed man, he is a new man, he is a man who is born anew. Christ is in him. The Spirit is in him. Christians, in other words, are unique people because they share a common life. Peter says that, as members of churches we are living stones.
>
> The unity that is characteristic of the church, then, is an organic unity, it is a vital unity. Look at the obvious illustration. What is a body? Is it a mere collection of fingers and hands and arms and forearms stuck together

anyhow? Of course not. It is organic, it is one.

This is the church. Not an institution, not a mere gathering of people as such. These people are special because they have all undergone the experience of regeneration, sharing the same life.

This has got to come first because it is the only way to avoid a dead orthodoxy. You and I are living in this evil hour in the history of the Christian church very largely because of what became of our grandfathers. They held on to their orthodoxy, but many of them had lost the life. The only way you can safeguard yourself from a dead orthodoxy is to put life before even orthodoxy. All appeals for unity in the New Testament are based on life.

This is what makes schism such a terrible sin. It is not merely that you disagree with others, it is that you are dividing Christ, you are dividing a body. And so the Apostle brings out his mighty powers of ridicule in 1 Corinthians 12. He says, 'What would you think of a hand that said to a foot I have no need of you? You would say that is lunacy!' It is only in terms of this doctrine that he is able to show the character of the sin of schism. For brethren who are agreed about the essential of the Gospel, and who are sharing the same life, to be divided by history, tradition or any consideration, is the sin of schism, and it is a terrible sin.

This was what gave the Doctor so much of his power – his zeal for spiritual life. This was also why he was so involved in organisations such as IFES – they were filled with Christians who were alive, united across the denominational barriers in the service of the living Lord Jesus Christ. To him anything that stifled life was to be opposed. While he had reservations about much charismatic thought and practice, he always encouraged Anglican charismatics such as Michael Harper, or Pentecostal house-church leaders such as Terry Virgo, because he felt that their churches had a life that should be nurtured.

Denominationalism stunted true growth and if, in the very last years of his life, he spoke strongly against the position of Anglican fellow-Evangelicals, it was in part because they had, to him, in staying within a denomination that contained so much spiritual deadness, failed to come out to join those of their brothers and sisters in Christ for whom life, rather than status within a mixed denomination, was everything.*

Last days

In 1979 illness forced him to cancel his engagements. Early in 1980 he started to preach again – he preached his last sermon in Barcombe, at a thriving new Baptist chapel whose minister, Ray Gaydon, later became closely involved in the work of distributing tapes of the Doctor's sermons at Westminster. But in June he became too ill to continue any longer, and his great preaching ministry ended, fifteen years after most men retire.

He still gave advice to friends and others who sought it, and worked gently on his books, but by December 1980, his 81st birthday, he was forced to give these up too. He had firmly resisted all attempts to persuade him to write his memoirs, but he now decided to dictate his early memories (to the great delight of his family) to his close associate and publisher Iain Murray.

He now had to spend much of his time in hospital, at the Charing Cross where, with his still up-to-date medical knowledge, he agreed to have a particular form of modern treatment. It amazed many that a man in his eighties should be given such a course of chemotherapy. But the doctor in him felt that he should use it, and he also had the sure conviction that God meant him to have the extra months. He was fortunate in having a Christian surgeon, Mr Grant Williams, who not only understood the Doctor's spiritual motives, but also welcomed the willing co-operation from a fellow medical man.

In February 1981 Dr Lloyd-Jones told his family that his

---

*The chapter on Jim Packer will show the case for those Evangelicals who believe that fighting for life within a mixed denomination is possible.

earthly task was done. He ended the treatment, and cancelled his newspapers from February 28th. 'Don't pray for healing,' he asked the family, 'don't try to hold me back from the glory.' He died peacefully in his sleep on March 1st, 1981, appropriately both a Sunday and St David's Day, the national day of Wales.

Over 1,200 attended the funeral service in Newcastle Emlyn, in the church were his grandfather-in-law, Evan Phillips, had preached during the 1904 revival. The memorial service a month later in London had over 3,500 in the congregation, and more in the halls at the back. They were people who had come from far afield to thank God for the life and ministry of this extraordinary man. It was not a sad occasion but a joyous one as the thousands present, and still more throughout the world, knew that a great saint had gone to his rich reward.

God's Welshman

Martyn Lloyd-Jones was a rare combination of great intellect and fiery emotion, and it was these two strengths that gave his life and ministry its special power and impact. It goes back to his Welsh upbringing – indeed, he cannot really be understood in human terms apart from his Welshness. His background was that of the Calvinistic Methodists and, in a sense, that is what he was himself. He had the solid doctrinal base of Calvin, together with the passion of the Methodists of the great eighteenth-century revival. If the motto of his preaching career was 'logic on fire', it was a particularly appropriate one, because that is what he was himself.

This was why he had such a wide-ranging impact. He could appeal to both brilliant minds and simple ones alike. His preaching never had any of the gimmicks so often thought necessary to grip people's attention. While he had an effective voice, it was never the sound of it, but what it proclaimed that held the congregation. He had converts Sunday after Sunday without any choirs or altar calls. What drew the crowds was that the message he put forward was both reasonable – 'logic' – and urgent – 'on fire'. It was cogent, structured, yet filled with power, so that he would often get carried away himself. It was thoughtful but not arid, emotional but never emotionalist. To the Doctor, the proclamation of God's truth in Scripture was power enough to move the hearts of those who heard it.

Peter Lewis has described this well. He has written,

Some preachers make their hearers everything and the truth nothing. Others make their hearers nothing and the truth everything. Dr Lloyd-Jones eschewed both extremes of error in the pulpit. He preached to bring the truth to men and to bring men to the truth. His sermons were therefore Christ-centred and people-orientated. He never presented Christian truth before his hearers (much less out of their reach) with a 'take it or leave it' attitude, but he began where men and women were, that he might take them where they ought to be. You could call it incarnational preaching!

If he was a Calvinistic Methodist, he was also a Puritan. He brought the art of systematic, expository preaching back to the forefront – as he stated in *Preaching and Preachers*, all true preaching ought always to be expository, based on the Word of God. With this emphasis he reintroduced Reformed thinking and a solid doctrinal base to Evangelicalism. The Westminster ('Puritan') Conference, and the Banner of Truth, were all sustained by him. Reformed thought had been neglected since Spurgeon's death, and the doctor brought it to life again with a new zeal and relevance.

But the Puritans were more than just Reformed. They believed passionately in the 'experimental' side of Christian life, that truth should be experienced as well as known. With this the Doctor fully agreed – which was why he often called himself an 'eighteenth-century man'. As Peter Lewis has put it, he preached

the relevance of timeless truth and the vital importance of right thinking for right living. For him the 'victorious life' was not based upon experience (assumed or real) but upon a right understanding and possession of Christian truth and a true grasp of one's new status as a child of God. Christian doctrine . . . was inseparable from Christian life, and was the foundation of all our peace and joy. The Doctor showed a whole generation of young Evangelicals the 'power of Spirit anointed expository and doctrinal preaching'.

Truth and life together – 'eloquent reason', as the doctor described his preaching – these were the twin facets of his personality and message. His emotional side came from his Welshness; the power of his intellect, although present from birth, was refined by his medical training at Bart's.

It was his ability to make complex doctrine simple and understandable to the ordinary Christian that accounted for the breadth of his appeal. As his friend Philip Edgcumbe Hughes has said, one of the most outstanding features of Martyn Lloyd-Jones was the sheer quality of his mind. Yet this same characteristic was also of exceptional help in his pastoral ministry – in the Chapel, in IFES, and as the pastor's pastor. He could, by using the Socratic method, preach a brilliant sermon on the spiritual health of a Christian or a nation. He would then use the same means to help a young Christian, a minister or an IFES staff worker in acute spiritual distress. Almost uniquely, what made him so great in the pulpit made him equally able outside it.

He was a man filled with a great vision – that of a united body of Christ proclaiming the message of Jesus Christ to a fallen world. If his dream of a united Evangelical church did not turn out quite as he had hoped in his own country, that same vision was outstandingly successful in the International Fellowship of Evangelical Students (IFES), which he helped to establish and nurture through its early days.

If he could be said to have monuments, one would be his books, which are the edited transcripts of his sermons or lectures. Another would be the IFES, which was the embodiment of all that he stood for and believed in. His mind made it possible to see the issues that really mattered and to set out the priorities that would establish the infant movement on a sound, secure base.

Furthermore, IFES was an organisation that grouped together all the different kinds of true believing Christian, regardless of denomination, colour or nationality in the common cause – the Gospel of Jesus Christ. It was a positive, Christ-centred unity of the kind that Martyn Lloyd-Jones fought for all his life. The ideals of IFES were created by him, and long after he is forgotten, they will continue to be held by *all* Evangelical Christians who love and wish to serve their Lord as he did. But perhaps above all, his greatest monument will be the many thousands of Christians whose lives he changed, either directly or through the IFES and his books.

Martyn Lloyd-Jones was buried in his beloved Wales, in the cemetery of the Phillips family in Newcastle Emlyn, not far from Llywncadfor, the farm from which his mother's family came. The words on his gravestone symbolise the one thing in his life for which he wished to be remembered, the motivation for his entire career. They are from Paul's first Epistle to the Corinthians:

For I determined not to know anything among you save Jesus Christ and Him crucified.

FRANCIS SCHAEFFER

Early life
Francis August Schaeffer IV, the pastor to modern youth and interpreter of the twentieth century, was born in America on January 30th, 1912, the son of a labourer of German ancestry and of his wife Bessie, whose family originally came from England. His father was a caretaker and although the Schaeffers were eventually to have enough money to be respectable, it was, in Susan Schaeffer Macaulay's words, 'very much a working-class family'. It was a home with no books or culture and the big treat was a day trip to near-by Atlantic City. Young Francis helped his father with the carpentry and, on going to Roosevelt Junior High School at the age of 11, he chose woodwork and technical drawing as his main subjects in order to please his parents.

He then moved on to Germantown High School where he began to feel dissatisfied with life. He went hiking in the countryside each Saturday. To reach it, he related, 'I used to save a couple of miles by tramping through the city dump. I have never forgotten this. It was a place of junk, fire, stench. It has helped me tremendously to think back on that place, because even as a boy I realised that I saw there almost everything people spend their money for.' His poverty of upbringing gave him a rawness of outlook that enabled him not only to see life directly, but also what his second daughter Susan has described as a 'blank-slate searching mind', an ability to learn about the wider world without any of the preconceptions that go with a more privileged background.

At 17 he started working part-time on a fish wagon. But he found himself being introduced into another world through having to teach English to an exiled White Russian

Count. The book that the Count chose to learn from was about Greek philosophy. Francis had read a little philosophy at high school, but this text aroused his curiosity in a powerful way. His family was not at all Christian and the only church he knew, a very liberal one, had given him none of the answers for which he had been seeking. So he began to read the classics, and Ovid in particular. But since he had also noticed that the American culture in which he lived was based on Christian thinking, he decided to study the Bible too.

He would read passages of Ovid, then of Scripture, starting in the book of Genesis. He discovered that the Bible gave him the answers to all the questions he had been asking, and over a six-month period he became a Christian. On August 19th, 1930 he wandered by mistake into an Evangelical church, where he heard evangelist Anthony Zeoli. He realised that there were other Christians who believed the same truth as he did and by September 3rd, 1930 he was able to write in his diary that 'all truth is from the Bible'.

Student days

The same year he graduated from high school and went to the Drexel Institute to study engineering. But he was already faced with a dilemma. He wanted to please his parents by becoming an engineer. At the same time he felt in himself a strong calling from God to enter the ministry to proclaim to others truth he had found. He worked part-time in a factory, then on a grocery delivery round. By December 11th he decided that his true vocation was to be a minister. His father, who had hoped that his son would be a fellow craftsman, was hostile, but eventually his parents relented.

So in September 1931 Francis Schaeffer enrolled at Hampden-Sydney College in Virginia. Life was hard there for a northerner, and even worse for ministerial students, who were bullied, especially by the heavy drinkers. But young Schaeffer obtained good grades and, as well as winning over the bullies, managed to pick up valuable experience through helping out at a near-by Sunday School for blacks. He became president of the Student Christian Association and in 1935 graduated magna cum laude.

That summer he was married to Edith Seville whom he had known for four years. Edith was the daughter of eminent former missionaries in China now returned to the USA. As one of the Schaeffer daughters has said, the freshness of insight of Francis' working-class background, merged with the culture and refinement of Edith's, combined to give their marriage the unique power and effectiveness in God's plan that was, twenty years later, to make the work of L'Abri possible. To start with, they had three children – Priscilla, born in 1937, Susan in 1941, and Debby in 1945.

'Come out of her my people . . .'

Francis Schaeffer went on to become a graduate student at Westminster Theological Seminary in Philadelphia, then still under the leadership of the great Dr Gresham Machen. But not long after the young couple's arrival in Philadelphia, the dispute on the truth of Scripture broke out. This led to Machen, and others who stood firmly by it, leaving the Northern Presbyterian Church and forming a totally Evangelical denomination of their own. Schaeffer followed Machen's lead, but he subsequently came to regret the harshness that ensued from the split. He later described his feelings on this issue:

> To be really Bible-believing Christians we need to practise simultaneously, at each step of the way, two Biblical principles. One principle is that of the purity of the visible church: Scripture commands that we must do more than just talk about the purity of the visible church – we must actually practise it, even when it is costly. The second principle is that of an observable love amongst all true Christians.

Those who stayed within the doctrinally mixed denominations, he felt, developed a 'co-operative latitudinarian-

ism', always pushing back the bottom line of what they were
prepared to put up with before being obliged to resign.
Those who left, by contrast, often adapted a harshness of
spirit and a bitterness towards those who had refused to join
them. Neither way of behaving was truly Biblical.

Schaeffer, in the light of his own experience in 1936,
always had immense sympathy with those Evangelicals
such as Martyn Lloyd-Jones who felt that separation from
doctrinally mixed denominations was a crucial issue. But
he himself was never to feel that it was *the* issue:
the doctrine of Scripture being more important – the
'watershed' as he has called it. Christians, he maintained,
should in their doctrine of the Church be imitators of the
character of God. The holiness of God dictates that true
Christians depart from those in the professing Church who
have ceased to teach and believe in the truth. But,
simultaneously, they should also practise the love of God
which, in practice, meant that they should continue to
show love and fellowship to those of their fellow Evangelical Christians who had, albeit mistakenly, opted to remain
within the mixed denominations.

This Biblically based response to such a thorny problem
was to be of considerable help to Schaeffer's continuing
ministry later on. Those who did not agree with his
denominational separation continued to listen to him when
he spoke out on the urgent doctrinal and social issues of
the day, in a way that became impossible for those who
made the narrower church issue the key test of orthodoxy.
By placing a positive emphasis on truth at such an early
stage in his career, and on the Biblical revelation of the
character of God, Francis Schaeffer was arguably not only
totally right in laying down his own priorities, but also
establishing a firm base for the greatness under God that
his subsequent ministry was later to show. He felt that
his life was like being on an escalator, with God taking
him on up to ever wider responsibilities, his own duty
being to follow wherever he was led.

Early days in the ministry

Following the denominational split, he attended the newly formed seminary – Faith Theological Seminary, in Wilmington, under Dr MacRae. Then in 1938 he became the first-ever minister to be ordained into the new Bible Presbyterian Church – the 'Covenant Presbyterian' in Grove City, Pennsylvania, a church which had seceded from its now liberal denomination. In 1941 he moved to another Bible Presbyterian Church, in Chester, Pennsylvania, which had similarly left its previous denomination. Many of his congregation were working class – shipyard workers, truck drivers, shop assistants and farm labourers. With his own working-class background, he found he was able to reach them, and in a straightforward way which they could understand.

Both intellectuals and workers seemed to him to be asking the same basic questions, the only real difference being that the more highly educated asked them in a more articulate way. He always made sure to preach in a way that could be understood by all members of his congregation regardless of background. When talking to working-class people individually, he took care not to be too intellectual, but at the same time he was never condescending, especially since their origins were the same as his own. He often felt that highly educated people sometimes were condescending, and underestimated the ability of working-class people to understand complex issues.

He later said that in the same way as Hudson Taylor learnt Chinese in order to work with Chinese people, so he would put over the identical truth in a manner that could be clearly comprehended by whoever was listening. In later years not everyone who came to L'Abri was an intellectual, and the training he received as a pastor, coupled with the ability to change gear in personal conversation, was to be of immense value for the future.

Edith Schaeffer also gained experiences that were useful in future years. In 1942 their church organised a summer camp for people of all ages in the Blue Ridge Mountains. A total of 118 turned up, but not the caterer, and Mrs Schaeffer found herself having to organise all the food single-handed.

The Call to Europe

The following year the Schaeffers were called to the Bible Presbyterian Church in St Louis, Missouri. Here they began, in their own church, the Christian outreach organisation Children for Christ. As a result of this, Francis Schaeffer developed an interest in seeing the state of youth work and of the Church generally in Europe, which by 1947 was slowly recovering from the devastating effect of war. His denomination's mission board therefore gave him special leave of absence to go and discover for himself what was happening.

He first travelled around France – Paris, Bordeaux, Nîmes, Marseilles and Aix-en-Provence – and in July 1947 arrived in Geneva, where he felt aware of the 'great heritage' of the Reformed faith. After visiting pastors in Lausanne, he stayed at the famous Emmaus Bible Institute, where both he and the director, de Benoit, found themselves agreeing clearly on the Evangelicals' 'need of separation' from the growing Ecumenical movement.

This conviction of standing fully for Biblical truth was reinforced in Schaeffer's mind when he reached Oslo, in order to attend the Young People's Congress of the World Council of Churches. The Presbyterian groups there struck him as being in the 'most unhappy' state and, after hearing the eminent theologian Niebuhr, he wrote home to his family, 'The whole conference makes me desperately lonely for some Christian contact.'

Indeed he found on the Sunday that when he worshipped in a local Baptist church he 'understood them better in Norwegian than the World Council people . . . in English'. He told his family that he prayed 'for the filling of the Holy Spirit' as he had 'never prayed before'. Liberalism was not, he decided, changing, so much as putting on a new face. But the truth of God was never worth compromising, a view strengthened in his mind after meeting the great Norwegian Evangelical leader, O. Hallesby.

He went on to visit several more European countries, finishing with Britain, where he had a warm meeting on September 30th with Dr Martyn Lloyd-Jones, who fully shared his concern about the World Council of Churches, and returned to the USA in October to continue his usual ministry. But a sense of God's calling him to Europe grew ever stronger in his mind. By Christmas he was asked to go there again, by his denomination's International Board, to help set up events for the International Council of Christian Churches gathering in Amsterdam in August 1948.

'Our nomadic life had started' . . .
He felt a 'dense fog ahead' when he and the family set out for Europe in February 1948. Mrs Schaeffer was later to comment, 'Our nomadic life had started'. After staying in the Netherlands, where Francis Schaeffer was to meet his lifelong friend and collaborator Hans Rookmaaker, they travelled to Lausanne in Switzerland where they rented rooms in a small pension at near-by La Rosiaz.

Schaeffer used the pension as a base for going around Europe, preaching on the dangers of liberalism, including those of the teachings of Karl Barth. It seemed to him Barth had introduced existentialist thought into theology in the same way that Sartre and others had introduced it into philosophy. The old, rationalistic, liberal theology had become bankrupt. What Barth brought in was a new idea – neo-orthodoxy. On the one hand, Barth taught a view which claimed that the Bible contained mistakes, and on the other that it none the less contained religious truth in it anyway. To Schaeffer such a thesis was 'pure existential methodology using theological terms', and he exposed it as such to all his audiences.

Meanwhile he and Edith continued to help strengthen the churches, and to establish Children for Christ.

In February 1949 the children – Priscilla, Susan and Debby – fell ill in La Rosiaz and it was suggested that the family move to a healthier part of Switzerland. After a trip to the Netherlands and France, they visited Champéry in

Switzerland and liked it so much that they came back intending to stay there for a short while, but eventually remained there for several years. They set up a Children for Christ work in the area and a parallel, but totally independent, work among English girls in the near-by finishing schools.

Schaeffer himself began to write articles, one of which proved to be the germ of his famous book, *The God Who Is There*. He spoke out strongly against the Bible Presbyterian Church joining the Reformed Ecumenical Synod and continued to lecture on the dangers of the neo-orthodox, Barthian view of the Bible. But at the same time he stressed in his articles the need for a balanced Christian approach, of sticking faithfully to the truth on the one hand, and of remembering to be loving in seeking solutions to differences on the other.

He was soon asked to speak all over Europe, as his resolute Biblical stand on the issues became more widely known. As well as attending the ICCC Conference in Geneva in 1950, he travelled to lecture in Scandinavia, France and Germany. He attended the Assumption of Mary proclamation in Rome, which provoked him to write the article 'The Bible is Our Authority', where he argued that Christians should act in the light of that truth and fight for it too.

'The Hayloft Experience' and the Origin of L'Abri

In 1951 the family moved to Chalet Bijou, still in Champéry. In its hayloft Francis Schaeffer was to have a major spiritual crisis without which, he was later to maintain, he would never have been able to start the work of L'Abri. He had felt a 'strong burden to stand for the historical Christian position, and for the purity of the visible church'. He was now suddenly struck with 'the problem of reality' – the fact that so many orthodox Christians exhibited in their lives so few of the fruits that 'the Bible so clearly says should be the result of Christianity'.

It forced him to reflect that his own faith was now less real to him than at his conversion. 'I realised,' he has written, 'that in honesty I had to go back and rethink my whole position . . . I told Edith that for the sake of honesty I had to go all the way back to my agnosticism and think through the whole matter.' He paced around, both in the mountains and in the hayloft of their chalet.

I walked, prayed, and thought through what the Scriptures taught, as well as reviewing my own reasons for becoming a Christian . . . I saw again that there were totally sufficient reasons to know that the infinite-personal God does exist, and that Christianity is true. In going further I saw something else which made a profound difference in my life.

I searched through what the Bible said concerning reality as a Christian. Gradually I saw that the problem was that with all the teaching I had received after I was a Christian, I had heard little of what the Bible says about the meaning of the finished work of Christ for our present lives . . . This was the real basis of L'Abri. Teaching the historic Christian answers, and giving honest answers to honest questions are crucial, but it was out of those struggles that the reality came, without which a work like L'Abri would not have been possible.

As Schaeffer said, 'True Christianity is a balanced whole.' It is 'not only intellectual, it is not only our cultural responsibility. Christianity is being born again on the basis of the finished work of Christ, his substitutionary death in space-time history.' As he puts it in *True Spirituality*, the book which he now feels should perhaps have come first, the only way to be converted is by 'accepting Christ as Saviour. No matter how complicated, educated or sophisticated we may be, or [even] how simple, we must all come the same way, in so far as becoming a Christian is concerned . . . the most intellectual person must become a Christian in exactly the same way as the simplest person.'

There is, he writes, 'no way to begin the Christian life except through the door of spiritual life'. Furthermore, that same Christian life is no mere mechanical, intellectual exercise. It is, as Schaeffer saw with such freshness again in the hayloft, above all a personal relationship in obedience to God – a 'moment by moment communion, personal communion, with God himself . . . letting Christ's truth flow through me through the agency of the Holy Spirit'.

Christianity is no mere system, but rooted in the 'substitutionary work of Jesus Christ in history', and its life is no passive acceptance such as that practised by the Eastern religions, but a fully active one, lived in the 'power of the crucified, risen and glorified Christ, through the agency of the Holy Spirit, by faith'.

In addition, and to Schaeffer this applied equally to Christians corporately, 'There is to be moment by moment supernatural reality for the group as well as for the individual', for, as Schaeffer had seen in the hayloft, the Church tragically did not exhibit what it preached.

L'Abri has often been misconceived by Christians as a place purely for intellectuals. Schaeffer himself has been thought of entirely as a philosopher. While, as will be seen later, he has dealt with the problems raised by twentieth-century thinking, he has been equally emphatic in stressing what the Puritans described as the 'experimental' side of Christian life, regardless of the mental ability of the individual.

Edith Schaeffer has said of her husband that he is 'really . . . a very emotional person'. Much of this side of his character became evident to the many who came to L'Abri over the years, through the immense care he took with each one of them. As his son-in-law Ranald has put it, Schaeffer had compassion for the 'little people'. Truth mattered to him, and he would occasionally get very emotional and sorrowing at the sight of so many who did not know it through Jesus Christ. In later life, in his campaign against abortion, the thought of the loss of so many human foetuses would sometimes reduce him to tears. He has also always been a close family man, and his increasing numbers of descendants look forward each year to the annual family reunion.

The vision of L'Abri that was forming in his mind at this

time was not of an academic forum for discussing ideas in the abstract but of a place where he could help the needy that God sent to him, including those confused young people with the kinds of intellectual doubt that the churches often seemed either unable or unwilling to resolve.

The work begins

Schaeffer has described the beginnings of L'Abri in *Reclaiming the World*. The 'essence of L'Abri', which is the French word for a shelter, was, he stated, 'a desire . . . in my mind' and his wife's, 'to demonstrate that God exists. That is really the heart of the whole thing. It was that specific historic situation that we found ourselves in in contrast to what we had seen. We moved ahead one step at a time . . . it was not our calling abstractly, but on the basis of my wrestling with the truth of God being there.'

They proposed to live by prayer and, within that sphere, operate on four guiding principles – they would not ask for contributions but rather make their needs known to God alone; they would not recruit but rely on God to send them the right staff; plans were to be made from day to day and not far ahead, in order to allow for God's sovereign guidance to them; and lastly, they would not publicise themselves but trust the Lord to send them those people truly seeking and in need.

In so doing, the Schaeffers were taking an immense risk – as he later commented, 'we were really on a limb'. By venturing out alone, they were abandoning all security. 'But', Schaeffer said, 'I had enough leading so that I was sure that we, and I as the father of a family, would have been disobedient not to step forward'. He was not claiming that this was a 'higher way'. It was 'our calling' . . . someone else can feel called in a completely different way.

Between 1951 and 1954 Francis Schaeffer had continued to travel all over Europe, as well as a furlough in the USA, in which he spoke 346 times in 515 days. But when they returned to Europe in September 1954, Francis Schaeffer decided to turn their chalet into a shelter for those searching

'to come to for help', and L'Abri was born. In November
he founded the International Presbyterian Church.

Many young people had already come, among them several girls from near-by finishing schools. One of them was
Deirdre Ducker, now an artist and designer in Britain. She
had heard Schaeffer speak at a local English church and with
other girls had warmly responded to an invitation to attend
regular Thursday night Bible studies. Several of them were
converted, and when L'Abri was formally set up, Deirdre
kept in touch.

By 1954 visitors were coming from as far afield as Asia
and Central America. As Francis Schaeffer recalled, he and
his family 'never sought to be far-reaching in our work . . .
We simply did the job that was given us . . . Gradually it
grew. There was no great propaganda. It has grown constantly from one person telling another . . . a root system.'

The Crisis

But in 1955, after only a few months, it seemed that their
vision might be shattered. In February the local cantonal
government told them that their foreigners' residence per-
mits were to be cancelled and they were to leave the country.
In January Edith had read in Isaiah that 'the Lord's house
shall be established in the tops of the mountains' – a perfect
description of L'Abri. Her husband determined not to
launch a campaign, but to pray instead. 'Do we,' she records
him asking, 'believe our God is the God of Daniel?' The
family felt certain that somehow God planned for them to
stay in Switzerland.

The local US consulate proved hopeless, but the consul
in Berne, the capital, had been at school with Francis
Schaeffer and arranged for the American ambassador to raise
the issue with the chef du Bureau des Étrangers in Vaud.
He told them that if they could find a house in *his* canton,
they would be permitted to stay *there*, in Vaud. So Edith
Schaeffer began the task of hunting for a place, losing a vital
day in the process through having to nurse a sick Czech
émigré. She discovered various chalets in the Villars area,

but they were all too expensive, and were for rent not for sale.

The Schaeffers deliberately kept to their principles of not publicising their plight. But, in order to help with the needs of L'Abri, they did establish a 'praying family' of close friends who would pray for the work on a regular basis. These friends naturally prayed for them through what Francis Schaeffer has described as 'those rough days in 1955'.

The prayers were answered, for a remarkable series of coincidences occurred that surely show beyond doubt the sovereign hand of God in the final establishment of the Schaeffers' lifelong work at L'Abri. Edith Schaeffer met an estate agent in the street who took her to the near-by village of Huémoz, where there was a place to buy: Chalet les Mélèzes. The deadline for their possible expulsion was getting closer, and matters became increasingly urgent. Then three letters arrived for them, all of which contained unsolicited money.

An American couple sent $1,000, but $8,000 was still needed. Almost immediately $8,011 arrived unsolicited through the post. Then the removal company backed out. Once again, friends came to the rescue. Then the local committee for religion and education, who had to make the final decision for the Vaud permit, had their decision speeded up by a man who bumped into Francis Schaeffer by chance.

By April there was only the decision of the Swiss Federal Government still to come. Edith Schaeffer had to make several telephone calls, and discovered a telephone in a pension owned by two elderly maiden ladies. She told them of her family's plight, and they promised to contact their brother who was not only Switzerland's national Defence Minister, but also the current President of the country! She then happened to meet a retired pastor, who also offered to help, by informing his nephew – the head of the Bureau des Étrangers in the capital, Berne!

By June every permit that could be given had been granted, and with young people already on the doorstep and the necessary money coming in, the Schaeffers were able to start. On June 4th Francis and Edith resigned officially from their Mission Board in the USA, and the real work of L'Abri finally began.

Scenes from L'Abri

There was one firm rule for discussion – it was to be based on ideas, not organisations. Francis Schaeffer has expanded on this in *True Spirituality*. The 'real battle for men', he wrote, 'is in the world of ideas, rather than in that which is outward. All heresy, for example, begins in the world of ideas. That is why, when new workers come to L'Abri, we always stress to them that we are interested in ideas rather than personalities or organisations.' This rule was not inflexible however – if a student (to use the L'Abri term) had a particular problem in relation to the teaching of an individual or organisation, then the workers could discuss it with that student, mentioning the names of the people involved.

Preaching, which Schaeffer also carried out on Sundays, was about ideas too, 'flaming ideas, brought to men as God has revealed them to us in Scripture. It is not a contentless experience internally received, but it is contentful ideas internally acted upon that make the difference.' L'Abri was not just about ideas, but changed lives. Christ, not the intellect, was the 'integration point'.

Many of the young people coming to L'Abri had terrible psychological problems. But it was Christ's message that saved them, and gave them a 'substantial healing of the whole person'. As Schaeffer commented, 'Find me the faithful pastor in the old village, and I will find you a man dealing with psychological problems on the basis of the teaching of the Word of God, even if he has never heard the word psychology or does not know what it means.'

Few leading Christians have stressed the importance of the mind more than Francis Schaeffer. But he has always made clear its true function under the totality of the Lordship of Jesus Christ.

L'Abri expands

The work at L'Abri soon started to expand at an ever-increasing rate.

By the first month, students were coming from England, the Netherlands, Germany, Canada, Greece, Portugal and the USA, as well as from Lausanne University, near which Schaeffer would hold discussions in a café. There were existentialists, liberal Protestants, Roman Catholics, Jews and humanists. Those converted at L'Abri would tell their friends, and they would then come and become Christians too.

In April 1956 two American opera singers studying in Italy turned up. One of them, Jane Stuart Smith, was converted after a conversation which had only taken place because she had narrowly missed a bus. A discussion group in Milan followed not long after, and Jane was to start an association with L'Abri that has lasted ever since. In July Hans Rookmaaker came, with the result that he was made L'Abri representative in the Netherlands, and many Dutch students found their way over to Huémoz.

The message of L'Abri

Francis Schaeffer would always take seekers coming to L'Abri right back to the basics. Edith Schaeffer has recorded four of the questions he asked one student who was interested. First, did she believe that God existed – the God as clearly revealed in the Bible, who was infinite, and yet could be known personally? Second, did she recognise that she was a sinner in the light of His standards? Did she believe that Jesus Christ truly came in what Schaeffer described as space, time and history? Did she bow to Him, and accept what He, Christ, did for her individually by taking her deserved punishment on the Cross?

In talking to the students, Schaeffer would always also try to see what lay *behind* each question. As Os Guinness, later a close colleague, has observed, his Germanic mind enabled him intuitively to go for the whole picture, and see the context of the enquiry, the 'gap between the clouds' that helped him to delve to the root of the issue. He and his wife were emphatic that they were not simple answer givers. Each person was treated separately.

As he has written, 'we cannot apply mechanical rules . . . we can lay down some general principles, but there can be no automatic application. If we are truly personal, as created by God, then each individual will differ from everyone else. Therefore each man must be dealt with as an individual, not as a case, a statistic or a machine.'

With the immense success that L'Abri started to enjoy, onlookers in the Evangelical world often felt that he must have developed a pattern that worked to order. But he was quite 'mystified' by all this talk of 'Schaeffer's apologetics'. There is, he has written, 'no set formula that meets everyone's needs, and if only applied as a mechanical formula, I doubt if it really meets anyone's needs'. Had he been in prison with Paul in Philippi, he would not have spoken with the gaoler on the problem of epistemology. But if dealing with someone who had 'honest problems' in this area, that was another matter. He would 'keep talking in the way they need'.

The facts of reality necessitated the answers that only Christians could provide. Scripture's 'emphasis is that there are good and sufficient reasons to know that Christianity is true, so much so that we are disobedient and guilty if we do not believe it'. Christianity is founded on historic facts, not the idle speculations of human thought. As a result, it appeals to an individual 'no matter what his level of education' – a stress Schaeffer insisted upon, as seen earlier. Non-Christians were lost, in need of Christ as Saviour.

But the great task which God, in His providence, had given L'Abri was to reach people for whom such concepts were meaningless. Schaeffer has described the three types of students who came to L'Abri. The first were what he has classified as 'twentieth-century people', that category, mainly of University age, devastated by the humanistic relativism of modern thinking, who believe that truth and sin are non-existent. Most of those arriving in L'Abri in the fifties and sixties were in this group.

Then there were young people from Christian back-grounds, who had been turned against Biblical faith, either because their churches or youth groups had demanded that they believe without any answers to their legitimate questions, or because they had been antagonised by seeing no Christian love in their church or group. The last category were older Christian workers who realised they were no longer able to cope with the questions raised by modern youth – many of this third group were in L'Abri on sabbatical leave.

Schaeffer understood an important truth about the first category that many churches either failed or refused to recognise. He wrote,

What we must realise is that these people do not realise that they are lost evangelically. How could they? They do not believe that there is right or wrong, they do not believe there is a God, they do not believe there is an absolute, there is no reason for them to see themselves as a sinner. Few people believe in guilt any more . . . How much meaning does our talking about accepting Christ as Saviour have for such a person?

He went on to elaborate his reply. 'This lostness is answered by the existence of a Creator. So Christianity does not begin with accepting Christ as Saviour', but with 'In the beginning God created the heavens and the earth'. (As will be seen later, Schaeffer has fought resolutely for the truth of Genesis 1–11.) 'That,' he continued, 'is the answer to the twentieth century and its lostness. At this point we are then ready to explain the second lostness (the original cause of all lostness) and the answer in the death of Christ.'

Faith, he explained to all the confused of the fifties and sixties, was not the leap in the dark that the existentialist philosophers were teaching them it was. There were good reasons to believe the Bible's picture of man's condition. Furthermore, whereas in all human religions – such as the Hinduism and Buddhism in which many of these young people believed – man had to do everything, in Christianity God did it all: 'We can do nothing for our salvation because Christ did everything.'

This meant that what he was telling the students was a total contradiction of rationalism – though, ironically, this was exactly what many Evangelicals who did not fully understand his purpose at L'Abri accused him of preaching. The rationalist was a man who started with himself and worked outwards. Christians, however, believed in God revealing His truth to humanity, the 'very opposite of rationalism'. Schaeffer always carefully distinguished between rationalism, which was wrong, and rational thought, which was thoroughly Biblical, based as it was on antitheses, like good and evil.

To him, his work was essentially 'all pastoral'. As he has said of himself, 'What I really am is an evangelist', dealing with the specific problems raised by those whom God had sent to him, and which were mainly intellectual. He would deny that he was an academic philosopher, while at the same time insisting that his philosophy was accurate. Many Evangelicals had, he argued, a platonic view of spirituality – that their faith applied only to matters entirely spiritual.

One of his greatest achievements has been to show that this opinion is utterly false. The Bible clearly taught that 'Christianity is the truth of all reality'. God in Scripture decisively answered all the major problems, in a way that 'no other system does'. If Christianity really was absolutely true, what Schaeffer called 'true truth', then it logically followed that there was no area of life which it did not touch, and no area whose problems it did not answer.

Life was not watertight compartments, and this principle applied equally to evangelism, and to apologetics. Christians, especially those espousing the kind of teaching that placed experience above content and sound doctrine, were as guilty as the existentialists of living in what he has described as the 'upper storey', belief without using God's gift of reason.

Consequently, when the young people flocked to L'Abri, he found that

my talking about metaphysics, morals and epistemology
to certain individuals [was] part of my evangelism just as
much as when I get to the moment to show them that they
are morally guilty and tell them that Christ died for them
on the Cross . . . It is not that suddenly, for some strange
reason out of nowhere, if you accept Christ as Saviour you
are in. Christianity is a system . . . It has got to be the
whole man coming to know this is truth, acting upon it,
living it out in his life, and worshipping God . . . Thus
apologetics, as I see it, should not be separated in any
way from evangelism. In fact I wonder if apologetics
which does not lead people to Christ as Saviour, and
then on to their living under the Lordship of Christ in
the whole of life really is Christian apologetics . . . Our
primary calling is to the truth as it is rooted in God,
His acts and revelation.

He found himself aware, however, that dealing as he did
with intellectual, or cognitive, issues, there was a danger
that in opposing those Christians whose faith was based
purely on experience – 'Christian existentialism' – both he
and L'Abri could slide into the other extreme of 'sheer
intellectualism'. His 'hayloft experience' had been crucial in
this regard. But he still wanted a way of expressing the
balance in his own mind.

One day he and Edith took one of their usual hikes up
into the mountains. It was pouring with rain. Then, as they
were having tea, a notion struck him and, drawing out a
pencil, he scribbled on to his napkin,

If the basis of your Christian faith is *only* the experiential
then that base is not strong enough, and when the winds
of adversity come your faith will blow away. But if you
turn Christianity into a pure intellectualism, then when
the winds of adversity come, it will also blow away.
However, the *base* must be the content and not the experiential. Then Christianity involves the whole person, but
the base is the cognitive.

In other words, the mind comes first, and then the will and heart.

Daily life at Huémoz

But the work at L'Abri was far from being solely a matter of discussion. Two other factors played a vital part in the overall pattern of evangelism. One was the sheer beauty of the surrounding countryside. The spectacular views of the mountains from wherever one looked made the students realise that there must be something – or someone – beyond the despairing existentialist philosophies they had brought with them to Huémoz.

But the key partner to all the discussions was love, not just as a concept, but as an emotion, that showed that Christianity was not just a set of correct propositions, but something true in experience as well as theory. This was why Schaeffer insisted on dealing with each person as an individual – 'Love', he said, 'means meeting the people where they are.'

There was more to it than that. L'Abri's success had, he thought, 'no human explanation'. With his Reformed theology, Schaeffer was very much aware of the Sovereignty of God, and of the power of the Holy Spirit being at the heart of all salvation. But, he felt, 'in some poor way, it's been this interrelationship between the intellectual presentation of the truth and simultaneously showing love' to the lost. Os Guinness has summarised this: 'Truth mattered and people mattered and these were the two secrets of L'Abri.'

Joe Martin, a former L'Abri worker, felt that the 'pastoral touch', the 'sense of love for the individual' that Schaeffer 'always had', was what made the difference, and this can be seen first in a general description of life at L'Abri, and then in terms of three very different testimonies, dating respectively from the fifties, the sixties and the seventies.

Deirdre Ducker, who with her husband Richard acted as houseparents for the newly acquired chalet of Beau Site, observed that Schaeffer used three methods in dealing with those who came. Firstly there were the sermons, which were usually kept as simple as possible so that even children could understand. He would take his text and go through it logically in an expository way, building up the total picture so that the essential truth in each passage would be revealed. Every sermon was an entity in itself, unlike his second method, the lectures, which were delivered in series. These would be far more complex in language, and frequently formed the material for his later books.

Then there were the one-to-one conversations with seeking people, where his incisive mind and 'immense compassion' would be seen in action side by side. He would listen carefully to the questions, and then, as he worked out where that person's own position was, would pose probing questions in reply. He would lovingly lead them to see the logic of their own position, and convince them of their own error. In human terms, Deirdre felt, 'they convicted themselves'.

The students soon decided that he had 'thought about practically every angle to life . . . as each fad came along he was aware of what it was'. He read as widely as possible, from books and magazines and, as Joe Martin has recalled, always picked the brains of knowledgeable visitors, such as when some of the pupils of the eminent existentialist theologian Heidigger visited L'Abri.

Learning at L'Abri
Schaeffer also learned and taught from discussion and seminars. As the work grew, the long-term students would be added to in large numbers every weekend. Many short-stay visitors would arrive in the bus on Friday night and on 'Saturday they'd flock'. The Saturday evening meal would be outside, the tables carefully arranged by Mrs Schaeffer. Vivaldi's *Four Seasons* would be played in the background to 'set the tone'. Workers would have been trained to guide the conversation to appropriate subjects, then Francis Schaeffer would appear, and everyone would adjourn to the living room of Les Mélèzes for hot drinks around the fireplace.

Everyone was invited to contribute to the discussion. 'No questions were disallowed' – as Schaeffer briefed the workers, 'We must never be shocked.' He would 'put the question into the broad Christian framework', thereby drawing further questions in turn. No clichés and, as seen earlier, no mention of personalities or organisations, were allowed. 'What', he would ask, 'are the issues?'

There would be many different nationalities, and a wide variety of backgrounds. Joe Martin recalls 'a lot of individuals who found their questions answered in an individual way'. Schaeffer would himself learn from the contributions how the young people were thinking, and this, many workers felt, was a strength in that it enabled him always to be contemporary. But he would never let changing fads alter his message, which remained resolutely the same. 'Unless our feet are anchored in truth,' he has said, 'it's very easy to go along with what is chic.'

Many of the students were rebels against society. He sympathised with their rejection of the artificial, 'plastic' Christianity, which was more middle class than Christ-like. But he equally realised that many of them, in being rebellious, were, paradoxically, being totally conformist, rebelling because it was the trendy thing for their age-group to do. 'Christians,' he thought, were 'the real rebels.' In 1970 he wrote, 'The only way to reach our young people is no longer to call on them to maintain the status quo, but to teach them to be revolutionary, as Jesus was revolutionary equally against both Sadducees and Pharisees.'

Christianity changed the whole person, unlike the dead end message of the hippies. It was a 'revolution based on truth', a living faith that was 'true to what is really there', based on a personal saving relationship with the risen Jesus Christ. The fashionable Eastern cults, with their pessimistic view of reality as an illusion, gave no hope. As a result Schaeffer, by sticking unashamedly to the conservative faith of the Bible, was able to reach precisely those people who were the most anti-conservative in their own societies.

Many of the students who came to L'Abri and were converted there wished to study the issues in greater depth.

As a result the Schaeffers used some gifts which they had been sent in order to establish a place where such research could be carried out. It was named Farel House, after the great Swiss Reformer.

One of its first inmates, Deidre Ducker, described it as 'jolly hard work'. As well as their own private studies, the students would listen to in-depth talks given by Schaeffer himself. He lectured on the book of Romans, on Hinduism and, Deidre remembers, on the vital tasks faced by Christians in today's world. The students should be 'aggressive, fighting for our Christianity . . . because it is so urgent'.

The start of the tapes . . .

Many of the workers felt that the content of his lectures was so important that each talk ought to be preserved for others to hear and benefit from them. A tape recorder was sent over from the USA, but Schaeffer himself disliked the idea, as he felt that to record the seminars would be to spoil their spontaneity. So the recorder sat in the office for months.

Eventually, in order to preserve an especially good conversation Schaeffer was having with a group of American college students, one of the workers, with Edith Schaeffer's agreement, hid a microphone in a plant while tea was being served, and recorded the talk. The next morning all the students wanted copies, and the great tape ministry of L'Abri was accidentally begun. Schaeffer's Farel House lectures were then taped as a matter of course – assisted initially by Richard Ducker, who drilled a hole in the ceiling through which to slip the microphone.

Francis Schaeffer, as senior tutor, chose the tapes best suited to the needs of each student, many of whom also prepared talks which were then discussed by Schaeffer himself along with the others. In no time the tapes were being sent abroad, and several of the series – *True Spirituality*, *The God Who Is There*, and *Escape From Reason*, were to end up as books.

. . . and of the books

Originally, Francis Schaeffer never intended any of his lectures to be published. As with the tapes, the books appeared at the request of others. He had gone on a major speaking tour of universities in Europe and the USA, lecturing on the place of historic Christianity in the twentieth century. As a result of the many questions put to him, the material became gradually modified. Then he delivered an address to the students at Wheaton, Illinois, and it was so well received that the college asked if it could be turned into a booklet. Schaeffer relented on condition that only the students would have it.

But when he read it himself, he saw that it contained the germ of a book that he had a responsibility to bring out. He therefore carefully reworked the material and it appeared as *The God Who Is There*. Not long afterwards, Oliver Barclay of the IVF asked if the talks he had given in Swanick to British students could also be published, and so *Escape From Reason* appeared.

These books, the contents of which will be looked at later, became famous for the new terminology they introduced into the vocabulary of many Christians – the Line of Despair and 'Upper Storey' thought. These derived in part from the diagrams in the books which Schaeffer used to convey his basic points more clearly. Grace – the spiritual, and Nature – the created, had over the years become separated, especially since the time of Aquinas. Thought was now divided by a vertical line: *Grace – God the Creator, Heavenly things, the Soul, etc.*

Nature – the created, earth and earthly things, Man's body. By the time of the Renaissance, and especially by the era of the eighteenth-century Enlightenment, secularism had gone so deep that rationalism had taken over. The line was now like this:

Freedom

Nature (This will be explained in more detail later.)

Then came the nineteenth century and Hegel. He completely altered the way in which Western man thought. Instead of antithesis – all that is A is not non-A – came synthesis. God and the spiritual ceased to play any part in thought – indeed many ceased to believe in God altogether. This universe – the observable – became all that there is. Man noticed the particulars of life, and from them derived his theories about what was universally true. The universe, instead of being seen as God's creation, was now seen as a closed, mechanistic system. Man was a machine. Absolute truth, based on God's revelation, had gone, and only relativism remained.

As a result, the thought processes of the new generations were totally different from what had gone before. They took a while to work themselves through into the different areas of life, but could be represented diagrammatically thus:

Faith
Rationality   This was the Line of Despair.

What was above the line was the 'Upper Storey', below the 'Lower Storey'. Rationally it seemed that 'man as man is dead' – indeed had never really been alive. Above was a non-rational experience that provided the only hope of being able to prove to oneself who one really was. This philosophy was existentialism in secular thought, and Barthian neo-orthodoxy in the theological field.

Schaeffer expounded his thoughts and criticisms of the way in which modern thinking had developed in more detail in the books that followed and in the conversations he had with people at L'Abri. Many young people found in the books the answers for which they had been seeking. Often their churches had been unable, or, sadly, even unwilling, to help. Through the books, the casualties of twentieth-century thought found that there was a place where they would be listened to by people who cared for them, who understood their struggles, and who would be able to tell them what they were yearning to know.

Portrait of a Shelter

The books changed L'Abri. More people than ever now came to Huémoz. The hippy era was at its peak, and the group of chalets that made up the community were filled with students demanding what Os Guinness has called tough answers to their passionate questions. The atmosphere at the time has been described by Michael Diamond, a former Farel House student and now an Anglican vicar in Cambridge, and his wife Sylvia.

They arrived in May 1969 as houseparents of Chalet Bethany. There was an 'open door policy', and the chalets were swiftly crammed to capacity, with twenty-four overnight and thirty to meals in the one chalet alone. Some students had to sleep in camp beds in the corridors, and at weekends there were people perched for the night on the balconies. (The Swiss authorities were later to clamp down on the overcrowding.)

Breakfast was always eaten in the assigned chalet, and students were farmed out to different chalets for other meals. Everyone had to help with the chores, and hardened city types soon had to discover the art of life 'from scratch' – gardening and peeling potatoes. Mealtimes were often spun out for several hours, especially so at the Schaeffers', where lunch could last until 4.30 or later. (This remains true today – one lunch in 1983 lasted till as late as 5 p.m., to the delight of the students, but to the despair of those cooking the meal!) The reason was both in order to foster a family atmosphere in each chalet, and also so that the houseparents could stimulate a useful discussion on whatever the students had been learning that day.

The varieties of young people who came were now even wider, as L'Abri's fame spread. Some travelled from as far as Japan, and a very large number of Malays appeared. These were from Moslem backgrounds, and their conversion meant that they had to make the 'colossal sacrifice' of never returning home because the conversion to Christianity of Malay Malaysians (as opposed to those of Chinese ethnic origin) was forbidden. Schaeffer intervened on their behalf with the Swiss authorities, and took immense care to follow them up.

The largest category of visitors was American 'college kids', many of whom were on the notorious drugs trail to

India. Drugs were banned, but some of the 'way out hippies' caused a few problems at Huémoz, which, till L'Abri's foundation, had been no more than 'a little farming village'. Despite the 'slightly anti-bourgeois feeling' of many of the students, the Schaeffers managed to preserve good neighbourly relations with the solidly respectable local Swiss.

In Summer, under Edith's influence, most meals were eaten outdoors, and a former helper vividly remembers the rather Bohemian atmosphere she created with her love of music and insistence that even the table settings should be regarded as works of art.

Indeed Os Guinness has said that 'Mrs Schaeffer is the secret of Schaeffer'. It was not just the Christian witness of a happy marriage. As seen earlier, much of the evangelism at L'Abri was the visible love shown to the seekers. Part of this was the corporate life of the helpers and workers – a 'community modelling the truth'. It was, Sylvia Diamond noticed, one based on 'real life', and the powerful witness of 'real experiences of answered prayer'.

Deidre Ducker has expanded on this. Prayer was seen as 'absolutely essential', the 'mainstay of the whole work'. Francis Schaeffer had instilled in everyone 'such a Biblical emphasis on the Holy Spirit', especially in his sermons. The prayer side of the community was organised mainly by Mrs Schaeffer. As he would take people off for evangelistic treks in the mountains, she would arrange for the prayer for God's blessing down in the chalets. There would be two prayers at meals, and if a crisis occurred, everything would stop for prayer. Day to day life at L'Abri, for all the intellectual discussions happening there, was a 'visible walk with the Lord'.

The Schaeffers, in establishing their work, had done so in order to prove that God was no illusion but really existed. Consequently, they stuck firmly to their foundation principle that they would have no publicity and no appeals for funds. Edith's father, old Dr Seville, helped distribute her family prayer letters, which described the work to concerned friends, many of whom contributed faithfully. Many a little old lady, who had probably never heard of the word existentialist in her life, kept the work going. But financial crises still continued and it became apparent to all that prayer alone was the answer.

One Christmas, Deidre Ducker remembers, the situation was particularly desperate. No less than $3,000 was needed that month. The same year, the son of a wealthy Swiss Armenian family had been spared in an accident and had invited everyone at L'Abri to join him and the rest of his family for Christmas. After an excellent meal, the young man handed the Schaeffers a donation – of exactly $3,000! No one outside L'Abri had known of the urgent financial need. It is not surprising that so many young people were converted. As Deidre Ducker said, it is a shame that those who only know the works of Francis Schaeffer from his intellectual books did not see the prayerful, deeply dependent on God, atmosphere that made everything possible.

Three memories of L'Abri

Francis Schaeffer was an intellectual, but he was more than that, and three testimonies bring out the different sides of his character. The first is from the fifties, that of a young European (who asked not to be named) from an orthodox but narrow Christian home. Francis Schaeffer gave him a challenge that his own church did not provide. He found him 'gracious and patient', and was soon converted. Schaeffer, he noticed, talked to students at their own level, and possessed an ability not just to communicate with them but to learn from them as well.

Most American missionaries in those days enjoyed a high standard of living, and the fact that the Schaeffers refused to own a car, or to have the latest gadgets, made an enormous impact on young Europeans. His burden for souls, the innate seriousness that made it so precious when he laughed, the sense of prayer, and the casual, relaxed atmosphere at L'Abri struck them as 'immensely refreshing'.

Schaeffer was, the European recalled, marvellous at the informal chats around the fireside. Everybody would sit on the floor and he would take on anyone. He never feared comeback, nor was he ever cornered. Schaeffer was big-hearted, making each student feel important. The climax of an individual's visit could be the trek up the mountain, 'walks with a purpose' that were 'real business sessions on a one to one basis'.

The amount of people there could increase dramatically from 30 to 130 in a flash, but Edith Schaeffer would cope. Countless conversions took place. Occasionally the Schaeffers would tire, and slip down to the apartment of a Swiss-English couple, Jacques and Frances Beney. (It was some time before L'Abri developed a methodical system of days off.)

By the late sixties, everything was even more hectic, and this was when Sylvester Jacobs came. (His story has been published as the book *Born Black*.) He had been to Bible college in the USA, where black people such as himself were still treated badly even by professing Evangelicals. He had come to England with an Operation Mobilisation team and, at the orientation conference, heard Francis Schaeffer on the 'phenomenon of our post-Christian West'. This lost Jacobs in the 'first sentence'.

All seemed very intellectual until Schaeffer mentioned that he had taught a Sunday School class for black kids while he was a student in the South at Hampden-Sydney. 'We were able,' he said, 'to talk to one another as human beings', and he spoke of their 'common humanity'. This bowled Sylvester Jacobs over. When the lecture finished the crowds gathered round Schaeffer but he, instead of speaking to them, went up to Jacobs, invited him to L'Abri, and asked him about himself. As Sylvester Jacobs relates, it was as if Schaeffer knew 'how to read the spaces between people's words'.

Not long afterwards Sylvester Jacobs and the rest of the OM team set off to Trieste, Italy. En route they stopped at L'Abri. It was the middle of the night but, despite the time, they were welcomed by Edith Schaeffer (who vividly recalled the event sixteen years later). 'I couldn't figure this place out,' Sylvester Jacobs wrote. 'It didn't seem like an intellec-tual community; more like a real homey home.' Some time later, when back in England, he heard a Francis Schaeffer tape. The talk was not 'preaching at people', but 'explaining it to people', despite all its quotations from philosophers. So he decided to go again, but this time for a proper visit.

He stayed at Chalet les Sapins. His initial impression was that L'Abri was indeed a 'brainy place'. But, unlike his earlier experiences back in the USA at Bible college, the white people here were both friendly and natural, and he felt that they genuinely embodied the 'common humanity' to which Francis Schaeffer had referred. All its possible variations seemed to be there too.

Sylvester Jacob's love of photography had in the past been frowned upon by Christian acquaintances. Here he was told, by Os Guinness, to stop being a 'hair-shirt Christian'. Os amazed him by saying that not only was it perfectly permissible for him to own a camera, but he should also develop his ideas on how best to use it. More important, he discovered that if 'I, a black, matter to these people, could it be because I matter to God?' In his talks with Hans Rookmaaker and with ordinary people there he found that he could trust them.

When Martin Luther King was assassinated, the 'whites dripped sympathy that spring morning'. Udo, who was married to Schaeffer's youngest daughter, told him that he could take decisions that counted, just as whites did. L'Abri helped Sylvester Jacobs to accept himself. They 'didn't quote memory verses; they gave me Biblical ideas to work with'. He met his future – and white – wife Janet there. At Bible college mixed dating had been forbidden: at L'Abri the Biblical teaching that there were no barriers of colour, race or class was fully practised. With initial help from Hans Rookmaaker, Sylvester Jacobs was able to go on to be the well-known photographer he is today.

Another person changed by L'Abri, this time in the early 1970s, was the popular poet and rock journalist, Steve Turner. The hippy era still lingered on – the students discussed drugs, violence, the trip to India. Rock music played a crucial role in everyone's life, and all the basic values were deeply questioned. 'What is truth?' was the burning issue if, indeed, such a thing as truth could be said to exist. It was for people such as this that Schaeffer coined his expression, 'true truth'.

Most of the young people were Americans, taking time off from study, and over 70 per cent of all the students were non-Christians. For the first six weeks of Steve's visit Francis Schaeffer was away – he became, to those who had never met him, a somewhat 'mythical figure'. In his absence everyone concentrated on listening to his tapes. When he finally arrived, all the students crowded in to hear him, especially at his informal seminars where, as always, anything could be asked in a relaxed atmosphere. He possessed an 'ability to see what was behind a question', and impressed the motley bunch of rebels against society sitting around him by the way in which he 'discussed relevant issues in a relevant way'.

Schaeffer had an openness to what mattered to young people at the time and an understanding of the subtleties of contemporary life. Unlike many of the churches of the day, who dismissed rock music wholesale, he had listened to many Beatles records, for example, and was able to distinguish between what was important or valuable and what was not. It was, for him, 'not a simple case of acceptance or rejection' – Evangelicals could have differing levels of response to the great events around them.

Because Evangelicals had been simplistic in their approach, young Christians such as Steve, who wanted to know how to react to the culture in which they lived, were 'not given a framework' in which to respond. L'Abri, and Schaeffer in particular, served this purpose for many similar searching people. It was 'not there to tell people what to say, but to provide a structure in which they can do their own thinking'. Schaeffer would lay the Biblical foundation for them, upon which they could build, ready to enter into whichever part of the modern world God called them.

Furthermore, Francis Schaeffer showed that the historic, Evangelical Christian faith had an integrity of its own that meant one did not have to abandon one's intellect on becoming a Christian. He was a 'man thrown up by the needs of that time'. The old answers that society had traditionally given, and to some extent Christians too, were no longer relevant to the deep questions being asked by the young people. Schaeffer on the one hand was able to explain what was going on to bewildered older Christians who cared enough to listen; on the other hand, he showed the youth of that confused generation that Christianity had the answer to the root questions they were asking.

Family life

Other events took place in the Schaeffer family's life that were of equal importance to them personally. There was now a son – Francis Schaeffer V or 'Franky'. Each of the daughters – Priscilla, Susan and Debby, got married in turn, and each to a man fully committed to the work of L'Abri. Priscilla married John Sandri in 1957 – the service was conducted by Martyn Lloyd-Jones who, with Mrs Lloyd-Jones and Ann, was a guest at L'Abri. (The Doctor discovered that Francis Schaeffer was, like himself, a man who enjoyed good conversation till the early hours of the morning.) Susan married Ranald Macaulay, soon to help found English L'Abri and later to become an increasingly important and influential figure among the younger generation of British Evangelical leaders. Debby married a German, Udo Middelman who, along with the Sandris, stayed in Switzerland to help with the work there.

L'Abri comes to England

In 1958 the work the Schaeffers had begun in Switzerland began in England. A Jewish girl converted at L'Abri sent Deidre Ducker some money so that the Schaeffers could come over. Arranging all the details, Deidre recalls, was 'sheer murder'. They met a wide cross-section of people, including a group of Cambridge students. One of them had heard of the Schaeffers through a converted cousin, and came to the tea to see what this couple were like. Francis Schaeffer spoke on 'The Supernatural is right here', which, the ex-student remembers, hit all those listening as 'brand new stuff'.

Several of them went to Swiss L'Abri as a result and got Francis Schaeffer back to lecture again in 1959. Michael Diamond, who first heard him in 1961, was deeply impressed with the way in which he dealt with the major theological issues of the day. Schaeffer, he felt, displayed a 'terrific insight' into Barthian thought, and after exposing its existentialism showed conclusively that one could be both an intellectual theologian and hold to the conservative view of Scripture that the liberals had rejected. 'We were,' said Michael Diamond, 'given a background to be able to cope with the Honest to God debate.'

Schaeffer's influence in Britain grew – until his books were published it was probably greater in England than in the USA. Ranald and Susan Macaulay set up an English L'Abri, first in Ealing in London (not far from the Lloyd-Jones's home), and then, in 1971, in an old manor house in Greatham, Hampshire. A major turning point was when Francis Schaeffer was asked to speak at British IVF student conferences. He was able, as Robert Horn (now editor of the *Evangelical Times*) has explained, to give an 'overarching view of Truth'. On one occasion his lecture 'took the place by storm'. He showed how certain trends were slowly permeating different aspects of life and how these events fitted into an overall pattern. He proclaimed an 'integrated view', a 'sense of wholeness', but with a strong practical emphasis on the 'reclaiming of the World for God'.

This, as Professor Mark Noll of Wheaton College has pointed out, was a thoroughly Reformed, 'Augustinian' view, both in its desire to put the whole of culture under Christ's Lordship and in its 'realism about the state of the natural person and the need for redemption'. To be Christian was to be fully human – an emphasis that was most important in counterbalancing the prevailing pietism of English Evangelical life.

In many ways, some have felt, Francis Schaeffer and Martyn Lloyd-Jones closely complemented each other. Martyn Lloyd-Jones established the solid doctrinal basis on which Francis Schaeffer was able to lead the way in restoring the importance of God-given creativity into Biblical Christian thinking.

Travels abroad

Schaeffer's fame spread. In 1971 he and his wife met Congressman Jack Kemp and his wife Joanne – who was later to set up a Schaeffer study group in Washington DC. Then in 1972 they embarked on a world speaking tour, being invited to Hawaii, Hong Kong, Singapore, Malaya and India. Two years afterwards Schaeffer was asked to address the International Congress on World Evangelism in Lausanne which, as will be seen in the chapters on Billy Graham and John Stott, was a conference that changed the face of international Evangelicalism. He had come to feel, as his book *The Church Before the Watching World* makes clear, that the 'real chasm' in the outward church was not that between the denominations, but between Bible-believing Christians and everyone else. He now expanded on this theme at Lausanne, in order to remind delegates of the basics. The 'crucial area of discussion for Evangelicalism in the next several years will be Scripture. At stake is whether Evangelicalism will remain Evangelical.' There was 'no use' in 'Evangelicalism seeming to get larger and larger if at the same time appreciable parts of Evangelicalism are getting soft at that which is the central core, namely the Scriptures'. While it was wrong to be simplistic, there was a danger of compromising the truth, of Evangelicalism 'not holding to the Bible as being without error in all that it affirms'.

This clearly included the literal interpretation of Genesis 1–11. Jesus himself believed in it as a 'historical statement', as did Paul. Christians, Schaeffer reminded them, should not panic in the face of science, and 'must reject' the notion that 'scientific truth will always be more true' than Biblical truth on such matters. The Bible's teaching about history and the cosmos was as true and inerrant as its teaching about anything else. (Schaeffer elaborated on this in *Genesis in Space and Time*.)

Scripture, and 'holding to a strong view of' it 'or not holding to it', was 'the watershed of the Evangelical world'. Otherwise an 'existential methodology' would prevail, in which spiritual truths were divorced from the real world, and Christianity a mere irrational experience like any other.

The inerrancy issue will be dealt with more fully in the chapter on Jim Packer, but it could be said here that in making Scripture the essential test, Schaeffer was surely right. His emphasis on it in recent years has lost him some of the support he once had, from those who have ceased to take a stand on inerrancy. But unlike those who lost influence in insisting on making ecclesiastical purity the dividing line, Schaeffer has been able to retain influence over a wide spectrum of Evangelicalism, including those who, while not agreeing with him on whether Evangelicals should pull out of mixed denominations, still warmly support him on the more important issue of Scripture. Indeed some of the people who most appreciated him at Lausanne were those who had split on the church issue, but who found they could unite as Evangelicals together in defence of Scripture.

New Beginnings
By 1974 the era of intellectual debate which had reached its peak in the late 1960s, and which had inspired so many young people to travel to Huémoz, had come to an end. Many wondered what the continuing purpose of L'Abri should be – some of the staff even suggested closing it. One of them commented, 'Swiss L'Abri went to seed'. Others, while feeling that such a view was rather strong, none the less agreed that Huémoz had, for the time being, lost its sense of direction. This did not seem to be the case with English L'Abri or with the new work that had been started in the Netherlands.

Schaeffer completely disagreed. L'Abri, he argued, had been set up to help people and to show that God existed. In the sixties these had been students with particular intellectual problems. The fact that the climate of thought had changed, and that apathy was widespread, did not in any way alter

L'Abri's basic purpose – helping and guiding the lost to the God who was there. All that had happened was that the problems were now different from before. All who came seeking help would be assisted in the same way as the intellectuals had been.

For a time in the seventies, L'Abri became a place on the spiritual tourist map of Europe, a place on the American College kids' itinerary. One day some Germans came, found a 'hippy', took a few pictures of him, and left. Several of the original staff resigned, albeit most amicably. But an era had ended. In some ways this was helpful. Some restructuring took place: chalets were made more self-contained, so that a much better sense of belonging was able to grow up in each of them. With not so many people, everyone was able to enjoy a more 'family' atmosphere.

By the early eighties Swiss L'Abri had found its feet again. Students continued to come in, many of them from Australia. While the debate might not be so passionate, it was equally sincere, and conducted with the kind of seriousness that marked the prevailing 'new realism' mood of the eighties.

L'Abri was different in other respects too. First, Schaeffer himself was there much less often. He had begun to travel abroad on speaking tours. But the end of the sixties era was, arguably, for him the equivalent of the illness that Martyn Lloyd-Jones suffered from in 1968. Dr Lloyd-Jones took his illness as a sign from God that God wanted him to go on to do different things. It could be said that now Schaeffer too had to look for something else. Some critics alleged that he had gone 'over the hill', with nothing new to say. But he was in fact about to begin the most influential part of his career, which would bring him to a far wider audience than he had ever had by the fireside at Huémoz.

Second, the work of the different L'Abris had, because of his absences, become independent of him. His youngest daughter Debby and her husband Udo Middelman turned the new family chalet just up the valley in Chesières into a mini-L'Abri in the old, smaller style. The English L'Abri, in an old manor house at Greatham in Hampshire, prospered under the leadership of Ranald and Susan (Schaeffer) Macaulay and, under the dynamic team that Ranald assembled there, began to play an increasingly important role in the mainstream of thinking British Evangelical life. The same happened in the USA, at Southborough, under the leadership of Dick Keyes. The books of close L'Abri associates such as Jeremy Jackson and John Whitehead proved to be influential contributions to the revival in awareness of public issues by American Evangelicals in the late seventies and early eighties.

The origin of the films

Francis Schaeffer had always believed his life to be like an escalator, with God taking him ever onward and upward to new areas of concern. With the changes in the intellectual climate becoming more marked, new opportunities to spread his ideas in a different format than before seemed to be the best way forward.

In August 1974 Franky Schaeffer approached his father with the idea of putting his thoughts into film – a major series on Western culture. Schaeffer considered it and, during a walk with Edith, formed the basic outline. The title, *How Shall We Then Live*, came to him while reading the book of Ezekiel and acted as confirmation to him that God wanted the series made. It would be a way to 'blow the watchman's trumpet' in an age that had lost its way.

The aim was for the films to be a 'study guide . . . for Christians to get a better understanding of the basics, for non-Christians to get a better understanding of what humanism is all about, in contrast to what Biblical teaching gives as a base to understanding the Universe and life'. It was not intended to be directly evangelistic, something which not all the Christians watching it later fully understood. The project lasted two years, and involved much research, filming in many places, and a lot of effort by many people. Naturally this proved a very expensive process and it became necessary to appeal for money.

This upset some of the old L'Abri workers, who remembered that a founding principle had been never to advertise or ask for money. One of them (who asked not to be named) wrote to Schaeffer, 'Where did all the commercialism come from? What happened to you? . . . You used to say that numbers weren't important but that God would bring his own people to hear without advertising. You and Mrs Schaeffer gave up years of your family life to demonstrate it. You used to deplore religious commercialism, castigate appeals for money and denounce a preacher star-system. What happened to you?'

His reply was that 'nothing had happened to us or to L'Abri'. In establishing the no-appeal principle, they had never claimed it was a *better* or spiritually superior system, but something that God had called them to in that particular situation. The series was a different situation, with different needs. Furthermore, the film series was not a part of L'Abri, but was made by a separate company, Gospel Films. 'Each person,' Schaeffer wrote, 'in each Christian work must follow the Lord's own leading for them' and stands before God in relation to that alone. The books, the tapes, and now the films, had all marked changes from the small beginnings in Chalet les Mélèzes.

The ex-worker replied that it was not that Schaeffer had ceased to be spiritual that concerned people – everyone knew that he was spiritually unaffected by it all – but that he had been unwittingly sucked into a commercialist, thrusting world, with 'ballyhoo' and 'Personal Appearances', etc., a 'stone of stumbling' to many of the old L'Abri folk. He had acted with 'the best will in the world', but made a mistake in doing so.

Schaeffer felt that he was aware of the dangers, and was taking steps to avoid them. God would judge whether he had been right. But 'with the world on fire, when one has the opportunity to speak, one has a responsibility, and when so much of Evangelicalism has on one side the devaluation of Scripture . . . and on the other side such trashy material, and then suddenly one can speak where it counts (or at least where one hopes it can count), where to say no and where to say yes is not always easy', but he tried. Evangelicals, and he has repeated this since, now had a voice as never before, and it was his responsibility to use it.

The films reached more than he could ever have done in L'Abri. Yet, as he has said, if he felt God calling him to return to the fireside at Chesières, and to go back to the old work of helping small numbers of people as in the early days, and no more, he would do so without hesitation.

The series, as the accompanying book explains, 'in no way' made a 'pretence of being a complete chronological history of Western culture', but rather analysed 'the key moments in history which have formed our present culture'. There was, Schaeffer demonstrated, a 'flow to history and culture' which was 'rooted and has its well-spring in the thoughts of people'. Each person's presuppositions stem from the way he or she thinks.

The film aimed to show the effect of this process on a larger scale, starting with ancient Rome, on to the Middle Ages, and next to the Renaissance and the Reformation. The Renaissance saw man as autonomous from God: the Reformation, which witnessed the 'removing of the Humanistic distortions which had entered the church', restored God and the Bible as the real answer to man's problems.

But the Enlightenment followed, with a silent God who never acted. Science had begun with a Christian basis of approach – uniformity in an *open* universe created by a God who acted. But the heirs of the Enlightenment created a closed, mechanistic universe, without God, and with Darwinian evolution as a substitute. Philosophers began the slide down the 'Line of Despair'. All was relative – God, the original ultimate reference point for man, had been abolished. Rationality now led only to despair, in a universe that had become deterministic, based on an impersonal beginning and evolved by chance. So there was an *escape from reason*, to existentialism, a philosophy which separated reason from meaning and reduced religion and belief to a non-rational part of life, which Schaeffer called the Upper Storey.

From this flowed liberalism and Barthianism in theology – which stipulated that Christianity was true even if many of its founding historical events had never happened. In secular philosophy, mysticism and the whole drugs/hippy phenomenon were the consequence of the same existential outlook. In the seventies, with the clear failure of the hippy alternative, people simply escaped into what Schaeffer has called 'personal peace and affluence'. Each person just gets on with his or her own life, enjoys his or her own pleasures, and ceases to care about anyone else – so long as his or her own security is not threatened. This view is a form of materialism, and its danger is that it prevents people from realising the threat posed to their basic freedoms by the growing power of secular humanism.

Humanism, Schaeffer made clear, was a Godless system that was replacing laws based on Christian moral absolutes with 'sociological law', and had terrible consequences in areas such as abortion and euthanasia, both of which were becoming legal and acceptable. Through the media and Government, secular humanism was taking over society and abolishing the Christian consensus on which post-Reformation society was based. With the old consensus gone there was a severe danger of a takeover of society by an authoritarian system – whether of the Right or the Left.

Schaeffer has not been one to see endless conspiracies, although he feels some humanists may have plotted to make their views predominant. The real worry to him is that a humanist minority, in the media, education system, and so on, have, by putting their materialist views across, altered what is 'thinkable' by the average member of society, so that what was unthinkable a generation or so back is now regarded as quite acceptable. Humanists, whether clear or 'hazy' in spreading their views, have been able to exercise influence out of all proportion to their numbers – which is why Schaeffer has felt so deeply that Christians too should play an increasing role in public affairs.

The films soon became a major topic of conversation among the many Christians who saw them in Britain, the USA, and farther afield. They made a favourable impression on most of the people who saw them, especially in the USA. Some, while totally sympathetic to Schaeffer's views and aims, wondered whether film was the best medium for expressing his important message.

Much of his appeal in the past, they thought, had been the man himself, especially his obvious love for people, particularly those who came into personal contact with him at L'Abri and elsewhere. One ex-L'Abri worker put it: 'Schaeffer's special qualities can't be put on film.' The series, they felt, was depersonalised. It gave ammunition to those Christians who had wanted deliberately to misunderstand his message, especially those who were suspicious of any kind of Christian involvement with the Arts. Sadly some of the critics were followers of Dr Martyn Lloyd-Jones who failed to remember that the Doctor took Calvin's view of the Arts as lawful, and part of God's creation to be enjoyed.

The fact that Schaeffer wore his usual Swiss mountain clothing on screen enabled his opponents to ridicule him and dismiss him as a would-be Christian guru. They maintained that he was saying that *all* Christians had to be aware of the latest developments in art and philosophy, and that those who were not were second class. All this was, of course, both untrue and unfair, but the films made openings for the critics in a way that the books had not. Another problem was that the mass publicity and the enthusiasm of many of the Christians who watched the films led to an image of Schaeffer as *the* great expert, even though he never saw himself as anything of the kind.

As Professor Mark Noll of Wheaton College, USA, has written, 'Francis Schaeffer has been one of our most effective evangelists and apologists. The American tendency to transform leaders of one field into another, however, has not served Dr Schaeffer well.' While Schaeffer has not encouraged such tendencies – far from it in fact – the films and the need of Evangelicals to have a figure whom they can use to put up against the non-Christian world outside has caused exactly such a transformation of image in the eyes of many people.

Part of the explanation is the rather tragic and totally unjustified inferiority complex suffered by too many Evangelicals today. Instead of basing the defence of the faith on their own study of God's word, and instead of resting secure in the confidence that comes from relying on the power of the Holy Spirit, they rely on big names to bandy about in order to show to non-Christians that Christians, too, can have famous intellectuals and rock stars as well. They depend on making the Gospel credible to non-believers not through its message and through the person and work of Jesus Christ, but on the existence of authoritative people within the Christian church.

As Steve Turner has put it, Francis Schaeffer taught him how to think and argue for himself, but the new generation now growing up sometimes use Schaeffer in order not to have to think the major issue through for themselves at all. Tragically, this is the exact opposite of all that Schaeffer has taught.

The other problem arising from the films concerns the nature of film itself, a restriction that applies not just to Schaeffer, but to anything that appears on TV and in the cinema. Films can, by definition, portray only that which can be *shown*, whereas books can both discuss complex ideas and illustrate them, if necessary, with pictures – as is the case with the books that accompany each of the films. (These also give footnotes, which give greater detail than could ever be possible in a short snippet of film.) So it was inevitable that some specialists, in seeing the episode in the series that covered their own particular expertise, should find what they saw to be slightly simplistic. This was not so much the fault of the films, or of Schaeffer, but of the very nature of the medium in which the ideas were being expressed.

Susan Macaulay has described her father as having a 'polymathic mind', and this has considerable relevance to the making of the series, which some have found simplistic. Schaeffer has been defended on two grounds. The first is that we are today plagued by overspecialisation – what Os Guinness has called the 'footnote mentality'. Schaeffer's panoramic view of the important issues in their wider perspective gives an important picture that would otherwise be lost. He sees the forests where the specialists only see the twigs. Above all, he shows how today's developments fit into a pattern that can readily be appreciated by the ordinary person.

Professor Wayne Boulton of Hope College, USA, has written, 'Schaeffer is less a scholar than a thinker. The scholar,' he comments, quoting Harry Blamires, ' "cannot endure exaggeration . . . hesitates to praise or condemn; he is tentative and sceptical". The thinker, on the other hand . . . "hates indecision . . . is at home in a world of clearly demarked categories . . . [and] works towards decisive action".' In saying this, he is surely right. Not only does Schaeffer have a comprehensive view of truth, but he also believes that it should not merely be studied, but acted on as well.

The other defence has been made by people such as Michael Diamond and by Schaeffer himself. The overwhelming majority of those watching the films have not been specialists, but ordinary Christians who have been confused by all that is happening around them. For such viewers, the series have been very helpful, in introducing them to topics which they might not otherwise have considered, and in giving them a courage that they might not otherwise have had. So long as they do not ascribe to the films attributes that they do not possess – the series never claimed to be an exhaustive or definitive account of modern culture – then no harm is done. As for the specialists, academics can always be reached by other means, such as high-powered books, discussion seminars, and so on.

Schaeffer could see the validity of many of the criticisms. But he believed that it was vitally important to get the message across to as many of the people as possible. Only a limited number of listeners could ever hear him at L'Abri, and the films have helped him to reach more people than ever before. This includes, some feel, those who found his earlier books hard to understand. His message is for everyone, not just the select few of intellectuals.

Many of the showings have been accompanied by seminars, attended either by Schaeffer himself, or by close associates, in which the issues raised only briefly can be discussed more fully by all present. The accompanying books also give greater detail. All agree, critics and supporters of the films alike, that Schaeffer's message is one that needs urgent consideration by Christians and non-Christians alike today.

The Abortion Debate

The Schaeffers embarked on a major US tour, speaking in over eighteen cities where the films were being shown. They were screened in hundreds of other cities in Britain and the USA, too, in local churches and similar locations. Francis Schaeffer also spoke to the Biblical Inerrancy Council meeting in Chicago. As he wrote to one of his family, Evangelicals in the USA were 'not making a clear line between those who hold the historic view of the Bible being without error in all it teaches, and those who are holding to the neo-orthodox view in the name of Evangelicalism'. He feared lest, in order to keep the peace, Evangelicals might compromise, and by losing their doctrine of Scripture cease to be Evangelical at all. Christians were 'in danger of having the ground really cut from under them'.

Schaeffer then invited Dr Everett Koop, the surgeon, to L'Abri. Koop's talk in Huémoz convinced first Franky and then Schaeffer himself that another series ought to be made, this time on the issue of human life and the attacks which secular humanism was making on its sanctity – especially its promotion of abortion, euthanasia, and maybe even infanticide.

As always, Schaeffer did not just deal with the issues themselves, but with the basic humanist, materialist philosophy behind them. He showed that they were a part of the process whereby humanism was corroding the basic Christian structure and value system of Western society. Much of the subsequent film series was taken up by expounding purely Biblical material – Schaeffer has called chapter five of the accompanying book the clearest exposition of the Gospel that he has ever made. As usual the films, entitled *Whatever Happened to the Human Race* were accompanied by seminars, often led by Schaeffer and Koop, one dealing with the basic moral side, and the other with the medical.

During the filming of one of the scenes in Israel, Schaeffer fell ill. He returned to Switzerland and Edith contacted the

Mayo Clinic in Rochester, Minnesota, USA. After filming had finished (by Autumn 1978) he went there for a check-up and on October 12th was told that he had malignant cancer of the lymph system. Major treatment was necessary, and he underwent chemotherapy.

By May 1979 the lymphoma seemed to have vanished and so he launched into a new series of seminars, the aim of which was not just to alert Christians to the attack on human life that was spreading in the West, but actually to co-ordinate action to do something about it. In February 1980, however, the cancer returned, as well as water on the lungs, and the lengthy process of treatment had to begin all over again.

Despite illness he battled on. He now had a hearing in high places. In Washington DC his seminars were attended by congressmen and members of the White House staff. Not long after, a major L'Abri conference was held in Rochester with 2,000 people from all over the USA and from other countries as well.

The debate over abortion began to raise more fundamental issues in his mind. He remembered how Nazi Germany had disregarded the sanctity of life, and developed a system in which arbitrary, or purely functional, 'sociological law' had taken over. He feared lest the same system should start creeping into the USA through the increasing humanist control of the medical, educational, legal and news media establishments there.

His interest in politics had 'gone back a long way'. But when making *Whatever Happened to the Human Race* and *How Shall We Then Live* he found himself thinking about the political implications of his Christian world view in a deeper way. All his books had been centred around the theme that Jesus Christ is the Lord of the whole life. So far he had dealt with the implications of this in the areas of philosophy, art, music, and so on. But he now saw that Christians ought to start asking the question: 'If our country and culture are the way you say they are' – increasingly dominated by humanist values – 'what should be the Christian's attitude towards our Governments?'

This led him to write *A Christian Manifesto*. In one
sense his ideas had developed naturally from his two film
series – abortion to civil affairs. But in another sense, he
felt, the views he now took were implicit from the very
beginning, and had 'grown . . . through the years, culmi-
nating in' the two film series and the *Manifesto*. He was
not, therefore, leaping on any bandwagon, but working
through to its logical conclusion in the area of politics the
view he held on the Lordship of Christ over the whole of
life.

He noted, in the course of his thinking, that the great
Scottish thinker of the seventeenth century, Rutherford,
had in his work *Lex Rex* propounded the view that the law
was above rulers, who had no right to ignore its basic
principles. Schaeffer had been aware of Rutherford's views
from as early as the sixties. Christian commentators of the
seventeenth and eighteenth centuries had pointed out that
the Bible clearly taught moral absolutes.

This climate of thought had had a decisive influence on
the political leaders of the day, in particular those of the
USA, the Founding Fathers who drew up the American
Constitution. If not Christians themselves, they lived in a
Christian dominated society and were imbued with Biblical
thinking and principles. The USA had, therefore, a Christian
heritage based firmly on Reformation values.

In the last forty years, however, America had lost this
Christian underpinning through the rising power of humanism with its base in a Godless universe founded on materialism and biological chance. The question was, what should
Christians do about it? They had failed to act for the past
forty years, and the rot had now gone a long way through
society.

Schaeffer's controversial response was that Christians
should, if necessary, engage in civil disobedience on issues
such as abortion. 'The bottom line,' he wrote, 'is that at a
certain point there is not only a right but a duty to disobey
the state . . . In almost every place where the Reformation
had success there was some form of disobedience or armed
rebellion.' Citizens had a 'moral obligation to resist unjust

and tyrannical Government'. (The criticisms of this view, and Schaeffer's reply to them, will be looked at later.)

Today, he continued, 'the whole structure of our society is being attacked and destroyed'. The silent majority had lapsed into 'personal peace and affluence' and failed to see that an 'exclusivist, closed system' was taking over. The reality of the situation as it had now developed was that 'one either confesses that God is the final authority or one confesses that Caesar is Lord'.

Schaeffer was careful to emphasise that Christians should be guarded in their actions – talk of civil disobedience was 'scary', as there were plenty of 'kooky' people around. Furthermore, the bottom line should be drawn fairly low. He was aware that the principles, although still applying, might need different ways of implementation in Communist countries. But 'if there is no final place for civil disobedience, then the Government has been made autonomous, and, as such, it has been put in the place of the living God'.

Christians should, however, not act against things without showing clearly that there was an alternative. Schaeffer emphasised that he was not trying to set up a theocracy, and added that Christians 'should not wrap Christianity in our national flag' – he was advocating truth, not a spiritualised all-American patriotic programme. What he wanted was to return to the open, Christian ethos upon which America was founded. Only this, with its firm belief in moral absolutes, could provide *true* freedom. In this America there would be 'freedom for all religion' (not just for secular humanism, which the exclusivist humanists wanted) in which 'Reformation Christianity could compete', uncensored by the humanist media, 'in the free marketplace of ideas'.

Many Christians who had passionately supported Schaeffer for many years and who had warmly backed his cause now found themselves sorrowfully disagreeing with him for the first time. There were two reasons for this. First there were those, mainly in the USA, who disagreed with Schaeffer's interpretation of history. His book, entitled *A Christian Manifesto* was published in early 1982. In the following November a *Newsweek* article attacked it and described him as the 'Guru of Fundamentalism'.

The onslaught from the humanists was predictable and the piece was in a way a tribute, showing that he was now seen as an enemy to be reckoned with. Unfortunately it quoted some Evangelical thinkers out of context, and one of them wrote to Schaeffer to clarify the situation. Professor Noll, a historian at Wheaton, felt that the book had not interpreted American history accurately, and that Schaeffer was thus damaging the cause in which both he and Noll believed. Schaeffer replied that Noll and others, by casting doubt on America's Christian origins, were playing into the hands of the humanists who wanted to claim a secular foundation for American values in order to justify the humanist state which they were now establishing. In doing this, 'the difference between the past and the present was obliterated, and students especially were harmed in not seeing the change which had taken place'.

The debate then became semi-public, as the participants shared the correspondence with friends and then with the Evangelical press. Much of it was conducted at a specialist level, on the extent to which, for example, Witherspoon was an Evangelical and, if he was, the degree to which his Christian commitment affected his political thinking. Some, like Gordon Marsden of Calvin College, a Schaeffer supporter since the sixties, felt that he was not applying as vigorous a test of orthodoxy to the Founding Fathers as he had consistently done with the other thinkers that he had examined over the years. The danger of the 'designating' of 'large sections of the American heritage as more-or-less Christian' was that it had 'helped lower the guard of Christians in distinguishing what is truly Biblical from what is merely part of their cultural heritage'.

What disturbed Noll was that Schaeffer was 'compromising his message . . . that only in Christ and only through a Biblical world and life view can we truly glorify God in all areas of life'. Noll was 'especially distressed when an erroneous reading of history takes the place of solid Biblical insight in the promotion of political action in the present'.

He felt that Schaeffer's 'impact for the cause of Christ in the twentieth century has been very great', and that he had done 'Evangelicals the world of good over the course of his career'. He was 'particularly impressed with Dr Schaeffer's willingness to struggle with the major ideas of history' and 'of contemporary culture, and with the imperative themes of Scripture'. But if Schaeffer built his case on shaky history, his more important message for today's America could be lost if its historical base was shown to be false.

The *Presbyterian Journal*, which discussed the correspondence, consulted Professor C. Gregg Singer of Atlanta, a leading church historian. Singer supported Schaeffer's interpretation. On the Founding Fathers Singer commented: 'Although no one has the right to judge these men as to their salvation, there can be no legitimate doubt that they were religiously literate and that the Scriptures made a deep impression on their thinking even if we do not see precise Biblical quotations in the political documents they produced.'

Singer concluded that Schaeffer's whole basic approach was indeed 'firmly based on the most Biblical theology available . . . Schaeffer speaks with great force and insight on behalf of the cultural mandate found in our heritage of Covenant theology'.

To those not living in the USA these arguments are, perhaps, not so important. If they do have a weakness, it is that as they deal with American history it could give the impression that the book is designed for a US audience, concerned solely with the current internal American political debate which followed what Schaeffer and others have called the 'open door' to Evangelicals in US politics after Reagan's victory in 1980.

In fact Schaeffer's urgent prophetic message to become involved in society surely applies to all Christians everywhere. It is relevant even if a Christian's country never had a Reformation heritage to save in the first place, or lost it so long ago that its Christians will have to start social action afresh. Some of Schaeffer's supporters feel that this point could have been made more explicitly in his book. Schaeffer's call is not just for Americans, and it would be tragic if all the long discussions on Witherspoon and the Founding Fathers were to give a false impression.

Schaeffer's words can apply to Christians living in any democracy:

> This is our moment of history and our responsibility: not just to write and talk of far-off ideals, but to struggle for Scriptural and practical means of what can be done in a fallen world to see people personally converted *and also* [Schaeffer's italics] to see what our salt and light can bring forth in the personal life and the political and cultural life of this moment in history.

Many of those who have agreed with Schaeffer over the years fully support his plea for Christians to be involved in the world in which they live – including the political sphere. But they find themselves disagreeing with him over what exactly the 'practical means' should be and in particular whether civil disobedience can ever be justified.

Robert Horn, in the *Evangelical Times*, has outlined the reservations that these people feel about this part of Schaeffer's message. First, he writes, Schaeffer is right to say, following Romans 1, that 'evil results are inevitable from a godless world view'. But his proposal 'can only deal with the results'. The New Testament 'never allows that anyone's outlook can be changed by external "compulsion or restraint": the very reverse. It is only by persuasion, by the truth, by the work of the Holy Spirit that a person's life-outlook is changed.'

Second, the early Christians did not *actively* oppose the state on civil matters, only on religious, and then without violence. As for the Reformation period the Bible, not what the Reformers did, should be our guide. Third, while there is a 'clear case for Christians to use all legal democratic processes to try to right wrongs', Schaeffer, he feels, 'fails to show that the existence of an injustice requires Christians to engage in civil disobedience', an instrument that can lead to coercion.

Fourth, he thinks that on the 'most vital question' of Scriptural teaching, Schaeffer is mistaken. Matthew 22, Romans 13 and 1 Peter 2 all seem to show to the commentator that Christians have no right to go against the state even if it is arbitrary, which is what it was in New Testament times. Only in defence of the Gospel itself and its proclamation may Christians disobey. Lastly, when Schaeffer 'argues that armed force ensured the success of the Reformation he is leaning on' precisely the kind of theocratic state 'argument to which he says the NT is a stranger'. Christ rejected the zealot option – it was *inward*, spiritual change that he was seeking, a change that 'only comes about through the word of God, the Gospel'.

Schaeffer's reply is that 'God has established Government but He has not made it autonomous. Thus if the office-bearer commands that which is contrary to God's Law, his authority is abrogated. At this point it is the Christian's duty not to obey.' Disobedience should 'be on the appropriate level – at the "lowest level" possible. The Bible does not only call for obedience to the Gospel in a narrow sense. It also includes loving my neighbour as myself. This calls for our stand for justice in this world, and standing against injustice', against internal and external oppression in countries ruled either by the Right or the Left.

What is appropriate, Schaeffer feels, 'depends on the circumstances' in 'each place and time', and 'What would be extreme in one place might not be in another', but Christians should be very careful to guard against what 'crazy people' might do. Just because civil disobedience can be misused – in the same way that anything in 'the fallen world can be twisted' – it does not mean that Christians should not engage in it. 'It is more important to stand by the principle, and then resist the wrong use of it, than to fail to teach, and live, the principle, as most of the Church is doing now – so as "not to rock the boat".'

Christians should, he feels, both evangelise the spiritually lost and 'teach people to live on the Bible's teaching', partly for their 'individual salvation, but also [because] there can be no solid base for a lasting change in society without a changed ethos which would come from such a base'. However, Christians cannot, he thinks, wait for such an ideal change to occur. 'We are too far down the road' and 'must act now and do what can be done now'. There should be no tension between evangelism and social action – 'between doing both' – 'while at the same time not confusing the one with the other'.

The debate that Schaeffer has started on this issue continues still, and more can be said on both sides. Even though both sides disagree on the 'practical means', both concur that it is the Christian's duty to be salt and light in the world, as Jesus commanded. As with other issues, Schaeffer has caused people to think, and that is important in and of itself, especially in an age in which all too many Christians have shown signs of retreating back into the ghetto from which they emerged after 1945.

In January 1983 I went to Swiss L'Abri myself, in connection with this book. I got off the train at Aigle, and found myself on the bus to Huémoz next to a wide-eyed American student. She was only going to be able to visit L'Abri for a few hours, but was ready with her camera, and looking forward to an afternoon's worth of 'meaningful experience'. When we arrived at Chalet les Mélèzes, I discovered that Schaeffer himself was resting, which gave me plenty of time to settle in. As the Schaeffers were living in the next village up the valley, Rod Miller, Priscilla Schaeffer Sandri's son-in-law, arranged for me to stay in the ski resort of Villars, in the pension of Madame Dubois, a Christian lady well known to all at L'Abri.

I spent most of my first day travelling round L'Abri itself – now a cluster of chalets spread around Huémoz. The students there were more serious than the one I had met the previous day. They were mainly – as always – from the USA, but there was a fair sprinkling of Europeans, Canadians and Australians. The Australians were to the 1980s what young Americans were to the sixties – travelling around the world, staying in different countries often for months at a time, and thus able to get the maximum benefit out of a prolonged stay at L'Abri. The chalet system was now tightly structured, everyone belonging to one in particular, but intervisiting for meals and study.

Most of the students were Christians, seeking how to reach the young people of their own age group back home, or to find out what area of life God really wanted them to enter. As one of the long-term staff, Ellis Potter (a crew-cut, knowledgeable and articulate converted Buddhist monk) told me, one of his main jobs is to teach people how to think, so that they can then start to look for the answers to their questions.

One of the students I met during my stay was Tom, an earnest young fine-art history student, an American living in Spain. He was also a Taoist. Some of the discussions he was able to provoke, in a gentle way, over the mealtimes in the different chalets, got many of his fellow students, not to mention some of the younger workers, tied up in glorious knots. He met his match in Ellis Potter, however. He made the mistake of quoting a poem of Edgar Allan Poe which, he said, expressed much of his own view of life. Ellis proceeded to quote the rest of the poem and proved to him that his view was totally untenable both from the context and generally.

Perhaps more typical of the students at L'Abri when I was there was Becky, a science graduate from Kansas. She had spent much of her youth in Europe, and was now taking a year's leave there before returning to carry out research work back home. She was spending some months in L'Abri to think through the relationship between her Christian faith and her scientific studies, before going on to university in Paris, where she would be helping with an IFES outreach team for overseas students. Her time in Switzerland was giving her the time she had lacked in college in the US, and the fact that Schaeffer was himself originally a scientist was proving of great help to her. Like the others at L'Abri, she was in the library every day, the headphones on, notebook on the desk and pencil in hand; she learned in the mornings and discussed over meals with her fellow students the issues that had been raised in her mind.

One of the meals to which she and I were invited was at the

chalet of John and Priscilla Sandri – Priscilla was naturally
interested to meet the grandson of the man who had conducted their wedding service. By now the snow had fallen (how
no one broke their legs with all the ice I shall never know) and
the views of the surrounding mountains was breathtakingly
majestic. The Schaeffers' youngest daughter Debby lived
with her husband Udo just up the valley in Chesières,
where, according to one exhausted student I met, they made
everyone in their chalet study and work twice as hard as all
the others down in Huémoz.

The news came that Schaeffer was ready to see me, so
early one morning I braved the heavy snowfall and trudged
the thickly covered path from Villars to Chesières (I was
later shown the short-cut, which avoided the main road) to
Chalet le Chardonnet, the Schaeffer family's private home.
Francis Schaeffer was there to greet me. He wore the Swiss
mountain costume made famous in so many of the films – in
the cold January weather, it was exactly the right clothing
to have on. He looked, as many who had been to L'Abri
had said he would, both serious and warmly welcoming.

We talked about my grandfather, sitting in front of the log
fire in the downstairs drawing room. Much of the subsequent
conversation forms the nucleus for a large part of this chapter. We ended up spending almost all the hours of daylight
together as he reminisced about his past, the state of the
world today, and that of the Church, as well as other more
private matters. His mind was as acute as ever and, although
he was evidently not as strong as the Schaeffer of the early
days who led treks across the mountains, he would occasionally amble up to the fire, put on a few logs, stoke the embers,
all the while discussing some matter of high theology or a
scene from his past.

Throughout he was warm, friendly and relaxed – serious,
but with a sense of humour sneaking to the surface (in a way
very similar to my grandfather Lloyd-Jones). It was the same
a few days later for the famous Sunday lunch – which has
become an institution at L'Abri. Selected students were
given a lift up from Huémoz after the Sunday morning
sermon (preached by Ellis Potter) to Chesières. The long

table was laid immaculately by Edith Schaeffer, who had
also prepared the meal. Schaeffer himself sat like a paterfami-
lias at the head of the table, with the students like children
listening to what he had to say. I was positioned near him,
but in fact everyone could hear him quite clearly.

The food – three and a half courses – was excellent, but
it was Schaeffer whom people wanted. The conversation
varied immensely, from the Tao of physics to the story of
Isaac and Abraham on Mount Moriah. This last topic had
turned into a major issue for some of the students, especially
after seeing it raised in one of the films. Down in Huémoz
everyone involved in the debate had got tangled up in
existential knots, unsure of why God would ask Abraham to
sacrifice Isaac. One student (Becky, the Kansas physicist)
had tentatively suggested that the story was a picture of
Christ's sacrifice on Calvary – the ram in the thicket was the
'other sacrifice', and Christ was both God's only Son and
the Lamb of God to take away the sins of the world. This
was far too simple for most people. So, without giving
away the earlier conversations, with all their references to
Kierkegaard and other existentialists, the students at the
lunch asked Schaeffer what he thought. Well, he replied, it
was all very simple – the story of Abraham and Isaac was a
marvellous foreshadowing of the death of Christ for our
sins . . .

Kierkegaard cropped up eventually in the discussion, of
course. The Tao of physics, raised by a young American
scientist, revealed how much reading on that subject
Schaeffer had done – the polymathic mind that his daughter
Susan had described to me. But the earlier incident also
revealed the extent to which the caricatures of Schaeffer
were untrue. For it showed that if the question had a simple,
Biblical answer, then that was the reply that Schaeffer gave.
If, as the Tao of physics discussion made clear, the issue
was a complex one, with a lot of preliminary groundwork
needed before bringing in the Gospel, then Schaeffer would
give a longer answer, using the kind of language that he
employs in his books. It illustrated the truth mentioned to
me by Joe Martin and Os Guinness: Schaeffer would always

take people where they were, and talk to them in the way that met their individual, special needs.

L'Abri legend proved true – lunch continued until 5.30 p.m.! The students returned to Huémoz while I stayed on, for some of the time in the study at the top of the chalet, to conclude my interview with Schaeffer. The study contained not only books but magazines, some piled neatly on the floor, and also some of Franky Schaeffer's better-known drawings. We also spent some time talking in the Schaeffers' personal room, with Francis Schaeffer under a rug on the sofa, discussing the state of world politics and the sheer lack of understanding shown by many Evangelicals in relation to the threat of totalitarianism to our society.

The time came to leave, and he bade me goodbye warmly. Eleven months later, he fell badly ill – and himself left Chalet le Chardonnet for ever, to live permanently in Rochester, near the Mayo Clinic. My visit had thus been more special than I could have known.

After an unexpected recovery from serious illness in January 1984, Schaeffer embarked on a mammoth tour, in connection with his latest book *The Great Evangelical Disaster*, and Franky Schaeffer's film of the same name. But when he returned to Rochester, it was discovered that his cancer was worse than before, and after a few weeks he left the clinic for his new Rochester home. He lived there tended for by his family, who had come over to join him. His frequent words to them were 'His grace is sufficient'. He died, with his family near by, early on May 15th, 1984. Many hundreds attended his funeral in Rochester, Minnesota.

Francis Schaeffer has been a major prophet of our time. In an age where secular thought seemed to dominate society, he fought back and has shown that the Bible has the answers as much in the twentieth century as in the first. When many Evangelicals cowered in the trenches, he strode out to battle in the front line. They could only see the symptoms of what had gone wrong and were frightened by what was happening around them. Schaeffer, by contrast, was able to grasp the *causes* of the twentieth-century climate, to diagnose the illness in a way in which they could not.

Consequently he was unafraid to face the issues, and was to confront them. He also realised that apparently isolated events and opinions were all part of a system, originating in a fallen, Godless view of man and the universe. Everything fits together. He was thus able to attack the very roots of humanism in a way impossible for those Christians who insist on dealing with the problem piecemeal.

He provided, for those who agree with him, a framework upon which they can base their own assault on secular culture – in fields as diverse as art, ecology, theology or particle physics. Many Christians have learned the totality of God's truth at L'Abri. For Schaeffer realised that the whole of creation is under the Lordship of Christ and should be reclaimed for it. There is no area to which Christian principles do not apply. Too many Evangelicals have become mere Christian existentialists, relating their faith solely to their personal lives and forgetting the clear Biblical teaching which shows that Christians are commanded to be the salt of the earth in whatever part of it God has placed them.

For the same reason, Schaeffer was able to help those confused young people whom the churches, by their escapist attitude, totally failed to assist. He saw, as many Evangelical leaders have not, that the whole climate of thought had changed, and that the Christian base on which the West had originally been founded has been massively eroded by secular humanism. Biblical terms such as sin – which imply the existence of God and of moral absolutes ordained by Him – no longer mean anything to such young people. To reach modern youth with the eternal Gospel of Jesus Christ one has to go right back to the very beginning, and in a language which they can understand.

As a result, many young people have been saved at L'Abri – and as much by the warm Christian love shown to them there as by anything else. For the Schaeffers did not just believe in truth as a cause to be fought for, they demonstrated that it was something to be lived as well. By these means, Francis Schaeffer taught that the message of Jesus Christ is, without compromise, the most urgent and only remedy for the needs of the twentieth century and one which, from art and philosophy to abortion and politics, touches the whole of life. Schaeffer has been a faithful prophet in our 'space and time'.

JAMES PACKER

Early life

James Innell Packer, the theologian, was born in Gloucester in 1926, son of James Percy Packer, a clerk with the Great Western Railway Company, and his wife, Dorothy Mary Packer, a schoolteacher. He was an introverted, bookish, clever child who preferred reading and study to being sociable with other children. His family was originally from Oxfordshire before moving to Gloucester, which is on the edge of the West Country – even today Packer has retained that region's distinctive burr. His grandfather was the keeper of the New Red Lion in Chalford in the Stroud Valley, and his grandfather had been a gentleman farmer in Oxfordshire, who lost all his stock in a terrible cattle epidemic.

He was brought up in an Anglican home, but as he told me (most of the early part of this chapter is based on his recollections to me), 'we didn't talk about Christianity'. He was not forced to go to Sunday School, but attended church with his parents. He was 'stirred to interest' in Christianity by the son of a Unitarian minister, with whom he played chess. Although at 15 he rejected Unitarianism, he none the less found himself thinking more deeply. He 'never doubted the reality of God', read the Bible and other religious works in the local library and defended the Anglican creeds in debates with atheists at school.

When he was 17 he read two of C. S. Lewis's famous books: *Mere Christianity* and the *Screwtape Letters*, but Christianity remained a set of ideas for him – he had 'no personal relationship with God at all'. An old schoolfriend became a Christian while at Bristol University (the young Packer was still at school, studying to enter Oxford) and tried to explain what had happened to him. But Packer was in complete perplexity about his friend's experience, though he did promise to contact the Christian Union when he got to university. In 1945 he won his place – at Corpus Christi College, Oxford.

Oxford and Conversion

'By the time I went up to Oxford I wanted reality.' He initially studied Greats: Latin and Greek language, history and philosophy. During his first term he played in a jazz band, the 'Oxford Bandits', as their clarinettist. He was (and still is) a great jazz enthusiast, and he found making music a very emotional experience. King Oliver and Louis Armstrong, Morton, Bechet and Bunk Johnson were among the musicians he enjoyed, and he has felt since those days that the New Orleans jazz of the 1920s was the most valuable cultural product to have emerged from North America in the twentieth century. He shared this taste with Hans Rookmaaker, Francis Schaeffer's close friend and collaborator. Packer's Oxford contemporaries felt that he enjoyed jazz, as opposed to orchestral music, because it reflected his introvert personality. But to him, and to Rookmaaker, jazz was fellowship music, an attraction that increased its appeal.

Packer did not just play music and work hard in libraries, however. He kept his promise to contact the Christians at the university and so went to the evangelistic services run by the Oxford Inter-Collegiate Christian Union (OICCU). There, listening to a sermon preached by the former Keswick preacher, the Revd Earl Langston of Weymouth, 'the scales fell from my eyes . . . and I saw the way in'.

It was, he remembers, 'an ordinary conversion' – nothing spectacular – but it made him realise 'where I wasn't and where I ought to be'. He gave up playing in the jazz band partly because he felt that he was not playing well enough, but his new-found faith also made a difference. He was now 'identifying heavily with the OICCU', who met for Bible lectures, known as 'readings', every Saturday night. This clashed with the band, which played the same time. The last reason for his decision was based on the principle in 1

Corinthians 6: 12 that while it would be quite lawful as a Christian for him to continue as a jazz musician, it would not be expedient, because he had become very emotionally attached to the music: he now had other priorities.

He was helped to faith by C. J. B. Harrison, of the Honor Oak Fellowship (Harrison was known to many generations of students as 'Harry Bean'), and by his college's OICCU representative, Ralph Hulme. Hulme attended St Aldate's, then regarded as less reliable than St Ebbe's, which was more narrowly Evangelical, and was also the church where most members of OICCU worshipped on Sundays. So although Packer was heavily involved with OICCU, his decision to follow Hulme to St Aldate's on Sundays meant, he later recalled, that he was thought of as being 'unsound'. Consequently, when James Houston (later to be founder of Regent College in Vancouver, where Packer is now a professor) proposed him for election to the OICCU executive, he was rejected as 'unreliable', which seems astonishing to us today.

Discovering the Puritans

He had, however, got a good academic reputation. When the Revd C. O. Pickard-Cambridge, an elderly clergyman who was going blind, gave a large number of theological volumes to the OICCU, Packer was appointed their junior librarian, as he was known 'to be interested in books'. Among them was 'an uncut set of John Owen', the great Puritan of the seventeenth century. It included his famous treatises on 'indwelling sin', which spoke directly to Packer's needs. This was to be a major turning point in his life, one which was to influence the whole of his future. Doctrine, he discovered, was no mere arid science, but the totally practical study of the living God.

There was much false teaching in Oxford at the time, including some in the OICCU, which implied that even those who were converted needed to go on to a further experience, when they received 'sanctification by faith', and then all the struggle would be over. The young Packer knew this not to be true either to life or to his own Christian experience, but he was at this time a 'very isolated person', and all this wrong doctrine made him 'very anxious'. He felt the 'odd man out'. The followers of these teachings were, he later concluded, either 'very insensitive' or, more to the point, 'very good at kidding themselves' that they could obey all God's laws. In the chapter entitled 'Those Inward Trials', of his book, *Knowing God*, Packer makes out the Biblical case against such doctrine.

Owen, however, 'did me good'. Packer then read Bishop Ryle's great book on *Holiness*, in which he discovered that Ryle based much of his teachings on the Puritans. 'Their insight into the human heart', he found, was unrivalled, and gave him a deepened spiritual interest.

Other students had also discovered that the Puritans gave them the same kind of solid, Biblically based, true doctrine which they had been seeking. They included Raymond Johnston, later to be director of Care Trust, and Elizabeth Lloyd-Jones, my mother and elder daughter of Dr Martyn Lloyd-Jones. They met regularly in the 'British Restaurant' (alas no longer there) to discuss their findings and debate theological issues – and have kept in touch ever since.

The call to the ministry

Packer began to sense that God was calling him to full-time Christian ministry and to a 'teaching role in it'. The idea crystallised over a three-month period and, on 'one long Sunday afternoon with the Lord', he concluded that he 'must enter the ministry'. Like Martyn Lloyd-Jones he felt that the ministry was no mere vocation, but a call from God which one was constrained to obey if summoned. His remaining hesitations were whether, being an introvert, he would be able to deal with the pastoral work. He read the Puritans, and they ministered to him and encouraged him in his resolve.

Then, just before he graduated in 1948, an offer came 'in the good Providence of God' from the Anglican theological seminary at Oak Hill, near London. They wanted a classical languages teacher for their intermediate students, as well as someone to teach Greek. Packer had originally intended to go straight to Wycliffe Hall in Oxford to start ordination training for the Anglican ministry. But he had begun to feel 'Oxford getting under my skin', and that Wycliffe would be an 'airless room' were he to go there immediately.

Oak Hill, he knew, would be different, especially as he then discovered that he would have to teach some philosophy at degree level as well. It was a 'great year'. He also taught Ephesians to those reading for the General Ordination Exam, and all his students graduated. 'I found,' he recalls, 'that I loved teaching . . . teaching was in my genes . . . nobody ever taught me how to teach.' At Oak Hill he also became close to Alan Stibbs, a fine Bible teacher whose *Search the Scriptures* has been used by countless generations of students for their personal Bible studies.

After a year he returned to Oxford. The influences that were to shape his thinking were slowly forming in his mind. First, there was the pietistic, evangelistic influence of OICCU, which emphasised outreach and personal holiness. Then there was the 'practical, pastoral impact of reading the Puritans', such as Baxter and Owen. This linked Packer to Free Church circles, such as that of Martyn Lloyd-Jones. Third, there was what Packer has described as 'the Protestant Evangelical heritage in the Church of England', which he received both from St Ebbe's (where he now went) and from John Reynolds, the senior OICCU librarian.

This heritage, Packer felt, had two strands in it. First, the 'National Protestant' strand – one which was anti-Roman-Catholic and anti-Tractarian (the Tractarians were an Anglican faction that tried to bring back ritual in the last century), pro-1662 Prayer Book and in favour of maintaining the distinctively Protestant worship traditions which that book contained. Packer, however, felt that this group sometimes forgot that the real distinctiveness of the Anglican Church was in its defined doctrines, not in its ceremonies and worship forms.

The other strand was the 'pietistic Evangelical', with its origins in the eighteenth-century revival. Such Anglicans concentrated on winning converts and placing them in fellowship groups, but 'sat loose to Protestant niceties under pressure' if the emphasis of distinctives got in the way of evangelism. Many pietists, because doctrine was underplayed, turned into theological liberals. They wished to keep the experience, but jettisoned the doctrine on which it was based.

Unfortunately the two strands of Protestantism and evangelism often did not intertwine with the result that the churches that were zealously Protestant did not evangelise, and the evangelising churches neglected solid, Reformed doctrine.

Packer noticed that in Bishop Ryle, the two strands, Protestant and pietist, had interwoven. Ryle's books influenced him enormously, and gave him an 'Anglican Evangelical stance' that he has, in many ways, maintained ever since. Above all they provided him with a framework of doctrine, pastoral care and evangelism on which to base his own thinking.

As Ryle and the Puritans were Calvinists, Packer has also inclined that way. But, like Martyn Lloyd-Jones he would call himself 'a Bible Calvinist rather than a system Calvinist'. After reading Hebrews several times, he turned to Romans, and it was his study of that great Epistle that, he recalls, 'made me a Calvinist'. As another distinguished Anglican of the same generation, Dick Lucas of St Helen's, Bishopsgate, London, has pointed out, all the problems that people had on this issue were unnecessary – it was just simply in the Bible. Packer also realised while at Wycliffe that 'God was going to make teaching at tertiary level' a great part of his career.

Another influence was Martyn Lloyd-Jones 'the Doctor', then, in Packer's view, 'on a plateau of supreme excellence' that was to continue throughout the 1950s. Packer heard him every Sunday evening in Westminster Chapel during 1948/9. He had 'never heard such preaching', which came to him like 'an electric shock'. The 'Doctor', Packer recalls, 'brought more of a sense of God than any other man' he had known.

The Doctor's sermons on Matthew 11 made him see what preaching was really all about. Listening to Martyn Lloyd-Jones was like hearing a full orchestra after a piano solo. Packer learned through him about the 'greatness of God and the greatness of the soul'.

New Horizons

The year 1952 was to be a major one in his life. The first important event was meeting his future wife, 'Kit', at a conference held on the North Downs in Kent. The main speaker had double-booked by mistake and so was unable to come. He felt obliged to find a substitute, so asked the already up-and-coming Packer if he would do the job.

Kit was a nurse at St Bartholomew's Hospital, London (where Martyn Lloyd-Jones had trained and where Sir Arnold Stott had been a physician). She was from Llandebie in Carmarthenshire in South Wales. The two of them married in 1954, the same year as his Oxford contemporary Elizabeth Lloyd-Jones married Fred Catherwood.

The Packers have three (adopted) children: Ruth, who is married herself and living in Bristol; Naomi, who is finishing a theology degree at Durham University; and Martin, who is at school in Canada. James Packer (who, as will be seen, is now a professor in Vancouver), comes back to Britain at least every second year to see his family including his sister, who lives in Reading. He also sees old friends including members of the Lloyd-Jones family, and new ones – from the generation who have been influenced by his many published works. Much of the information in this chapter was gathered in conversations I had with Packer on one of his trips.

Packer was also ordained in 1952. He became a curate to the late William Leathem, the gifted Reformed pastor and missionary statesman, in St John's Church, Harborne, Birmingham. In many ways, however, he felt closer to those holding his Reformed views outside the Church of England, in the Free Churches. He was actively involved from the beginning with Dr Martyn Lloyd-Jones in the Puritan Studies Conference, held annually in Westminster Chapel, and was soon associated with the revival of Reformed theology which the doctor was pioneering in Britain.

But he remained an Anglican because of that Church's Evangelical heritage, and stayed in it in order to work for true reformation and renewal from within. To him, all Evangelicals, whether Free Church or Anglican, were 'concerned about Godliness', and he has not regretted the decision that he made then. Apart from his views on ritual, which he now thinks is not an important subject, he told me of his thought in general that 'I had it in my mind by 1952, and it's there still'.

To some, especially those in the Free Churches who deeply admired his exposition of Reformed theology, his arguments for remaining an Anglican were special pleading. This issue will be examined in more detail later – it is important here because it remained a major issue until he went to Canada. While his Anglicanism has never been an issue for Packer himself, it became one in the 1960s when, as will be seen, Free churchmen such as Martyn Lloyd-Jones called upon their fellow Evangelicals in the Church of England to leave it and join the Free Churches outside.

A Leading Controversialist

Packer had always recognised that the parochial side of the ministry was not his primary calling, and in 1955 he entered his real vocation – teaching. He started as a lecturer at Tyndale Hall in Bristol, an Anglican seminary. But he was soon in demand, as a clear speaker on theology, particularly at Inter Varsity conferences. At the Theological Students' Conferences (a part of IVF), where he often took over from Martyn Lloyd-Jones, he was able to influence many generations of future ministers and professors.

Robert Horn, now editor of the *Evangelical Times*, has explained why this was. Until the 1950s, Evangelicals were wary of theology, partly because so many young Evangelical students seemed to lose their distinctive beliefs when they studied it at university or seminary. Consequently, Evangelicals had withdrawn into a pietistic, non-intellectual world of their own, and the major issues raised by the liberal theologians had only been dealt with in a 'piecemeal' fashion by the small number of Evangelical scholars then around.

Martyn Lloyd-Jones did much to dispel this inferiority complex and Packer complemented him, by inspiring young theologians and ordinands with a sense of intellectual self-confidence in the face of liberal theology that they had not possessed before. The fact that one could be fully Evangelical, with a conservative view of Scripture, and intellectually defensible all at the same time was 'an absolute revelation to a lot of people' as they listened to Packer's carefully prepared 'overall exposé of liberalism'. He gave an overall picture of the defence of Evangelical, Biblical truth which, until then, students had had to ferret out from many different sources.

Fundamentalism

The book that established his reputation and which has been the key to his high standing in Evangelical circles, was *Fundamentalism and the Word of God*, published in 1958. In it he gave a solid defence of the *Evangelical* position. The Billy Graham crusades of 1954–5 had aroused a new awareness of Evangelicalism, as had the rapid growth of Christian Unions in the universities.

This had caused a panic and sense of hostility to emerge from among the now threatened Establishment and their allies in the Church. All Evangelicals were tarred with the obscurantist, anti-intellectual brush of certain kinds of American fundamentalism. The sharpest critic was Michael Ramsey, then Bishop of Durham who, in order to argue against a John Stott Mission to Durham University, wrote an article entitled 'Our English Fundamentalism'. Other attacks followed which tried to show that Evangelical doctrine was a new phenomenon and was merely a reaction to modern Biblical scholarship and recent scientific discoveries.

Packer was asked initially by the IVF Graduates' Fellowship to give a talk rebutting that kind of reaction. At Tyndale

Hall, Packer realised that a longer reply was needed, and *Fundamentalism* was the result.

The book did not merely show up weaknesses in the liberal case. It also showed to Evangelicals that theirs was an intellectually tenable faith – indeed it was this aspect of Evangelicalism that differentiated them from the anti-intellectual 'Fundamentalists' and made the liberal portrait of Evangelicals such a ridiculous caricature. Packer aimed to make 'a constructive re-statement of Evangelical principles' in the light of the controversy and 'to fix the right approach to the Bible, to the intellectual tasks of the faith, and to the present debate'. He showed that Evangelicalism was not the 'loosely linked collection of isolated insights' that ecumenical, liberal theology was, but a 'systematic and integrated whole, based on a single foundation'.

The real liberal/Evangelical split was on the 'principle of authority', a point which the liberals had totally missed. 'Authentic Christianity is a religion of Biblical authority', he explained. Where Roman Catholicism had placed tradition, liberalism had placed fallible human reason. Both were perversions of the truth. 'Evangelicalism' was therefore, he argued, 'in principle nothing but Christianity itself.' Fundamentalism, as it had developed, had forgotten this, in its fear of the intellect, and had thus lost Evangelicalism's intellectually virile attitude.

'All truth is God's truth' he argued, 'and right reason cannot endanger sound faith . . . A confident intellectualism, expressive of robust faith in God, whose Word is truth, is part of the historic Evangelical tradition.' Evangelicals should reject the Fundamentalist label and simply call themselves Christian.

The liberals, in failing to see authority as the key issue, simply did 'not know what they are talking about'. Authority was important because 'Christianity is based on truth . . . on the content of a divine revelation', revealed to us by God's Word: Scripture. Evangelicals held the 'original Christian position' that Scripture was both complete and comprehensible, and that it was 'all of a piece', Old and New Testaments together. An implication of this authority was that 'the Bible itself must fix and control the methods of presuppositions with which it is studied'. The liberal position was totally subjective, based entirely on human reason.

It also failed to see that the Bible was simultaneously 'both a fully human and fully divine composition'. Scripture was 'the oracles of God', not merely a random series of books containing elements of truth. The Bible was propositional truth from God that was infallible and without error. Christ himself believed this, and such a view was far more edifying to the Church than was the liberal position. Further, the liberal claim that Evangelicals were obscurantist and irrational was false – it was the liberals that were refusing to 'face all the facts', by rejecting *Christian* reason. True Christians should be 'guided by reasoning faith'. Reason was to 'receive the teaching of God'. Proper reason, whether scientific or otherwise, was to 'appreciate objects for what they are', and to analyse Scripture as being something other than it really was would be unbelief.

Another part of reason was to 'apply the teaching of God to life'. Sadly many Christians had forgotten how to do this – 'God', Packer reminded his readers, 'forbade Christians to lose interest in His world.' As Christ told an enquirer in Matthew, he should 'love the Lord thy God with all thy mind'. Reason was also used in communicating the Gospel to others. It was not, therefore, a clash between faith and reason that was being waged, but a battle 'between a faithful and faithless use of reason', between authority and subjectivism. The mind of liberalism had been permeated by too much secular thinking, and this had warped their view of Scripture. This was true even of the 'New Liberalism', which recognised Christ and the supernatural, but, unwilling to accept the logic of its position and become Evangelical, still stuck to the old methodology and its subjectivism. True Christians recognised that they knew God and His truth only through His testament to Himself – the Word of God in Scripture.

For the beleaguered fifties' generation who read it, Packer's book was, Robert Horn recalls, a 'tremendous shot in the arm', that caused a 'distinct feeling of lifting up drooping heads'. For Packer had not only taken on the enemy, but done so in a way which gave Evangelicals a 'whole rounded doctrine of Scripture'. It expressed what young Evangelical theology students knew they believed but in a sound, doctrinal, systematic way. The book, and Packer's lectures at conferences, 'changed the mood of a whole generation' of students and, through the eminence they later achieved as ministers and professors, has altered the way Evangelicals think today. People could trust Scripture and had no need to fear reason. He 'made doctrine exciting against the popular view' that it was a boring subject best avoided.

Tyndale Hall

He was an effective lecturer at Tyndale Hall, too. Dick France, later a New Testament scholar at London Bible College, commented on his lectures, 'We really felt we were getting the goods.' Packer taught Biblical, historical and systematic theology, and students discovered that if they wrote quickly enough they could obtain a crystal clear, lucid outline of theology that made further reading easier. He would walk into the classroom, look across it, and start at once. In discussion, he could be ruthless with those not sticking to the point, and was always skilful in his handling of questions.

As an introvert he was not strong on the pastoral side of college life. An Anglican former student recalls that he was not the easiest conversationalist over meals and that he never publicly played his jazz clarinet during that student's time at Tyndale. But he had, like Martyn Lloyd-Jones, an astonishingly accurate memory for names. He was also much in demand at Christian Unions. Dick France has described a visit to the OICCU. On the Saturday night he gave a solid Bible lecture, as expected, then on the Sunday delivered a powerful Gospel message that was 'attractive and not at all egg-headed', which, given his cerebral reputation, was not what many expected. In all his talks, Packer taught people to think for themselves – perhaps one of his most important long-term contributions.

Evangelism and the Sovereignty of God

In 1960 a London University mission nearly collapsed and
Packer was sent in to rescue it. 'Missioning,' he felt, was
'not really my thing,' but the talks he gave on the subject
to the students produced a remarkable book: *Evangelism
and the Sovereignty of God*. Under the influence of Martyn
Lloyd-Jones and the Banner of Truth publishing house,
Reformed theology had once again become popular, especially among students. To such people the book was a
'godsend'. It was, Dick France remembers, 'extremely
useful', and made Packer into a 'champion of Reformed
Evangelicalism'.

The book clearly demonstrated that the idea that Calvinists, with their belief in Divine Sovereignty in salvation,
were thus not truly committed to evangelism, was patently
ridiculous, and that, by contrast, it was precisely because
they believed in it that they could evangelise most effectively.
Its 'aim', he wrote, was 'to dispel the suspicion . . . that
faith in the absolute Sovereignty of God hinders full recognition and acceptance of human responsibility, and to show
that, on the contrary, only this faith can give Christians what
they need to fulfil their evangelistic task',

Indeed it was 'nonsense' to believe anything else. Everyone believed in God's Sovereignty when they prayed. Did
those who claimed to reject the doctrine limit themselves,
when praying for non-Christians, 'to asking that God will
bring them to a point where they can save themselves,
independently of him? . . . Nothing of the sort!' Prayer
showed that it was 'not true that some Christians believe in
Divine Sovereignty while others hold an opposite view.
What is true is that all Christians believe in' it, 'but some
are not aware that they do, and mistakenly imagine and
insist that they reject it'. The reason for this 'error' was
'rationalistic speculations . . . a reluctance to recognise the
existence of mystery and to let God be wiser than men,
and a consequent subjecting of Scripture to the supposed
demands of human logic'. Such people were 'not content
to let the two truths' of Divine Sovereignty and human
responsibility 'live side by side as they do in the Scriptures.'

As he commented, while Christians 'should always remember that it is our responsibility to claim salvation' – Christ's command to go and make disciples of all nations was quite clear – they 'must never forget that it is God who saves . . . Our evangelistic work is the instrument He uses for that purpose, but the power that saves is not in the instrument, it is in the hand of the One that uses' it. If Christians regarded it as their 'job, not simply to present Christ, but actually to produce converts', their 'approach to evangelism would become pragmatic and calculating . . . terrifyingly similar to the philosophy of brainwashing . . . a proper concept of evangelism, if the production of converts was our responsibility'.

Part of the problem was that Christians had forgotten what evangelism was, a 'confusion' caused by the 'widespread and persistent habit of defining evangelism in terms not of a message delivered, but of an effect produced in our hearers', i.e. that 'evangelising is producing converts'. The New Testament teaching, however, was that evangelism was 'just preaching the Gospel, the evangel . . . a work of communication in which Christians make themselves mouthpieces for God's message of mercy to sinners'. Packer made clear he felt that the ultra-Reformed position which did not see the necessity to preach the Gospel at all was equally mistaken.

'Anyone who faithfully delivers that message, under whatever circumstances, in a large' or 'small meeting from a pulpit or in a private conversation, is evangelising'. The 'way to tell whether in fact you are evangelising is not to ask whether conversions are known to have resulted from your witness. It is to ask whether you are faithfully making known the Gospel message'.

Packer demonstrated his case from Paul's ministry and writings. He showed that if Christians were engaged in proclaiming the message of salvation in Christ, with the aim of making converts, then they were 'evangelising, irrespective of the particular means by which' they were 'doing it'. It was 'grievously astray' to 'define evangelism institutionally' as some were seeking to do. Packer added, in a paragraph that is as relevant today as then, a description of a church not using the hard-sell methods deemed so necessary by many. 'Imagine a local church, or fellowship of Christians, who are giving themselves wholeheartedly to evangelism by the' means he had outlined as proper,

> personal work, home meetings and gospel preaching at their ordinary services – but have never had the occasion to hold, or join in, evangelistic meetings of the special sort we are considering. If we equated the Christian duty of evangelism with running and supporting such meetings, we should have to conclude that this church or fellowship, because it eschewed them was not evangelising at all. But that would be like arguing that you cannot really be an Englishman unless you live at Frinton-on-Sea. And it would surely be a little odd to condemn people for not evangelising because they do not join in meetings of a type of which there is no trace in the New Testament. Was there no evangelising done, then, in New Testament times?

Sadly, many people, twenty years after Packer wrote this have precisely such regrettable ideas. Packer has occasionally called for a stop to all big meetings and jamborees so that the local Evangelical churches can simply get on in their own areas with their Biblical task, instead of relying on outsiders to do it for them. Tragically for Evangelicalism, far too few churches are listening to this prophetic call and are becoming lost instead in organisation, for the best of motives, instead of doing it in the New Testament way.

In the Holy Spirit's power

Part of the problem, Packer showed, was that Christians had lost the confidence in the power of the Holy Spirit that so marked the early Church and the great missionary journeys of Paul in particular. 'The Sovereignty of God in Grace does not affect anything we have said about the nature and duty of evangelism', nor does it alter its urgency. But, the

'Sovereignty of God in Grace gives us our only hope of success in evangelism', as it gives a 'certainty that evangelism will be fruitful.'

As Paul wrote, man is naturally dead in sin. Humanly speaking, evangelism is a 'hopeless task . . . We can organise special services and distribute tracts, and put up posters, and flood the country with publicity – and there is not the slightest prospect that all this outlay of effort will bring a single soul home to God.' Many realised that there was something wrong with the state of evangelism in Britain – unfortunately they wrongly attributed it to the doctrine of God's sovereignty in salvation.

Packer, however, saw that the real answer was a 'widespread neurosis of disillusionment' arising from the failure to see that evangelism as a *human* enterprise must fail. Evangelicals had come to see it as a 'specialised activity, best done in short sharp bursts', and had fallen 'into the way of assuming that evangelism was sure to succeed if it was regularly prayed for and correctly run (i.e. if the distinctive techniques were used)'. Churches presumed that 'intensive evangelistic mission' backed up by a 'routine of prayers' would do it, but 'well-planned evangelism' had not succeeded in the way they had hoped. Disillusion had thus set in.

Packer had the answer, and backed it up by a clear exposition of Scripture. His response is very relevant today. First, his fellow Evangelicals should 'admit that' they 'were silly ever to think that any evangelistic technique . . . could of itself produce conversions'. Second, they should recognise that man's heart is naturally impervious to the Gospel. Third, they should remember that the Christian's calling was to 'be faithful, not successful'. Lastly, 'they must learn to rest all their hopes of fruit in evangelism upon the omnipotent Grace of God. For God does what man cannot do.'

Packer demonstrated this from Ephesians, Acts and Christ's own words in John 6. It was this assurance that God saves that gave Paul the ability to continue in Corinth (Acts 18).

Paul's confidence should be our confidence too . . . There is no magic in methods, even theologically impeccable methods. When we evangelise, our trust must be in God who raises the dead. He is the Almighty Lord, who turns men's hearts, and He will give conversions in His own time. Meanwhile our part is to be faithful in making the Gospel known, sure that such labour will never be in vain. This is how the truth of the Sovereignty of God's Grace bears upon evangelism.

Christians should be bold, and not downcast if results were not instant. Above all, they should be prayerful – 'because the salvation of sinners depends wholly on God, prayer for the fruitfulness of evangelistic preaching is all the more necessary'.

As Dick France of London Bible College has said, this was 'an extremely useful book'. On the one hand it showed people that belief in the Sovereignty of God actually helped evangelism by giving confidence to those practising it, and by making them more relaxed. Packer has pointed out that Whitefield, with his Reformed views, preached no less than ten sermons a week on average throughout his career. The book also made clear to Reformed Christians that they were to get on with the task of evangelism with the application and urgency that Scripture commanded, something that they too often forgot.

Fighting for the truth

By this time, Packer was fighting new battles. 'Evangelism' had made him one of the leading exponents of the Reformed position in Britain, and he was still active, along with Martyn Lloyd-Jones, in the Westminster Conference for the Study of Puritanism. It was precisely his awareness of the Puritan tradition that led him to remain *within* the Church of England.

To Packer, Roger Beckwith of Oxford has said, Anglican Puritanism was genuine Evangelicalism. Packer saw himself in this tradition, and thus argued that his position of staying within was perfectly defensible. If to be an Anglican was right, it followed that the true, Evangelical foundation of the Church of England had to be defended, especially as it was now under attack. Archbishop Fisher and others were seeking to undermine its essentially Protestant base, by altering canon law, worship and even the founding Thirty-nine Articles themselves.

Latimer House and the Unity debate

John Wenham, a leading Anglican Evangelical New Testament scholar and vice-president of Tyndale Hall, had become worried by the trends and approached Packer after a debate at Oxford in 1958. He proposed an institute in Oxford to continue the fight against theological liberalism. Soon a list of supporters was drawn up and £18,000 raised. The committee decided that the institute should not be another theological research centre, on the lines of the already existent Tyndale House at Cambridge (run by the IVF), but a specifically *Anglican* centre, to help Anglican Evangelicals in their fight against liberalism within the Church of England.

It was named Latimer House, after the great Reformer and martyr. One aim, according to the present warden, Roger Beckwith, was to 'revive Evangelical Anglican scholarship', to provide back-up support for those in the front line. Originally, the staff was to consist of the distinguished theologian Philip Edgcumbe Hughes (who was one of Martyn Lloyd-Jones's closest friends) and another Anglican, Richard Coats. But difficulties arose and, to the loss of British Evangelicalism, Hughes went to the USA, where he became a visiting professor at Westminster Theological Seminary, Philadelphia. Coats started alone and in 1961 persuaded Packer to leave Tyndale Hall, Bristol, to go to Latimer House as librarian. Then Coats left, and Packer remained alone until Roger Beckwith went from Bristol to Oxford as his assistant in 1963.

One of their first tasks was to help those fighting the scheme to unite the Church of England with the Methodists. Many opposed this scheme because of the fact that Methodist ministers were not ordained by bishops. But to Evangelicals, the real cause of concern was not just that the Anglican Church refused to recognise Methodists as ordained, but chiefly because the Methodists had been so permeated by theological liberalism that the defence of the clear, Evangelical foundation of the Church of England would be made all the more difficult once the Methodists were in it.

Packer and others fully accepted that God's family should be seen to be united and enjoy Communion in one another's churches. But true, Biblical, unity was based on unity of faith, on oneness of love, and of a common commitment to the spread of the Gospel. Only when these three prerequisites were met could organic unity, of the type proposed, then proceed. Packer therefore kept raising the doctrinal issue in all discussions. To him the best unity was that of churches getting together in an area to proclaim the Gospel locally.

In 1963 the initial scheme was voted down by the Anglican Church's governing body. The main opponents of unity were the Anglo-Catholics, but Packer was appointed to a commission to study the idea further. The commission favoured union of the two churches in a two-stage scheme, but its report contained a note of dissent from Packer. He not only opposed the basis on which unity was to be achieved – one which reduced doctrine almost to a minimum – but also preferred a one-stage scheme that would confront the churches *now* with the major doctrinal issues which they were trying to avoid. As a result of Evangelical and Anglo-Catholic co-operation, the plan failed to achieve the necessary majority in the Church of England's governing body, and was therefore defeated.

Growing into Union

During the debate, Packer and the two Evangelicals most closely associated with him, Colin Buchanan and Michael Green, worked in harness with two leading Anglo-Catholics, Canon Eric Mascall and Graham Leonard (now Bishop of London). They felt that they had much common ground between them and that this was worth exploring more fully.

The result was that four of them (Michael Green was away) wrote a book entitled *Growing into Union*, and published in 1970.

It was to Packer an exercise in partnership and a good example of scholarly debate. It examined first the doctrinal basis of any future Church. The Anglo-Catholics, unlike the liberals, were quite happy to have the Thirty-nine Articles as their foundation. Scripture and tradition, the sacraments (such as Holy Communion), bishops and non-episcopally-ordained ministers, and the major doctrines of justification by faith, were all discussed in some detail. Points of possible agreement and co-operation were duly noted. The book then went on to look at unity schemes, and go into practicalities for a new united Church.

An attached memorandum (from 1969) made clear that the 'beliefs and practice of the united Church should be controlled by theological norms, with explicit reference to the Bible. The Church must confess its faith in the Christ of the Scriptures, and seek constantly to live under the word of God and to reform its way of life accordingly.' Unity locally should be mission orientated. Local congregations, the book stated, were extremely important (Packer and others felt that the supporters of union had been very elitist in approach to grass-roots opinion), and that true unity should be 'treated as dynamic, growing and flexible, thus marching in step with the concept of the Church as "semper reformanda" '. Indeed, reform was 'basic to reunion', something which Packer has felt very deeply.

One of the comments made in the book was that all four authors declared their

concern that unity should exhibit and retain diversity. If the body of Christ had many differing members, our church life should do justice to that. No doubt there are differences among members in which one is right and one sinful. The nature of church life must promote the healthy living together of such members (with a view to a better mind prevailing). But there are also differences simply deriving from the fact that God by nature and by grace has given different gifts to his different children, and he desires his Church to conserve and exploit the rich variety of abilities contained within it.

This view was natural to someone in a church as varied in its doctrinal emphases as the Church of England. But to many outside, in the Free Churches, Packer had gone too far in his search for ways of accommodation with the Anglo-Catholics. He had conceded too much on, for example, the issue of authority. To many Reformed men, the Anglo-Catholics were no different from their Roman Catholic brethren. Free Church Evangelicals had retained links with him after the split of 1966, and even after the Anglican Evangelical Congress in Keele in 1967, despite the fact that Packer had played a most active role in its proceedings. But the book marked the parting of the ways, and Packer's involvement with Reformed Free Church Evangelicals ceased for a long while.

But the real difference – though Packer would strongly disagree with this view – was that of approach. Packer was essentially an academic, to whom co-operation with those whose views differed from his own was quite natural. One could use some of the fruits of liberal scholarship, for example, without in any way taking a liberal position. To the Free Churchmen, Martyn Lloyd-Jones included, such co-operation was futile. One proclaimed the truth, and lived it, and sought to persuade those who rejected it of their urgent need of salvation – dialogue was just a waste of time. Packer believed in preaching the Gospel – and also in academic dialogue.

A parting of ways

This was not what Packer wanted. On the one hand he had been active in Keele, with those Evangelicals who had decided to remain within the Church of England to fight for its historic doctrines. Hitherto such people had neither been fully in nor fully out in relation to the Church. But, following their decision to reject the secession call made by Martyn

Lloyd-Jones in 1966, they believed that they should now try to work for a 'responsible Anglican movement' and for the truth as they saw it until a new generation arose in the Church of England more responsive to Evangelical truth.

Packer edited a book for Keele entitled *Guidelines*. It showed that Evangelicals such as himself accepted the implications of their Anglican identity, and dealt with the issues relevant to Anglican membership. To outsiders this was compromise, to Packer a sign that Reformation truths were still worth fighting for. Evangelicals like himself had not suddenly accepted all the things that they and the Free churchmen knew were wrong with the Anglican Church, but were seeking to reform from within rather than attack from without.

To men such as Martyn Lloyd-Jones, however, the idea that the Church of England could be reformed was entirely unrealistic. Simply to stay within at all would involve a massive degree of compromise, and they believed that Packer and others were making such compromises already. Francis Schaeffer also regarded Keele as a missed opportunity. But he also rejected the harshness that sadly followed the split between Packer and the Free Churchmen after 1970, when as a result of *Growing into Union*, Packer was asked to leave the Puritan Conference (which was reconstituted to exclude those Evangelicals who remained in mixed denominations).

Packer had always tried to adopt a 'consciously bilateral stance' – that of being an Anglican and a Reformed theologian simultaneously. He knew that he was closer to those who held to the Gospel of Jesus Christ than to those who did not – that he was certainly closer to Free Church Evangelicals than to liberal Anglicans. Yet he felt that to stay within the Church of England to battle for reform and renewal was right. Unfortunately it turned out to be impossible, in the aftermath of 1970, to enjoy fellowship with both kinds of Evangelicals. To the Free Churchmen, it was unthinkable publicly to associate with someone who remained in official fellowship with those theological liberals who denied the very basis tenets of the Gospel.

The situation was worsened when the report of the Church

of England Doctrine Commission, *Christian Believing*, was published. Packer was seen by other Anglicans as one of the foremost defenders of the Evangelical position and was invited to join it. He felt this was a good opportunity and, under Ian Ramsey's chairmanship, all went as he had hoped. Packer was able to help to defend the principle that members of the Anglican Church had to subscribe to the Thirty-nine Articles, and he was able to alter a report on prayer in the right direction.

But Ramsey (Bishop of Durham) died in 1972, and his successor was Professor Wiles of Oxford, a leading liberal. The radicals steamrollered a lot of their opinions through the commission, and created a report much of which was totally unacceptable to Evangelicals. He 'disliked it very much' yet to the dismay of many, Packer went along with the report. His reason was that it was an essentially 'phenomenological' examination of the different strands of thought then in existence – 'descriptive' rather than 'normative'. It had not been the useful guideline to doctrine that he had hoped for. But to have written an essay dissociating from it would have looked like censuring his colleagues. From the academic angle, it had been a useful exercise. He felt that open dissent would not have helped, so *publicly* he stayed silent.

To the separatist Free Church Evangelicals, however, the incident proved the utter futility of remaining within a mixed denomination, and confirmed their decision to exclude Packer from their circle. Once again, one sees the psychological difference between their approach and Packer's. In a sense, their reaction to his signature of the report was right. It is very difficult to see how he could have remained an Anglican. But it is equally arguable that if they had not broken fellowship with him, he might not have made the mistake and they could have realised that he was essentially an academic, whose own position was unchanged. His motives in joining the commission were pure – the defence of the Evangelical position in which both he and the separatists believed.

The whole business had proved Schaeffer's thesis. On the

one hand those who remain within have to concede much in order to maintain a tenable foothold within the denomination. Although such people do not compromise their own doctrinal stand, they have increasingly to shift the line beyond which they will not go and what they are prepared to tolerate from the non-Evangelicals who control the denomination.

On the other hand, those who pull out are, in Schaeffer's thesis, marked by an ever increasing hardness towards those who stay within. By so doing they cut themselves off from fellowship with Evangelical Christians who share the same Gospel as they do. In this way, the true church is split, and the separatists cease to be able either to help or to influence their fellow Evangelicals. To Packer, the Puritan Conference, for example, was a wonderful occasion at which *all* Evangelicals who wanted the spiritual life and better preaching could get together. Many feel it would have been better if he and other Reformed Anglicans had been allowed to stay within. This way, the Free Churchmen could have discussed the issues lovingly with their brother, and perhaps been able to persuade him to devote his efforts to other issues.

Just such a group of Free Churchmen is now arising, led by ministers such as David Jackman, Roy Clements and Ranald Macaulay (Schaeffer's son-in-law). While themselves outside the Church of England in the kind of purely Evangelical denominations advocated by the separatists, they have put the unity of the Gospel, and its defence, above everything else. They have extended a loving hand of fellowship to Packer despite their ecclesiastical differences.

Knowing God

The exclusion of Packer from Free Church Reformed circles became all the more sad when, from the mid-1970s onward he started to champion the cause of Scripture, not just against the liberals, as in the past, but now also against those who professed to be Evangelicals themselves. Like Schaeffer, but unlike those who devoted their energies to denominational struggle, he saw that inerrancy had turned into the watershed issue. His battle was all the more effective as he had, in 1973, published his most famous book, *Knowing God*. This was to sell 500,000 copies in its first decade, and it influenced many generations of Evangelicals, especially in the universities.

Part of the reason was that it was not a heavyweight theological tome but an eminently practical book which enabled readers to grasp many complex truths by seeing them logically arranged together in one volume. Its systematic format put together, in a way people could digest, key truths that had hitherto been spread through many books. It showed, in an age that often forgot the importance of doctrine, that the study of God was as relevant as ever. Five key truths opened the book. First that God has spoken to man and that the Bible is His Word for salvation; second that God is King and Lord over His world; third that He is Saviour, 'active in Sovereign love through the Lord Jesus Christ'; fourth that God is triune – 'the Father purposing redemption, the Son securing it and the Spirit applying it'. Last Godliness on our part is responding to God's revelation in trust, obedience, faith, worship, prayer, praise, submission and service. This was something Christians wanted to hear, and accounts for the book's remarkable – and still continuing – popularity. While many Christians have not read all of it, they have found it helpful as a source of reference, always with its accompanying study guide.

The book takes the reader through the attributes of God, not just to give doctrinal knowledge, but as 'a means to the further end of' Godly living. 'One can know a great deal about God,' Packer wrote, 'without much real knowledge of Him.' Those who truly know Him have 'great energy for' Him and 'great thoughts of' Him. They obey Him and have contentment in Him. We need to know Jesus Christ in order to know the Father, and knowing Christ 'involves going with Him, now as then'. This knowledge of God affects our 'mind, will, and feeling' – our emotion as well as our intellects. Further, 'we do not make friends with God' but He with us.

What really matters is that 'He knows me' that gives the Christian the 'unshakeable comfort' that 'no discovery can now disillusion Him about me' – a real incentive for worship if ever there was one. Packer then looked at idolatry, which dishonoured Him by obscuring His glory and reducing Him to our level. God is a God of revelation, not symbols, and above all through His word made flesh – Jesus Christ. This is at the heart of the New Testament, with Calvary at the centre. (The book examines all the different aspects of Christ's ministry on earth.) The Trinity, Packer felt, was a neglected doctrine, and he thus went on to describe the work of the Holy Spirit. Without Him there would be 'no Gospel and no New Testament'.

God is an unchanging God, from everlasting, whose ways and character never change. Nor do His truth, His ways or His purposes. Nor does Jesus Christ change – which means that the experience of Christians today should be the same as those of the New Testament. God is a majestic God, whose power is far greater than we can ever imagine. Wisdom is another of His attributes, and is linked to His omnipotence, and His purposes.

God has not abandoned His aim that man should live in fellowship with Him and to His glory. Christians should see 'all life in relation to Him' – just as Abraham and Paul did. God communicates His wisdom to men, through His word. We do not see all His strategy, but those parts of it we need to know, to mould us and to increase our trust in Him. Wisdom for us is to trust in and obey God and to enjoy His good gifts. God's word is truth. In Bible times, the King spoke in terms of decrees and in speeches that established a rapport with the people. God does the same with us – law, promise and testimony, as revealed in Scripture.

God is love. The fruits of His love are central, more important than the gifts. Revival is not just a time when the gifts are made evident, but when the 'longing that the Spirit may shed God's love in our heart with greater power' comes to pass. God is also the God of Justice and light – His is a 'Holy love'. While His love for us is the main attribute for Christians, He is not soft in relation to others. Above all,

His love is expressed in the gift of His Son to us as Saviour, bringing us forgiveness of our sins and into a new, covenant relationship with Him. Why do so many Christians grumble, divide and become half-hearted when He has done everything for them? Why do they not show love to others?

Packer then dealt with God's grace, the issue covered in 'Evangelism', before going on to show what the Bible taught on the subject of God as judge. This gave Christians a 'revelation of the moral character of God . . . imparting . . . moral significance to human life'. God's wrath was often ignored, but was an important Biblical teaching. It should not be a taboo area. His wrath was always judicial and righteous, and was 'God's resolute action in punishing sin'. The 'heart of the Gospel' was that in Jesus Christ on Calvary, God provided the one way of redemption from His wrath. He was not the 'Santa Claus' God of liberal theology. Propitiation was an unpopular concept, yet it was central to the New Testament message. 'When you are on top of the truth of propitiation', he wrote, 'you can see the entire Bible in perspective'.

The Christian's 'highest privilege'

After dealing in a clear way with the Gospel message, Packer then went on to deal with the practical side of Christian life – perhaps one of the reasons why the book has had such a wide appeal. He started with the glorious fact that God is the Father of all Christians. Adoption by God through the blood of Jesus Christ is 'the highest privilege that the Gospel offers'. Justification is the first blessing, but adoption is higher because 'of the richer relationship with God that it involves'. The Sermon on the Mount is the Christian family code. Adoption gives 'an ethic of responsible freedom' and is the basis of our access to our Father in prayer.

The New Testament could be described as 'adoption through propitiation'. It shows the glory of what God has done and includes the promise of an eternal inheritance, 'a share in the glory of Christ'. Packer then details many of the practical results of adoption, including the role of the Holy

Spirit. He deals with Christian morality, the thorny problem of guidance, and then with the 'inward trials' that so beset the Christian life.

With the memories of his own trials in Oxford in mind, he demolishes the kind of false, unwittingly 'cruel' teaching that says that Christians can know complete victory over sin in this life. The Christian is fighting a daily battle, he reminds readers; sin is part of the struggle. Endlessly to try to claim total victory over it is to put oneself under a new bondage, and 'sentences devoted Christians to a treadmill life of hunting each day for non-existent failures in consecration'. This produces either 'grinning, irresponsible' Christians, stuck in spiritual infancy, or a breakdown of Evangelical faith. It omits all Biblical teaching on chastening by God of His children and 'loses sight of the method and purpose of grace' which is 'God drawing us sinners closer and closer to Himself'. He does so not by mollycoddling His children, but by constantly bringing us back to Him through making us realise how much we need Him. 'Unreality towards God', Packer wrote, 'is the weakening disease of much of modern Christianity.'

There then follows a chapter, based on a clear exposition of Romans, on the 'adequacy of God'. This combines solid theology with practical application. There is now no condemnation for the Christian. He can stand all assaults with God as his shield. When problems seem to overwhelm, Packer, like Martyn Lloyd-Jones in *Spiritual Depression*, reminds Christians to 'let Evangelical thinking correct emotional thinking'. Calvary proved that God is our sovereign benefactor in whom there is complete assurance.

Christians therefore have no need to fear, yet often they do, because in their heart of hearts they are 'afraid of the consequences of going the whole way in the Christian life'. They have forgotten that 'He will give us all things'. Furthermore, 'no accusation can ever disinherit us' – as it is God who justifies, no one can challenge the verdict. Many Christians today have other priorities, but the 'true priority' of every Christian ought, as always, to be 'learning to know God in Christ'.

Knowing God dealt with these themes in far greater detail than is possible here. Packer has said that he is a Packer by name and a Packer by nature, with the result that each of his books is very closely argued. But because the book is primarily pastoral in aim, it is one that should be read precisely for the fact that it manages to put so much into one volume. It is perhaps typical of Packer that the *magnum opus* on systematic theology that so many Christians (not to mention Christian publishers) have been waiting for for so long will not be just a learned academic treatise, but also a practical book to help students in theological colleges. Many have lamented the fact that he has not produced such a volume before. But since the 1950s he has devoted a considerable part of his energy, and of his literary output, in helping the soldiers in the front line. His new book, while not written for the generals, will at least be the work that influences in a lasting way the thoughts of the generals of future generations.

The Battle for the Bible

One of Packer's constant refrains in *Knowing God* was that God spoke to people through God's word – the Bible. The 'Battle for the Bible', as it became known in America, thus had very considerable implications. For, if the Bible was known to contain mistakes, how then could it be trusted? If God's Word had error, then much of the *spiritual* teaching within it could also be mistaken. The defence of Scripture was therefore an urgent priority – something which Evangelicals such as Schaeffer and Packer clearly saw.

Although Packer, now (1971) back at Trinity College, Bristol (Tyndale had merged), was cold-shouldered by many in his own country, Evangelicals in the USA turned to him for help with increasing regularity. They had seen how vitally important the issue was. For it was not simply a case of saying that all Evangelicals should stick together in one group. The problem went farther back.

There were now many who claimed to be Evangelical, yet who rejected what had hitherto been one of Evangelicalism's most basic tenets – the infallibility and inerrancy of all Scripture as originally given. These neo-Evangelicals taught that Scripture was infallible on all spiritual and moral matters, but contained error when it came to historical and scientific matters within it – that the Bible was *not* inerrant. Much of this teaching came, according to an attack on it published by Harold Lindsell, from Fuller Theological Seminary in the USA, and those individuals influenced by Fuller thinking.

In 1965 a conference had been convened in Wenham, USA, to try to stop the drift. Packer addressed it, but discovered that the polarisation between the different views was exacerbated by the conference format, so that nothing constructive resulted. In 1973 a Presbyterian named R. C. Sproule called a meeting for the defenders of inerrancy. This time the conference yielded results – in the shape of the book *God's Inerrant Word*, to which Packer contributed two chapters. At a subsequent gathering Packer and others decided that something more permanent was needed. So the International Council on Biblical Inerrancy was founded. It was to have a 'two-pronged' strategy, designed to combat anti-inerrantist teaching. It would organise creative scholarship at the appropriate academic level and also start a popular education programme for use in churches.

Major conferences were convened in Chicago in 1978 and in San Diego in 1981. Inerrancy was tightly defined at Chicago, and its relevance made clear at San Diego. The Bible *could* be trusted. A further meeting for scholars took place in Chicago, in late 1982, on hermeneutics. Packer was a major draughtsman for all the statements – the most important of which forms the appendix to his book *God Has Spoken*.

In his essay 'Freedom, Authority and Scripture', Packer makes the point that inerrancy is a profoundly practical issue.

It is really about knowing, trusting, obeying and proving God as a way of life. It is an illusion to think that differences of opinion about the meaning and trustworthiness of the various strands of Biblical instruction make no difference to one's thoughts about God, one's relationship to Him, and one's moral practice. What is actually at stake is whether, or how far we learn the secret of supernatural living and of pleasing God.

Entry into such a life came through accepting and obeying the teachings of God as revealed in Scripture.

True freedom – freedom from sin, freedom for God and for righteousness – is found where Jesus Christ is Lord in living personal fellowship. It is under the authority of a fully trusted Bible that Christ is most fully known and this God-given freedom most fully enjoyed. If, therefore, we have at heart spiritual renewal for society, for churches and for our own lives, we shall make much of the entire trustworthiness – that is, the inerrancy – of Holy Scripture as the inspired and liberating Word of God.

Bristol and the Anglican identity crisis

In 1970 Packer left Oxford to become principal of Tyndale Hall in Bristol, but the following year the bishop arranged a merger of the three Evangelical theological colleges in Bristol, as part of the general rationalisation programme. So Packer found himself associate principal, working with Alec Motyer, of the new Trinity College. He discovered that, in a bigger college, he did not have the room to manoeuvre he had been able to enjoy at Tyndale. He had just reformed the syllabus there, and changed it into an organic teaching pattern, where the interconnections between the academic and pastoral training sides of the course could clearly be grasped by the students. At Trinity such linkage was not possible. He soon had at least ten hours of administration a week on top of his already arduous teaching and counselling duties. Time to sit back and think or write was scarce.

The follow-up conference to Keele – Nottingham '77 – was, to him, a 'non-event'. He 'did not believe in it as a Congress'. He argued that to hold it was unnecessary, but agreed to participate by contributing a paper on Christology and lending a hand in the planning. The exclusion order against him by many of his former Reformed colleagues meant that he was unable to pursue his bilateral course of remaining an Anglican and continuing close co-operation with Free Churchmen who held Reformed views like himself. He felt increasingly that the revival was what mattered, yet saw the opportunities for it in the Church of England ebbing away as his fellow Anglicans absorbed all their energies in meetings and congresses. Those that shared his passion for revival were often precisely those Free Church Evangelicals who had severed contact with him. It was a frustrating situation.

In 1978 he published a pamphlet entitled 'The Evangelical Anglican Identity Problem'. In it, he first proved to his critics that despite his participation in *Growing into Union* (which he saw as a Schaefferite exercise in co-belligerence) and the commission report 'Christian believing', he was still an Evangelical. On the fundamental doctrines of the faith, he reminded them, 'all Evangelicals are at one' – the Trinity, Christ's deity, grace and faith, justification by faith through Christ's substitutionary death on the Cross and so on. All believed in the authority of Scripture, and in the 'constant priority' of evangelism. All share a 'Christ-centred spirituality in which fellowship with the risen Lord by faith is central'. All other differences were secondary and were 'within the family'. However much *these* differences caused a strain, true Evangelical unity existed wherever the basic principles were found.

There was, none the less, an acute identity problem for those Evangelicals who stayed loyal to these basic principles and yet also remained within the Church of England, with its very broad span of belief. Packer analysed the historic position and the changing role of Evangelicals within the Anglican Church during the twentieth century. The problem was heightened by the fact that after Keele, Evangelicals had decided to seek a more active part in Church affairs. They should, he felt, understand the psychology of their problem, and by so doing 'affirm their identity by positive evaluative Biblical thinking' about their Church situation. They should also seek spiritual revival in the Church.

In the sequel pamphlet, Packer spelled out his own position more explicitly. The Anglican system had within it a degree of pluralism some might find strange. This view was a proper one, which people such as himself ought to recognise. But, he wrote, Evangelicals

> were right to approve the older type of comprehensiveness, based on common acceptance of the fundamentals of the creed, but that they cannot and, for a fact, do not commend or condone what historic comprehensiveness has now turned into. They accept it reluctantly and with sorrow, as in a fallen world and an imperfectly sanctified church they accept much else reluctantly and with sorrow. They accept it not as one of Anglicanism's special goodies [sic] but as the unavoidable result of Anglicanism's other qualities, namely its desire to rule out no questions and clamp down on no discussions, but to give every viewpoint which claims, however freakishly, to be in line with Scripture and reason, opportunity to make its claim good, if it can. Approving this quality as a mark of both human and Christian maturity they are prepared to show conscientious good will to a good deal of experimental theology which would, perhaps, be looked at askance in doctrinally unmixed churches. But in accepting Anglicanism's present doctrinal plurality in this way, their conscience is good and their commitment to doctrinal purity as an ideal

remained uncompromised for two main reasons.

First they saw that

> in the providence of God much insight, stimulus and help in understanding spins off from work done by good scholars whose claim to be interpreting Christianity is marred by some seemingly heterodox opinions . . . because of the great potential benefit of what the theological explorers do, Anglican Evangelicals think it right to be patient with them.

Heresy was better refuted by public analysis 'than from any
use of the big stick on the offending author'.

Second, 'Evangelicals see it as part of their own task in
the Church of England to serve present and future
Anglicans (not to say members of the doctrinally unmixed
bodies mentioned earlier) by themselves tackling off-key
views in debate and showing them to be inadequate.'
While Evangelical theology was pure and true, Packer felt
one could still learn from other positions in debate. There
was 'no solid reason to suppose that those Anglicans who',
like Packer himself, 'contend for the historic gospel are
fighting a losing battle'.

His own aim remained clear – 'Reformed theology, Reformed pastoral care of individuals and Reformed worship',
within the Church of England. But while these arguments
– the historical tradition of Anglicanism and the ability to
debate in a way constructive to growth – appealed to Packer,
they appeared to many, including those who greatly admired
all the battles he had fought for the faith, as 'special pleading'. They did not find in this work the majestic sweep of
Knowing God, of Packer at his brilliant best. Further, if he
was still seen by many as an Anglican, his much more
important general theological views could be ignored by
those who took a separatist position.

The call to Canada

American Evangelicals, however, because of his concern
about the vitally urgent issue of defending Scripture, were
increasingly asking him to visit the USA as a guest lecturer
to speak out in defence of the Bible. Whereas he was stymied
in Britain, these Americans were asking him to do 'things
that seemed to me significant'. People, he felt, 'tend to
pursue lines that open up'.

Regent College, Vancouver (Canada), a transdenomi-
national Evangelical college, asked him 'out of the blue' to
be a professor on their staff. He would have no administrative
duties, and not such a heavy counselling commitment with
students as he had had at Trinity. On the positive side,

he would have plenty of time for writing and for reflection, as well as being on the side of the Atlantic where his talents were better appreciated. The offer, he realised, would make him a 'perfectly square peg' in a 'perfectly square hole'.

All the frustrations he had been suffering in England would be over. He had wanted churches in Britain to get on with their proper Biblical task of being local churches ministering to the needs of their own areas, instead of losing themselves in meetings and jamborees. He did not feel he had succeeded in the task of persuading them of this. Too many of his fellow Anglical Evangelicals had in his view settled for being a mere wing of the Church of England with a distinctive view of their own. They were not interested in Reformation and renewal, but in being tolerated and allowed to get on with their own task undisturbed. Too many of them were not engaged in evangelism in their own churches, but relied instead on outside bodies to do it for them. In Canada, he would be away from all the frustrations that this sad situation created for him.

So in 1978 he accepted the offer and has been based in Canada ever since. He still comes to Britain, and in 1983 was invited by a group of Anglican and Free Church Evangelical ministers to address a conference on preaching. He spoke to them on the key issue – the defence of Scripture. He then added a plea for all Evangelicals to return to the unity which they had enjoyed in the 1950s, and to forget the splits on denominational issues which had kept them apart in recent years. Most of those present, especially those from the younger generation who represented thriving and growing churches, agreed with him. It was *Evangelical* distinctiveness that mattered, they felt, and it was Evangelical unity that would bring about the revival which all who truly loved the Gospel longed to see. Other issues, in comparison to those distinctives that made Evangelicals Evangelical, were less important.

Packer was being listened to again. Many feel that when his major systematic theology is published, his reputation will be established permanently amongst the majority of

Evangelicals, and confirm the standing that *Knowing God* had given him.

As his lifelong friend Raymond Johnston has said, Packer's eminence among Evangelicals is primarily due to the 'quality of his mind'. He gave 'total coherence' to Evangelical doctrine at a time when beleaguered theological students needed it most. Books such as *Knowing God* have, by providing a 'total architecture to Christian belief', given the same help to students and Christians generally of subsequent generations. Theological students no longer had so much to fear from liberalism – Packer had demonstrated its bankruptcy. He also, along with Martyn Lloyd-Jones, put Reformed theology on the map after it had suffered a period in the doldrums. He showed in theory, as Martyn Lloyd-Jones did in practice, that Reformed people were not only as committed to evangelism as those who held different views, but were in fact able to evangelise from a far more secure base. Although many disagreed with him on his decision to remain within the Anglican Church, he was able to give a solidly Evangelical rationale to those who followed him in this decision. Above all, in an era when the Gospel has been under attack, and at a time when Scripture has been assaulted not just from outside, but from within, he has demonstrated that the Evangelical position is the truly Christian one and that part of the defence of the message of Jesus Christ has been to affirm the total inerrancy of the Bible in all its states and reaches. He has shown that theology is no arid science when practised by men whose commitment is to revival in the Church, and that doctrine, far from being arid, is the key to the fullness of Christian experience that should be the joy of every Christian.

BILLY GRAHAM

Early life

William Franklin Graham – 'Billy' – was born on November 7th, 1918, the son of Franklin and Morrow Graham. The Grahams were of old Confederate stock, and farmed just outside Charlotte, North Carolina. His parents were initially not at all religious, but changed in 1933, particularly after Frank Graham suffered an injury. Then in the autumn of 1934 Billy's life was altered too, when the fiery evangelist Mordecai Ham came to town. Till then Billy had been a typical country boy – average at schoolwork, keen on games, always ready for fun. To start with he thought Ham was a 'wild fanatic', but slowly but surely he became convinced of his own sin. He discovered that one could 'know Christ personally', and, near the end of the crusade, went forward to commit his life to Christ. Although, as childhood friend Grady Wilson recalls, Billy was 'by nature very shy' he soon found himself speaking in public. In 1936 evangelist Jimmy Johnson persuaded him to give his testimony to prisoners, and his career as an evangelist without his realising it, had begun.

Billy originally intended to attend North Carolina University. But his mother had been impressed by evangelist Bob Jones, who ran a college in Tennessee, and so Billy decided to go there instead, to join his friends Grady and T. W. Wilson. To fill in time, he and the Wilson brothers sold toothbrushes. Billy was so sincere, Grady recalls, that he believed his own sales patter and nearly ruined his own teeth on the brushes. Bob Jones's College turned out to be a mistake. It was not academically credited and far too strict for Billy's liking. So he transferred to another place his mother had found – the Florida Bible Institute near Tampa.

There he spent three and a half happy years. By 1937, thanks to his tutor John Minder, he was given his first preaching engagements. He was slowly changing from being the carefree country boy into the serious preacher. Two Christians he admired were found guilty of grave moral slips, which made him realise the need to depend more on God personally; he was influenced both by the visiting speakers and by his then girlfriend and fellow student Emily Cavanaugh. To be a preacher would, he now saw, need total commitment. In March 1938, at a place called the '18th Green', near his Institute, he decided to become 'an Ambassador for Jesus Christ'.

His ministry begins

He began preaching with a new vigour, undimmed by Emily's rejection. He helped with street services in the rougher parts of Tampa and at the Tampa Gospel Tabernacle. He made up in zeal for what he would later say he lacked in quality. The Baptists specially liked him, and although he had originally been a Presbyterian, he was ordained a Baptist minister in 1939. The following year he moved to Wheaton, Illinois, to study anthropology at the famous college there. One of his fellow students was Ruth Bell, the daughter of the famous China missionary, Dr Nelson Bell.

By 1941 Billy Graham and Ruth Bell were engaged. Ruth, a Presbyterian, and from a more sophisticated background, helped to broaden his horizons. Her sound common sense (revealed most charmingly in her book, *It's My Turn*) and deep spirituality were to prove of immense help to him in the years to come. She provided him with the devotion and security he needed, but also gave him well-thought-out advice. She has been a model of what a Christian wife ought to be and the Grahams' marriage has been an example and encouragement to many. The wedding took place in 1943, just as his ministry was getting under way.

Graham's first pastorate was in Western Springs, near Chicago, but his ministry soon widened. He was asked to take over the commercial radio programme *Songs in the Night*. The soloist he hired was a popular Canadian-born singer, George Beverly Shea – the partnership has lasted ever since. He also spoke, at the request of the Revd Torrey Johnson, at a successful Youth for Christ rally in Chicago. Graham had decided to enter the Army chaplaincy, but fell ill and, rather than accept a desk job, resigned his commission in order to concentrate on working with Youth for Christ. He made a series of whistle-stop tours round the USA and Canada, then in 1946 visited Britain with Youth for Christ. The team were very American in their manner, and committed several gaffes, including that of staying in an expensive hotel at a time when many British people were short of food. But Graham learned a lot – including the need for cultural sensitivity, an asset that was a major factor in his later, highly successful, Third World crusades.

His career took another turn in 1947 when William Bell Riley, the octogenarian head of the Northwestern Schools in Minneapolis, asked Graham to succeed him. He was reluctant at first but, when Riley died within months of making the offer, reconsidered, and was appointed president with childhood friend T. W. Wilson as his deputy. The motto he chose for the school was 'Knowledge on Fire'. He quickly tired, however, of the frustrations of administrative life and, while retaining his post, soon set off again on evangelistic meetings round the country.

He revisited Europe where he met Dawson Trotman, the founder of the Navigators. This greatly influenced him as Trotman enabled him to see the crucial importance of following up the converts made at rallies, a policy that had been sadly lacking in mass evangelism, including Graham's own. He attended the World Council of Churches Congress in Amsterdam in 1948, showing, according to his official biographer, John Pollock, that 'he would not hesitate to break the taboos of his circle in order to further the Gospel'. This was a different view from that expressed by his fellow Evangelicals, Martyn Lloyd-Jones and Francis Schaeffer.

Some time after his return from Europe, Graham had

a spiritual crisis that was greatly to help his subsequent evangelism. He had never had a formal theological training and felt the need for a deeper level of knowledge than he then possessed. A friend of his, Chuck Templeton, had also become dissatisfied with a certain lack of depth in Youth for Christ and had gone to Princeton Theological Seminary as a result. But the prevailing liberal atmosphere there had caused him to doubt the authority of Scripture. He argued the case with his friend, and slowly doubts began to enter Graham's mind too. Was his faith as simplistic as Templeton maintained?

He went to a conference in California and decided to pray to God for guidance. As he did so he realised that he could not answer many of Templeton's intellectual queries, but he knew that from that moment on he would accept the Bible by faith as the Word of God. The phrase 'The Bible says' has become one of his most famous expressions. He has never had any doubt that his unashamed faithfulness to the Word of God, coupled with his totally sincere belief in its truth, has been perhaps the major factor under God in his success as an evangelist. To walk in integrity before God and His Word has been his 'greatest desire'. As he has said, 'I really mean what I'm preaching.' His simplicity and clarity when speaking may in no small measure be thanks to the fact that he never had his theology complicated by a seminary education.

The 'most successful evangelist' . . . in America

This transparent sincerity and trust now helped him to become almost overnight the most famous evangelist in the USA, and even more important, the most respected. The Los Angeles crusade started in September 1949, and was conducted without any drama. Billy Graham was already known in the Christian world as a man with a 'quick mind, facile tongue and a magnetic platform personality' coupled to a 'spiritual punch which has merited him unusually wide acceptance in different religious groups all over America'. He was well aware of his limitations, and told the magazine

Christian Life in July 1949 that he 'prayed years ago not to be a great preacher but a great soul-winner'.

It was his decision to extend the Los Angeles crusade that lifted it from being yet another event into a nationally known success. A well-known radio personality Stuart Hamblen, who had one of the rowdiest shows on the air, was converted. His broadcast testimony created a stir, as did the conversion of criminal Jim Vaus. These events made Graham and his team resolve to go on. Hearst, the newspaper magnate, ordered his reporters to 'puff Graham', and the North Carolina evangelist became an instant national celebrity.

As the magazine *Illustrated* noted on December 31st, 1949, a 'wave of religious revival', led by 'hot gospel' men of whom Billy Graham was the 'most flamboyant' was sweeping America. In the Los Angeles tent, it observed, 'he hypnotises the six thousand nightly by a blend of good showmanship, common sense and a fine voice'. The publicity preceded him to Boston, an area of the USA usually thought of as hardened against the Gospel. Yet, as Grady Wilson recalls, the visit was 'the closest thing to revival that I've ever seen'. He ended up preaching, the *Reporter* commented in its article 'How Beulah Land Came to Boston', to a total of over 100,000 people in seventeen days, including a record 16,000 on January 16th, 1950.

Further invitations for him to preach poured in. In Columbia, South Carolina, he spoke to the state legislature, and the crusade was attended by the famous Henry Luce, owner of *Time/Life*. As the *Christian Herald* noted, these three crusades meant that 'West, East and South, America is responding en masse to the old-time Gospel'.

The leading secular magazine, *Newsweek*, commented on May 1st, 1950 that Graham had 'clinched his title as America's greatest living evangelist'. The article was not sympathetic to his Evangelical Christianity, but it highlighted two key reasons for his success. Evangelism had become discredited in the eyes of many Americans – the 'Elmer Gantry image' (named after the fictitious evangelist in the novel). Many evangelists would abuse the names of local ministers, then alienate the audience further by blatant appeals for money – euphemistically called 'love offerings'. *Newsweek* noted, however, that 'Mr Graham, unlike many evangelists, will not visit a town unless invited by local ministers . . . Also . . . Mr Graham doesn't emphasise love offerings. His salary at Northwestern Schools is $8,500 a year – his main source of income.' The local committees guaranteed his expenses only, and those which 'lose money from his visits are reimbursed by those which profit'.

The secular picture paper, *Look*, observed on June 14th, 1950 that another reason was the 'impeccable behaviour of his revivalist team . . . Acutely aware of the sometimes shady reputation of revivalism as an occupation, Graham has struggled to keep his ministry clean.' His team, which now included the popular Cliff Barrows, were, like Graham himself, always smartly dressed. As *The Pathfinder* commented, his 'spellbinding oratory is as colourful and up to date as the flashy ties he wears'. To him, 'Christians are the only people in the world who have anything to be happy about' and evangelism ought to project an attractive image to help win people.

T. W. Wilson, Graham's long-time chief of staff, has stated that part of the team's success has been the providence of God at work. Even the secular press acknowledged that something special was happening. *Look*, in an article in January 1951, noted that it was 'doubtful whether, in any other age, Graham would have enjoyed his enormous success of the last two years'. The USA was being 'stirred by a religious consciousness the like of which it has not felt since the turn of the century'. It was 'Moody's old revival message warmed over the fires of contemporary events . . . All the substitutes for religious faith seemed to have failed when he appeared. The scientists had to confess that though they could control the atom, they couldn't control human beings. Communism and Fascism, which purchased human freedom with promises of security and happiness, gave neither in return. The failures of these ideologies sent people searching for a personal faith.'

Furthermore, it was Evangelical Christianity that the masses were turning to, not the liberalism that had prevailed between the wars. Noting the growth of Christian belief on the university campuses, the magazine went on to observe, 'In the present revival, the influence of the Modernists is almost nil. Once again, emphasis is on the Gospels as the Word of God, rather than the mortal records of a period in history.' Remarkable changes were occurring. Revival was crossing all class and racial barriers. In the segregated South, Baptists were beginning to treat black believers as equals for the first time.

Graham on his own success

Billy Graham was being hailed as 'the most successful evangelist in the world today'. Americans, as distinguished Evangelical theologian Lewis Drummond has commented, 'love a hero', and Graham had become one. But he himself had no doubts as to the real cause. He told *Christian Life* in January 1951 that 'all the glory and the praise and the credit must go to God the Holy Spirit. It is the Holy Spirit that convicts, the Holy Spirit that regenerates, and it is the Holy Spirit that carries on the work after we've gone. It is actually all a supernatural performance and a supernatural process. All we are is witnesses to the saving grace and power of the Lord Jesus Christ. And I sincerely believe that any man preaching a simple Gospel message in the power of the Spirit can expect results if he is speaking to unconverted people.'

Follow-up, especially by the local churches, was essential, as was solid doctrinal teaching to build the new converts up in faith. When it came to the invitation at the end of each message, he made it clear that 'I'm very much opposed to general invitations that call people forward for anything in order to get a move. We try to make our invitations straightforward, so that a person knows he is coming for conversion and salvation.' The real work was that of the Holy Spirit and, through him, the local churches, in salvation and follow-up. It was these emphases that made Billy Graham different and, under God, gave him the power that astonished even the most cynical of listeners.

The ministry expands

His ministry was expanding rapidly. In order to cope with this, and in order too to keep the financial side of his work indisputably clean, he established the Billy Graham Evangelistic Association. No more 'love offerings' were to be taken. Graham was to be paid a regular salary, at the same rate as ministers of big city churches, as a paid employee of the Association. The team would be paid in the same way. All their income would come from central funds, so that they could offer their services free to those inviting them. (The costs of each crusade, such as publicity, hiring of halls, etc, would be met locally.) One of the new, centrally supported, ventures was the nationally broadcast *Hour of Decision* evangelistic programme. Graham was initially reluctant to begin such a series, but the necessary funds arrived within the deadline he had set for guidance. The broadcasts, soon to be networked over 150 stations, began on November 5th, 1950.

The team also altered the terminology of evangelism. From now on, 'revivals' were given the more proper name of crusade, and 'counsellor' was used instead of 'personal worker' – terms that have stuck ever since.

One of the greatest contributions Graham has made to Christianity in the USA has been the cause of promoting genuine reconciliation and integration between black and white. The fact that he has been so active in this (often at the cost of losing considerable support from many white Americans) has been a major factor in the immense success he has enjoyed in Third World countries generally and in Africa in particular. The American South, where he was raised, had a terrible racial record, and it was not until he came to the North and studied anthropology at Wheaton, that he came to see that black people were his full equals. This same Southern background proved, however, to be of immense help when his crusades in the South began.

Southerners resented interfering liberal northerners ordering them to integrate with the blacks. But Graham was a white southerner like themselves, and when, at the Chatta-

nooga crusade of 1953, he demanded racially integrated
seating, his opponents could not accuse him of being a
meddlesome outsider. In the Dallas crusade, the local committee tried to enforce segregation. Graham, seeing a negro
aide in his hotel lobby, made his views clear by ostentatiously
taking him up with him in the lift instead of making him
climb up by the back stairs.

After the Supreme Court decision of 1954 that made
segregation illegal Graham was able to insist that all crusades
be fully integrated. His stand on racial issues was warmly
appreciated by President Eisenhower. It also had the effect
of bringing him into close contact with the then Senator
Lyndon Johnson, who was campaigning in Washington for
equal rights.

Billy Graham also took steps to improve follow-up at his
crusades. He persuaded Dawson Trotman of the Navigators
to take charge, and a counsellor training scheme was established. Those coming forward at the meetings would be
spoken to by qualified Christians, many of whom were
laymen, on a one-to-one basis. Counsellors were to see
themselves as 'spiritual obstetricians'. They were to remember that it was really 'Christ that saves' and that the 'great
follow-up agent is the Holy Spirit'. All decisions were to be
referred to local churches. At the same time, Graham's first
bestselling book was published – *Peace with God*. He began
writing a regular, syndicated column in newspapers, and
branched out into making films (though he refused offers to
star in Hollywood productions).

The international evangelist

Many evangelists have become successful in the USA, but
have failed to achieve fame outside it. Billy Graham showed
in 1954 that he had the ability to reach people in cultures
quite different from his own – a major achievement. He had
been asked by the British Evangelical Alliance in 1952 to
conduct a crusade in Britain. A venue was arranged – the
Harringay arena in north London. Prayer meetings were set
up worldwide. Much of the fund raising for the team's

flight and accommodation expenses was done in the USA. Unfortunately the team did not then have the superb knowledge of other countries that was later to be a hallmark of their overseas successes. As a result, the publicity brochure they produced created a storm of controversy that nearly overshadowed the crusade itself.

The final brochure ran, 'The England of history has been an England whose life, both national and individual, was ever centred on the things of God' – the recent Coronation having reinforced this emphasis. Nazi bombing had levelled many churches, and a disillusioned atmosphere now prevailed. 'What Hitler's bombers could not do, secularism with its accompanying evils has accomplished.' Hyde Park was filled with orators who spoke on many topics, 'but most forcefully they speak for Communism'. Over 90 per cent of Britons had no church connection. 'Only a religious revival,' wrote Graham, 'can give the English people the moral integrity and stability necessary to stand with us in the days to come.' Unfortunately, in the original brochure, the word 'socialism' had been used in place of 'secularism' and the press created an outcry when a *Daily Herald* reporter found this out.

As a result, Graham's visit got massive publicity, not all of it welcome. He had to spend some time on arrival explaining that he did not intend to be political, but had agreed to preach in England at the express invitation of local Christians. The crusade opened on March 1st, 1954 with a sermon by Graham on John 3: 16. The numbers attending slowly grew. Maurice Rowlandson, Graham's chief English associate, recalls the 'absolute thrill' that pervaded English churches as the audiences multiplied.

British evangelist Tom Rees had held many crusades from the 1940s onward, many of them fairly successful. They had paved the way for the kind of event that Graham was now holding. But as the number of people converted steadily increased, it soon became obvious that Britain had not seen anything like it since Moody's visit decades before. Graham's preaching had a 'certain Gospel simplicity at heart' that many found refreshing. It was, as Rowlandson said, 'a remarkable experience'. Billy Graham, John Pollock wrote, 'had released Britons from their reticence; it suddenly became easy to talk about religion'.

Not all Evangelical churches took part, for the reasons given earlier, but many of them, such as Westminster Chapel, were happy to take their share of the new converts. Martyn Lloyd-Jones, while sorry that Graham had liberal churchmen on his platforms, was quite happy to see Graham privately in Westminster Chapel and, when on one occasion Graham fell ill, took him to see a specialist he knew in Harley Street.

Billy Graham has always understood that non-participation in his crusades does not mean lack of commitment to evangelism, but a difference among believing Christians as to the *methods* of proclaiming the Good News. As Maurice Rowlandson pointed out, wise supporters of crusade evangelism never make the claim that their method is exclusively the best, but recognise that it is one of the methods that God has blessed. Non-participating churches such as Westminster Chapel proclaimed the Gospel faithfully every week and saw many conversions. When Harringay converts arrived on their doorstep, they were warmly welcomed.

By the end of the crusade over 1,869,000 people had heard Graham preach, and 37,600 had enquired about becoming Christians. He hoped, he told the *Daily Sketch*, that many of them would be 'those who will make an impact in years to come in London, the nation and the world'. But what had thrilled him most, he added for the *Daily Mirror*, was 'the support given by the churches'.

After trips to Europe, he returned to Britain in 1955, for a crusade in Scotland. Here for the first time an important system was used that has been an integral part of his work ever since. Operation Andrew, named after the Apostle, was a scheme whereby local Christians had to pledge themselves in advance to pray for and interest non-Christian friends, whom they would then bring along to the crusade meetings in order to be admitted themselves.

As at Harringay, many of the converts went on to become Church ministers. There are those who feel that the major impact of these crusades in the long-term has been the number of present-day clergy whose spiritual lives began in 1954 and 1955.

Evangelist across the globe

Two not so successful English follow-up missions, at Wembley and at Cambridge, were succeeded by a highly profitable and fruitful visit to India – the first major tour to the Third World that Graham had made. He realised, as Martyn Lloyd-Jones had done in IFES, that people are often best evangelised by those of their own culture and nationality. The Gospel would be seen to be true because of its claims and relevance, and would not be muddled with Westernism or anti-imperial resentment. The fact that he himself was from the rich West makes his perception, and Third World popularity, all the more impressive. At the Henry Martin School of Islamics he met Dr Akbar Haqq, whom he persuaded to become an associate and evangelist to Asia.

Back home . . . and away again

Meanwhile, his organisation had expanded still further, moving to new premises in Minneapolis. At the cost of much criticism, he installed the latest labour-saving office machinery, now made even more necessary by the founding of the magazine *Christianity Today*. This journal, under the distinguished editorship of Dr Carl Henry, the systematic theologian, was independent of the Billy Graham Evangelistic Association, but strongly supported by it. The staff and contributors have been called the 'intellectual vanguard of the Billy Graham movement'. Its establishment showed that Graham, although no intellectual himself, cared about the deeper issues, especially the need to combat theological liberalism in a cogent manner.

Two successful crusades followed – in New York and in Australia. In New York Graham found himself attacked by liberal theologian Reinhold Niebhur for his lack of social concern. Graham replied that such issues were, as always, vital, but that the *real* need was the same as ever – for sinners to find salvation in Jesus Christ. Nearly two and a half million heard him preach in sixteen weeks, but perhaps his greatest impact was in Harlem where many poor black people lived. He had for some time felt the need to have a fully racially integrated team in order to 'take a strong stand on race relations' in practice as well as in theory. The director of the missionary organisation, 'Word of Life', introduced him to Ohio pastor Howard Jones, a black preacher who had had experience evangelising in Africa.

Jones had long felt that Graham was 'something else' and was 'impressed with him straight away'. He agreed to work on the team initially for five weeks, but ended up staying for ten. Many whites resented Jones's presence, but Graham insisted on giving him full assistance, stating, 'I don't care how many stop supporting me.' Jones persuaded several black pastors in Harlem to co-operate, and when he and Graham arrived one Sunday at Salem Methodist Church, the place was packed – 3,000 inside, and 1,000 downstairs, all of whom had come despite the rain. When the sun appeared they flocked outside and by the time Billy Graham began his appeal there were 8,000 listening, as well as a further uncountable number watching from the balconies. As many as 10,000 heard him in Brooklyn, and many blacks decided to make the journey to the main crusade in Madison Square Garden.

Howard Jones was asked by Graham to join his permanent team, which he did a year later in order to help co-ordinate the work in Africa where, in 1960, Graham and Jones undertook a major tour. Billy Graham, Jones recalls, made a 'tremendous impact' on the Africans. His sincerity impressed them, and they also noted his refusal to visit South Africa because Howard Jones would not have been able to accompany him there. In 1972 Graham accepted an invitation to speak in Durban and Johannesburg, provided that the audiences were racially integrated. The government disliked this, but felt obliged to give way. Many black South Africans told Jones that they 'thought they would never see the day when people could mix together without racialism', but Billy Graham's meetings had shown it could be done.

Political connections

In the early 1950s many had considered Graham to be promising Senate material for his home state of North Carolina. He refused, but there remained those who wished to use his considerable talent for their own political ends. In 1960, American presidential election year, he tactfully stayed out of the country as long as possible. He wrote a non-committal article on Nixon for *Life*, but his Democrat friends begged him to withdraw it. In the end he composed a piece on why Christians should vote. On social issues generally, he later said at his friend Lyndon Johnson's inaugural in 1965, 'our problems are basically spiritual'. He felt that 'if the church went back to its main task of preaching the Gospel and getting people converted to Christ, it would have more impact on the social structure of the nation'.

On one issue he continued to be active – race. He had held crusades in Little Rock in 1959, and held another in Birmingham, Alabama in 1964, not long after the racial tensions had erupted there again. Graham and Martin Luther King were friends and Howard Jones recalls King telling Graham, 'Your crusades have done more to help race relations than anything else I know. You've helped me.' When Johnson launched his campaign to help the black poor in the 1960s, Billy Graham enthusiastically supported him. No President had done so much since Roosevelt, he thought, and what impressed Graham most was that Johnson 'really believed' in the programme. He was, he later remembered, 'with LBJ more than any other President'. He often stayed in the White House during Johnson's presidency (far more than when Nixon held office) and preached there several times.

More expansion in the ministry

In 1960 Billy Graham founded a mass circulation magazine – *Decision*. The *Hour of Decision* broadcasts and the now frequent televising of many of the crusades had shown him that a popular paper was necessary. *Decision* was an instant success. Another innovation was the school of evangelism, attached to every crusade. Seven theological seminary students attended the 1961 Philadelphia crusade and in 1962 twenty-seven were paid to join the one in Chicago in order to see evangelism in action. By the November 1962 El Paso crusade, a school of evangelism to teach seminary students (and later ministers as well) had become a fixture. Initially the team doubled up as its staff, but later on distinguished outsiders such as Kenneth Chafin and Lewis Drummond (now Billy Graham Professor at the Southern Baptist Seminary in Louisville, Kentucky) were brought in as guest lecturers, in order to give greater scope and depth.

The aim of the schools was to make local churches realise the importance of evangelism and ways of approaching it. But, as Graham told ministers in Los Angeles in 1963, it was fully realised that men could not organise revival. 'The longer I work in crusades,' he said, 'the more I am convinced that salvation is of the Lord.' One of Graham's greatest strengths is that he knows that neither he nor any other human could create a revival, but only God. Similar emphasis is made today by Drummond and by Joseph Aldrich at the schools of evangelism.

The BGEA also entered films in a bigger way than before. The film *Man in the Fifth Dimension* became very popular, as did two films made with Cliff Richard: *Two a Penny* and *His Land*. All these activities cost a lot of money, but even though millions of dollars were now needed, the BGEA carefully kept fund raising low-key. Billy Graham himself maintained his clean image by rejecting any salary increase for a long-time, and by continuing to live a relatively modest life in his family home, a large log cabin in Montreat, North Carolina. Team members such as Grady Wilson increasingly conducted smaller crusades of their own, especially after Graham fell ill for a while in 1963.

Britain – and Berlin

The years 1966 and 1967 saw new crusades in Britain. For that of 1967, the modern technological device of cable relay was used so that people could see Billy Graham on screen at relay points all over Britain. Coffee-bar evangelism was also tried – an art that was perfected by the New York crusade of 1969. Many of the counsellors were converts from the 1954 crusade, which proved to Billy Graham that the oft-quoted criticism of his crusades, that few of the converts lasted, was demonstrably false.

There were also small evangelistic events in Turin and in Zagreb, Yugoslavia. The Zagreb visit was Billy Graham's first preaching trip to a Communist country, and enthusiastic crowds listened to his sermon in an open field in the pouring rain.

But by far the most significant event was the 'World Congress on Evangelism', in Berlin in October 1966, and sponsored by *Christianity Today*. There were over 1,200 delegates from more than 100 countries meeting under the theme of 'One Race, One Gospel, One Task'. All different varieties of Christian leader were present, and the Congress received coverage in the secular press. The Church was now becoming *visibly* international and multiracial and, paradoxically, it was an American, Billy Graham, who was helping to speed up the process – a fact often ignored by the blinkered US secular critics of his ministry, who still insisted on seeing him only in American terms and as a product of southern US Christianity in particular.

The Christians, Carl Henry reminded the delegates, were a new race of people, something that the Church ought never to forget. They were, as Billy Graham pointed out in his address, 'ambassadors under authority'. The Gospel was the one hope for society, being relevant to all the needs of modern man. On Reformation Sunday, Graham, the delegates and 10,000 West Berliners celebrated that great event in the Wittenbergplatz church. The Congress showed that Graham had begun to be the world Evangelical statesman that he has since become.

God's ambassador

His new status was recognised by the Berlin regional follow-up conferences – in Singapore in 1968, Bogota in 1969 and Amsterdam in 1971. At Singapore, with twenty-five nations meeting under the title 'Christ Seeks Asia', Graham kept a low profile. The Congress established a permanent Co-ordinating Office for Asian Evangelism, with Bishop Chandu Ray of Pakistan as its first secretary. Graham spoke at Amsterdam and, as will be seen, conceived the idea that led to the Lausanne congress in 1974, arguably one of the most influential Christian gatherings since the Second World War.

But it was in the crusades conducted outside the traditionally Christian countries that he showed that he had turned into a truly international figure. As Henry Holley, the director of international crusades at the time, has remarked, 'Billy has an amazing credibility and acceptance' outside the USA. In sixteen years of crusades in Third World and similar countries, Holley found an incredible amount of co-operation. Indeed the crowds Graham drew in such lands usually exceeded by far those he drew in America.

In Seoul, Korea, in 'five days he spoke to 3.2 million people'. Furthermore, he always had to speak through an interpreter. How many Americans, Holley has speculated, would turn out to hear a Japanese evangelist, preaching in Japanese, translated into English? In terms of locally raised financial support, 'we've oversubscribed every budget', Holley recalls. The response to the message has, in percentage terms, been 'greater than in the United States', and this in countries like Japan, where only 0.5 per cent of the nation are Christian.

Some reasons why

Henry Holley has listed the causes, under God, for this success. The first is that as in the USA the local Christians 'know he'll proclaim a message without compromise that penetrates the hearts and minds of the people that are prepared for it'. Graham has a financially clean image too – all the funds for the crusades are raised locally. Then the fact that he is so famous makes 'his presence . . . an encouragement to the local Church' and can give the Christians in that country a status that they might not hitherto have enjoyed. This has been especially true in his overseas visits since 1974 when Graham deliberately stopped identifying himself with the USA.

But perhaps the main reason has been the considerable effort made by Graham and Holley to be sensitive to local feelings. 'Unfortunately,' Holley has pointed out, 'Americans do not always enjoy a good reputation.' Frequently in the past US missionaries have imposed American methods on places to which they were wholly unsuited, thereby antagonising local listeners. 'Each culture,' Holley and Graham have realised, 'is different', and the team have been 'very careful' to find out exactly how different each one is.

'I have a philosophy,' Holley has said, 'that we look at everything through their eyes.' The team therefore never give a package deal that local Christians have to accept or reject in order for Graham to come, but instead humbly offer suggestions based on tried and tested methods that have proved successful in a variety of countries – and which have often been used first outside the USA. The local Christians are then asked to adapt these to the particular circumstances of the country being visited.

'How would I react,' Holley tells his fellow Americans to think, if a Japanese evangelist was coming to the USA? The team must never have a 'made in America label' when they arrive, and must always adopt a 'very, very, low profile'. Holley feels that the Chinese sage Lau-tzu had a good principle. 'The best leaders' work is done', Lau-tzu used to say, 'when it's over and the people say "We did it ourselves".' If the national churches can say this about themselves in human terms when the Billy Graham team have gone then, Holley states, that is the team's 'best contribution'. Above all, both Holley and Graham believe that 'the Holy Spirit is the constant factor' in every crusade, and that He is the One who achieves 'all the goals'.

Japan, Nagaland and Korea

In 1966 the Japanese churches invited Graham to preach in
Japan. He accepted, and the Tokyo crusade took place in
1967. On the first night all the 15,000 seats were filled; by
the last, 36,000 were cramming in to hear the message.
Nearly 16,000 enquirers came forward during the whole
period. But more important was the impact on the local
churches. They engaged in massive preparatory activities before Graham arrived, and this had the crucial long-term
effect not only of boosting their morale, but of showing to
their fellow Japanese that not only was there a Church in
Japan, but that it was fully national in composition and not
at all a product of Western influence.

The visits of the Graham team have produced the same
result in other countries and, if the crusades have helped
kindle the kind of growth in these places that has gone on
to be self-supporting, then they have, for this alone, been
worth while. The greatest revival this century has been
taking place in the Third World nations, and where leadership has been local. Billy Graham has seen this, and his
encouragement of the Church in these areas (in the same
way that Martyn Lloyd-Jones did through IFES) could turn
out to be a far greater contribution to the spread of God's
worldwide Kingdom than anything he has accomplished in
the USA and in Europe. As Henry Holley said, Graham's
epitaph should read: 'Billy Graham – Evangelist to the
World'.

His continuing impact can be seen in two further crusades
which he conducted in Third World countries. The first, in
Nagaland, north-east India, in 1972, has been described by
John Pollock as the 'Kohima Miracle'. The area was one of
massive political unrest and violent conflict. The Indian
Federal Government were initially reluctant to grant visas
to Graham and his team, but eventually gave way. Tribes
from six Indian states converged on Kohima for the crusade
meetings. At one stage the political tensions grew so bad
that the team suggested cancellation, but Naga Christians
flew to see Graham in Bangkok, and persuaded him to come.
Over 100,000 people greeted him on his arrival in Kohima

on November 20th, 1972, and more than 4,000 professed conversion during the crusade. For the local church, this was a great revival.

The Korean crusade, in Seoul in June 1973, was entirely run by local Christians. It was also the biggest event in which he had ever preached. Over 500,000 heard him on the first night, and on June 3rd the audience numbered more than 1,120,000. Graham decided in his appeal to stress more than usual the cost of becoming a Christian, in order to ensure that those going forward truly grasped the implications of what they were doing. None the less, no fewer than 120,000 responded to the Gospel during the course of the crusade.

But, characteristically, Graham and the team realised that these enormous results were not, even in human terms, their own doing. They were the product of patient sowing by the local Korean Christians among their own people – the team were no more than reapers. This truth about so much of the success is strongly emphasised to ministers by members of the Billy Graham team. Inviting Graham, Stirling Houston his director of US crusades told a group of American ministers in 1983, is no short cut to the results unless the local churches have done their work first. Over 80 per cent of those converted at crusades were brought to them by believing Christian friends. This had been the case in Korea, and in everywhere else that Billy Graham has been. A Graham crusade can never be a substitute for evangelism done by local Christians in their own areas, and both Graham and his team continue to emphasise this wherever they go.

Watergate
One event still had to take place before Billy Graham could become a truly international Evangelical statesman – Watergate. As John Pollock has commented, the temptation to be deflected from his main task and enter the political arena still hung over Graham for a long time, and it took the trauma of Watergate finally to rid him of it. Billy Graham had many of the qualities that would have made him into an excellent political leader.

Senior politicians such as President Eisenhower regarded him highly, and he enjoyed talking with them, particularly if he felt he could influence them for the Gospel. President Johnson, who shared his vision of a genuinely multiracial America, encouraged Graham to use the crusades as a means of helping black and white come together. But Graham refused to participate in secular activities and turned down Johnson's request to be involved with implementing the civil rights programme, even though he believed in it. Johnson was always welcomed whenever he attended one of Graham's crusades, which he did more than once.

With Nixon, however, Graham found himself politically ensnared. He first met Nixon in 1954 – Nixon's mother was a keen Graham supporter. Graham then withdrew from endorsing Nixon in 1960 (and indeed became friends with some of the Kennedy family). But in 1968 he felt, as did numerous other American Evangelicals, that Nixon had the right moral character and family life to make an excellent President. It must never be forgotten that all that is now known about Nixon was completely hidden then. Although Graham did not publicly endorse Nixon, it soon became news that Nixon had offered Graham the Vice-Presidential slot on the ticket, and that the two men were close.

After Nixon's victory in November 1968, *Time* magazine wrote that 'Billy Graham's spirituality pervades' the White House. The Nixon–Graham relationship received huge press publicity, even though it was not as close as Graham's had been with Johnson (nor was Graham's influence with Nixon anything like as great). Graham's statement to a friend that Nixon had 'brought a sense of ethics to the Presidency . . . largely derived from the Christian faith as believed and practised by his parents' shows his own feelings quite clearly. Nixon paid a visit to the Knoxville crusade, and when Graham was honoured by his old home town of Charlotte, Nixon was there to see him accept the award. Graham, although internationalist in outlook, was also a strong patriot, and so to be honoured by the President's attention, regardless of who was President at any particular moment, was something he esteemed highly.

In 1972 Graham, along with the overwhelming majority of Americans, voted for Nixon – who therefore won by the greatest margin in US history. But, unfortunately in the light of future events, Graham made his support for Nixon public. His participation with the President and other American celebrities in the patriotic 'Honour America Day', which Nixon used for political ends, enabled hostile critics unfairly to tar Graham with the right-wing brush of pseudo-Christian American civic religion. Not only had he denounced such false belief, but his Third World success showed that his message was truly international. Nevertheless, his identification with Nixon and Middle America in the popular mind meant that commentators could dismiss him as a purely American cultural phenomenon by totally ignoring his activities elsewhere.

In many cases during this period, it was not Graham as a person that was being attacked, but his faith. Those who wished to deny true Evangelical Christianity used Nixon against him, especially once the Watergate scandal had broken into the open. Initially, like many Americans, Graham and the team thought the affair was a 'political frame-up' against Nixon by the Democrats. As the revelations piled up, Graham came to see it as a 'symptom of a deeper moral crisis' facing the USA. In reply to hostile questioning, Grady Wilson pointed out that there was 'a little bit of Watergate in all of us . . . Watergate is sin'.

Graham loyally refused to condemn Nixon outright, as he still sought to influence his friend for the good. This was misunderstood, and criticism of Billy Graham mounted, as it had done over his refusal to oppose the Vietnam war. As a senior team member recalls, 'We got our fingers burned' over Watergate. It was not until May 1974, when he heard the White House tapes and realised the full moral duplicity of Richard Nixon, that Graham finally saw that he had to speak out. He had been deceived by Nixon, who had portrayed to him a very different image from the real, inner Nixon as so shockingly revealed by the tapes. Graham's statement urged prayer, a lack of hypocrisy in the media, and the need to turn to God for forgiveness.

People now saw that Graham was human like the rest of them. His true gifts, his spiritual ministry, would now shine through more clearly and, with the temptation to be involved in American politics now banished, he could concentrate more effectively on his God-given task of proclaiming the Gospel to all the nations. Unfortunately the press failed to realise this. Marshall Frady, then a *Newsweek* journalist, wrote a hostile biography implying that after Watergate Graham was all but finished. Even ten years after Watergate, questions put to Graham at press conferences are primarily political, ostensibly to find out whether Graham will endorse such and such a politician or policy, but often really in order to try to find a means of tripping him up so that his Christian message can be discredited.

On the one hand, therefore, one must sadly conclude that over Nixon, Billy Graham was well meaning, but unintentionally naive. He had abandoned the neutrality that had until then been one of his major strengths, and thereby allowed himself to be manipulated for political ends by politicians who did not have his sense of integrity and honesty. On the other hand, he swiftly learned the lessons. He ceased to permit himself to be identified with any political leader or cause in domestic politics, and stopped identifying himself abroad with America and US interests. This gave him greater credibility in the Third World, where his ministry was increasingly to be focused, and also meant that he was less distracted at home. As so often happens, a mistake had led to the need of self-examination, and reflection had led to renewed strength. For those who were unprejudiced enough to see it, Billy Graham had now become a truly international Evangelical figure.

Lausanne

This new role emerged most forcefully at the Lausanne International Congress on World Evangelisation, held in Switzerland in July 1974, with over 2,700 delegates from more than 150 countries. Half of those present, including 50 per cent of the key planning committee and of the speakers, were from Third World countries. *Time* described it as a 'formidable forum, possibly the widest-ranging meeting of Christians ever held'. Various congresses had been held after Berlin, but Graham felt the time had come for another truly international gathering, and in 1971 he convened an informal group of leading Evangelicals, including the late Stacey Woods of IFES and Bishop Dain of Sydney, Australia.

The issues they had to discuss were vital for the future. Many Third World churchmen had called for a ban on any future Western missionaries in their countries, a deep worry to someone as evangelism-minded as Graham. There was also a concern that the World Council of Churches had become 'bankrupt of any real spiritual leadership' on the issue of the Gospel. On the other hand, Graham was aware of the true Third World Church and of the enormous revival spreading right through it. New and important figures, with immense potential, were emerging among the Christians there. A positive congress, that would not merely be a centre of opposition to the WCC, but would also show that Evangelical Christianity was both alive and growing, seemed an excellent idea. Stacey Woods and others agreed in principle, but successfully argued that the time was not yet ripe.

By August 1972, at the Los Angeles consultation, everyone agreed that action should be taken. Billy Graham was chosen as honorary chairman of the planning committee, Bishop Dain became executive chairman, and Don Hoke the executive director. The late Paul Little was made programme director, and Leighton Ford chairman of the programme committee. The main committee met six times in three years, and an office was established in 1973. Graham, Dain recalls, did not involve himself in the day-to-day details, but was 'constantly available' to give advice if asked. At meetings, he was 'never intruding', but 'always helpful'. The committee ran on consensus, voting only once in its history.

'Lausanne,' Dain remembers, 'would never have happened but for Billy Graham.' He ensured that the Congress would be grounded on a sound doctrinal basis, and that the delegations from each country represented a genuine cross-section of Evangelicals, including age and professional status. It would 'relate the changeless Gospel to a changing world'. The theme would be 'Let The Earth Hear His Voice', especially the 2,700 million who had 'yet to be evangelised'.

The Congress itself, Dain said, represented a 'wide span'. There was a basic theological unity common to all delegates, but a broad spectrum of background. Some were from wholly Evangelical denominations such as the Australian Baptists, others were from doctrinally mixed churches such as the Anglicans. There were radical 'angry young men' demanding political action in their Third World homes on the one hand, and wealthy, conservative Christians from the American Mid-West on the other.

Yet, as Dain has pointed out, they had all chosen to come. When, at the planning stage, Graham wrote to many leading Evangelicals to find out if they wanted such a congress to be convened, the 'overwhelming response' was favourable. Those against had been those who hoped that Lausanne would be primarily negative in emphasis, an anti-WCC caucus, as opposed to the positive rallying cry to Evangelicals to engage in world evangelisation that Graham had intended.

The Congress was a major landmark, in that it marked the official international recognition of the fact that the majority of Evangelical Christians were from the Third World. It was a watershed – an acknowledgment that the Western domination of the Church was over. This change was embodied in the 'Covenant', a document drafted from the many congress resolutions by John Stott, whose genius for diplomacy enabled all the very different groups there to agree on that document.

Lausanne showed that evangelism and social concern were not incompatible, and that Evangelicals could once again engage in the two without compromising either. Billy Graham spoke twice, but played a low-key role throughout. The Congress, he felt, 'accomplished far more than I had ever anticipated'. It is a tribute to his vision that a congress such as Lausanne, that put the Third World on the map of the Christian world, should have owed its origins to an

American. As John Pollock wrote, Billy Graham had now publicly become 'a world Christian statesman'.

Brazil, Africa, East Asia and more

More successful Third World crusades followed. In the autumn of 1974 Graham went to Brazil where he had been in 1960 and 1962. By that time the Protestant church was growing at a higher rate than the population, and the Pentecostals probably faster than virtually any other major denomination in the world. There were 125 Christian life and witness classes for trainee counsellors in Rio alone before the crusade even began – the average for most Graham crusades is 10. Although initial attendance was lower than expected, for the last two nights over 200,000 crowded into the Maracana stadium. Within a year of the end of the crusade, Brazilian pastors had been requested by local believers to provide over 100,000 New Testaments. The already expanding Church had been enlarged still further.

The Far East crusade – October 1975 in Taipei and November 1975 in Hong Kong – saw many young people profess conversion. More important, the crusade proved a massive incentive to local evangelists, whose own crusades reaped even more than Graham's own, much to his delight, as that was just the kind of effect he hoped for. In December 1976 he addressed the Pan-African Leadership Assembly in Nairobi, Kenya, then in late 1977 he conducted crusades in Manila in the Philippines and again in India.

In September 1977 Graham went to Hungary at the request of the Free Church Council and preached to 30,000 young people in Budapest, including many from the surrounding East European countries. He also attended a reception given by the American Embassy in his honour, as an 'Ambassador of Good Will', at which several senior Hungarian state officials were present. Then in October 1978 he preached in Poland at the invitation of the local Baptists. Once more, he was regarded as an international goodwill ambassador, and was seen by senior Communist Party and government officials. He visited the Roman Catholic Shrine of the Black Madonna at Czestchowa, in order to help bring Catholic, Orthodox and Protestant churches together.

Moscow

In 1982, Billy Graham accepted an invitation to Moscow, to address a conference of 'Religious Workers for Saving the Sacred Gift of Life from Nuclear Catastrophe', made up of Christian, Buddhist and other delegates from around the world. His visit caused an immense controversy, which will be examined later. Graham had been worried about the nuclear issue for some while. But he also felt that the invitation was 'a God-given opportunity for me to proclaim the Gospel in a country where I have not had this privilege before'. He would see top religious leaders and Soviet Government officials. He concluded: 'My purpose in going to the Soviet Union is spiritual, and it is not my intention to become involved in political or ideological issues.'

He spoke at one of the biggest Baptist churches in Moscow, to an audience all with special admission tickets. There was a demonstration by several local Christians, some of whom had unofficially managed to get in. (Just before his visit 50 Baptist families had been raided and their Bibles confiscated, and 12 of them had been imprisoned. Unfortunately Graham did not manage to see them.) At the conference itself, he made a Biblically-based plea for peace. He did not, however, join in a walkout led by a Dutch delegate on the refusal of the conference organisers to discuss Solidarity or Charter 77, the Czech freedom group. Graham stated that he did not wish to enmesh himself in politics.

He did however visit the 'Siberian Seven', the Pentecostals who were still refugees inside the US Embassy. Later, he claimed to be one of the people who helped in their eventual release. (The reaction of the Seven will be discussed at the end of this chapter.) Graham took immense care to do nothing to offend his Soviet hosts. Partly, he hoped that it would be possible for him to return to the USSR at some stage in the future, in order to conduct a crusade there. Needless to say, his decision to maintain a low profile caused considerable discussion among Evangelicals concerned about Eastern Europe, not all of whom agreed with his approach.

Czechoslovakia and East Germany

Graham's visits to East Germany and to Czechoslovakia in late 1982 proved not so controversial, however. Rolf Damman, General Secretary of the East German Baptist Union, commented that Graham's visit to the German Democratic Republic 'resulted not only in many conversions and rededications, especially among young people, but it has also given us a feeling of unity with other Protestant churches'.

A sympathetic account of Graham's trip to Czechoslovakia in the autumn of 1982 has been given by his interpreter for the visit, Stanislav Svek, General Secretary of the Czech Baptists. Graham was invited by the Baptist Union shortly after his Moscow trip, and he agreed to go if he could combine the timing with his East German trip. Official government permission was granted for him – the Czechoslovak authorities had been impressed with his views on the peace issue. In Prague he preached in the Baptist and Czech Evangelical Brethren churches, in a Hussite church in Brno, and in Bratislava, the Slovak capital, his sermon was relayed to the Baptist church near by. He met with the heads of the Bohemian Protestant Churches in Prague and with Slovak leaders in Bratislava, as well as with Cardinal Tomasek at a party held in the US Embassy. He held talks with Christian Peace Conference delegates (including many non-Czechs) and with Deputy Premier Mattei Lucam.

Both with political leaders and at official functions, such as laying a wreath to the victims of the Lidice massacre, he made clear that his main reason for coming was to 'preach the Gospel'. He even managed to do so on television, to everyone's amazement. He also emphasised the issue of peace. In his address in Bratislava at the memorial to Soviet troops who died in the war, he stated that the sacrifice of the blood of American and Russian soldiers to set people free from Nazism was a picture of the greater sacrifice made on the Cross by Jesus Christ to set sinners free. Peace, he said on several occasions, had three dimensions – between neighbours, between nations, and between Man and God. He preached regularly on all three.

Home again

Graham's overseas crusades turned him into an international figure of far greater stature than many of the evangelists who were able only to appeal to a home-grown US audience. Many commentators, especially the radical ones, have tried to show that his influence in the USA has declined. Moral majority, they say, has made Jerry Falwell, not Graham, into America's leading Evangelical. This is partly because Graham has wisely decided to stay out of US politics in a way that Falwell and others have not. Maybe, too, this is no bad thing, as it has given Graham and the Gospel he proclaims a credibility, in those countries in which Evangelical Christianity is growing, in a way that might not have happened had he remained a purely parochial figure always popping in and out of the White House.

His decision to oppose the arms race has, as veteran political commentator Henry Fairlie pointed out, reduced his following among more politically conservative Christians, as has his decision not to make abortion into the priority issue in determining for whom to vote. But this means that he is now seen increasingly as an evangelist first and foremost – which is what he had always meant to be ever since the time he dedicated himself at the '18th Green' to be an 'Ambassador for Jesus Christ'.

Amsterdam 1983

Lausanne had been one of the most important Christian conferences since the war – the recognition by the West that the Third World church had come of age. But it had not been quite the meeting which Graham had originally had in mind. As he told a meeting of Americans in Orlando, Florida, in spring 1983, he wanted to help his fellow evangelists of the Third World, who quietly got on with the task of spreading the Good News against what were often appalling odds. Lausanne had had too many establishment figures, mostly self-nominated – Graham now wanted a gathering of 'itinerant' evangelists, the front-line men, one which would garner in the people he really wanted to help and keep out the church ministers for whom evangelism was only part of their job.

So, a while before, Graham decided to hold a conference for such itinerant evangelists, to be held in Amsterdam, which was both easy to reach by plane and in a country for which it was not difficult to obtain a visa. Planning was firmly in the hands of the BGEA, under the chairmanship of Walter Smyth. Applications were to be on an individual basis, with eligibility to be determined by the Amsterdam office, under the directorship of Werner Burklin. This was to ensure that those who needed to come would be there, and that those countries present would be represented by all ages and denominations, something which had not always been possible at Lausanne. Over 11,000 applications came in, of which the office were sadly only able to accept 4,000.

By far the largest number of evangelists there came from the Third World – from Africa, India, South America and other places where the Gospel is growing fastest. These were the front-line countries, where Graham's ministry had often borne its greatest fruit, and where the churches are in many cases far more alive and active than those in the West. The itinerant preachers who listened to Graham's keynote address on July 12th, 1983, 'The Evangelist in a Torn World' were those who were playing a vital role in the process. Once again a conference inspired by Graham revealed the parts of the world in which God was at work, and evangelists from Western countries were deeply challenged by the contacts they made there. Many of the Third World delegates had never left their countries before, and as well as being able to contribute so much to the seminar groups into which the conference divided, they were also greatly encouraged by the experience, and by the knowledge that people were praying for them and concerned about them.

Whereas Graham had carefully kept a low profile in Lausanne, here he maintained an active role, staying on the platform and speaking over five times in ten days to the audience containing over 130 nationalities. Other speakers also took part, some from Graham's own team, others, such as the popular American evangelist Rebecca Manley Pippert, from outside. Third World evangelists were not only given cassette players to help in their ministry, but also clothing parcels from Dutch Christians (organised by Franklin Graham's relief agency, 'Samaritan's Purse').

As Graham pointed out in his final address, 'while the social needs of man call for our urgent attention, we believe that ultimately these needs can be met only in and through the Gospel. Man's basic need is to be born from above, to be converted to Christ. Man must be changed – man's biggest problem is man himself.' This accorded with the views of many from the Third World. As an Indian Christian said not long after, the real tragedy of India was not so much that it was poor but that it was Hindu – and that the poverty was caused by Hinduism. Reach India for Christ, and the poverty would decrease as the Gospel spread.

Graham has deliberately not nominated a successor, feeling that God will raise up His own men. Yet in many ways, the barefoot evangelists of the Third World could be said to be his true heirs, sharing his call to preach the Good News. His role in the growth of Christianity in that region has, in human terms, been one of his greatest achievements, and Amsterdam was proof both of the concern he has felt for such people and also of the affection which they feel for him.

Mission England

Although the Third World may have become the area where he has had greatest impact, Graham has not neglected the developed, non-Communist world. In 1979 he led a highly successful mission in Sydney, Australia, and in mid-1982 took part in a major crusade in New England, USA, where the response was far greater than any of the organisers imagined possible. Many in Britain hoped that Graham could come back to the United Kingdom, but Graham, fond of the British as he was, kept feeling that the time was not quite right.

He had visited Britain in 1980, to conduct missions in Oxford and Cambridge. The first, at Oxford, was to 'town and gown', and, according to John Pollock, Graham felt he was not as fresh as he was to be in his talks at Harvard two years later, maybe because of ill-health and an accident just before the mission. Nevertheless, many local clergy, such as Keith Weston, the rector of St Ebbe's, felt the visit had been worth while.

At Cambridge he was the official CICCU (Christian Union) missioner. He was most anxious to work closely in collaboration with the members, and amazed the president, John Barclay, the committee and the assistant missioners by his willingness to seek and pay heed to their advice. His first sermon, they felt, was too intellectual, so he carefully made all the others more straightforward. This was appreciated by the Overseas Student Outreach team, of which I was a member – many of the students we brought along had only rudimentary English, yet responded warmly to his addresses.

In addition, at the CICCU's request, Graham also scrapped the appeal to come forward, a sure sign of his sensitivity and ability to adapt. Great St Mary's was packed to capacity at every meeting and, as in other countries where he had dispensed with it, the response to the message was no less through the lack of an altar call. Significantly, the best results were often in the colleges where the Christian group was small and where the Mission had given a new impetus to evangelise.

Soon after Graham was handed an invitation, containing 100 signatures and organised by the Evangelical Alliance, asking him to return to conduct a full-scale crusade. Graham was seen by Clive Calver, of Youth for Christ, who pointed out that most of those who would be attending any crusade would be under 40 – as Graham himself had been when he led the Harringay crusade. So Graham asked that a small steering committee be established, five older and five younger members, plus Walter Smyth of the BGEA and

Maurice Rowlandson, Graham's London representative. Graham, however, felt that the timing was not yet right, a view he still held in 1981 when a group of British clergymen and Christian workers visited him in the South of France, where he was on a crusade.

The idea they put to him was a new concept in crusade evangelism – a three-year Mission England of which his visit would be a part. The first phase would be a full year of prayer, preparation and evangelism by local churches; phase two would be a series of missions by Graham himself in selected venues across the country; the final stage would be both follow-up from these meetings, plus further evangelism by the local churches. It would thus not be a Graham crusade but, as Graham quickly realised, a joint effort with him working alongside the local churches. So he agreed to set aside three months in 1984 while the committee tested the water.

Many churches proved positive and, after a warm response to his visit to the Christian Booksellers' Convention in Blackpool in February 1982 and his addresses to the mini-mission which followed it, he agreed to come in 1984 to be part of what was now officially called Mission England.

As Bob Williams, the BGEA liaison officer with Mission England, reported, it was agreed that the first phase should be for participating local churches to reawaken within themselves the need for evangelism. As in the Third World, the greatest long-term effect of a Graham visit is to do precisely this – the role of the local churches has, in human terms, often been the key to the success of a crusade. So two courses were instituted – 'Prepare the Way' and 'Is My Church Worth Joining?', the second course being seen as a crucially important instrument in waking churches out of their complacency, and challenging individual members so to change their life styles that they would be witnesses to the non-Christians around them. This was the factor that to Graham, Williams noted, made 'our involvement worth while'.

Mission England then, was to be 'much more than just an event with a superstar', a real exercise in collaboration. It was, Williams has stated, not so much to be mass evangelism, but 'personal evangelism on a mass scale', with the local churches the key to the whole enterprise. It was to begin with 'people praying for their own lives to be renewed', then going out and doing something about the lost in the areas in which they lived. To illustrate this, Williams used a human analogy that is often used by members of the Graham team: evangelists are the obstetricians, ministers the paediatricians, but ordinary Christians the parents. Billy Graham, to change the metaphor, is no more than the harvester, garnering in where the local churches have sown. 'You only get out of it,' team members emphasise, 'what you put into it', and as countries like Japan showed, the real results of a crusade are often most apparent a good year after Graham's visit is over.

The BGEA staff often find that the real beneficiaries of a visit are the 'little churches' and Williams discovered that this was true of Britain too. Much of the Mission England material was given to such churches for free. They find, Williams noted, 'a common ground at the foot of an empty Cross', a strength from the living Lord. The doctrinal basis for participation is reduced to the basic minimum – rather to the concern of many Evangelical churches, Mission England (as with Graham-run crusades as well) has no basis of faith. The team argue that 'it's not a theological exercise – it's a life saving exercise'. One may not agree with all the views of the crew of a lifeboat, but at least they are saving lives. (The theology of this view will be discussed later in the chapter.)

The popular author and Billy Graham Professor of Evangelism, Lewis Drummond, has shown from crusade statistics that over 80 per cent of those going forward at Graham meetings were brought along by Christian friends – and Williams added that 90 per cent of converts admit that they had had close contact with Christians before coming. 'People,' Williams commented, 'reach people.' In the church in Cleveland of which he was a pastor, there were 500 people after Graham's crusade in the city, and 800 three years later – many of the additional 300 were as a result of those converted in the crusade bringing their non-Christian friends along to church. Much of the fruit is a result of such activity, and also of prayer. When Billy Graham asks about a town he is to visit, his first question is not about organisation or finance, but 'are the people praying?' Stirling Huston, Graham's director for the USA, has said that the people who come forward at each crusade are the results 'of the power of answered prayer'. Finally, as Williams has pointed out, 'the real work begins when the public phase of the mission is over', in the follow-up by local Christians in their churches and Mission England nurture groups. Billy Graham does not even pretend to 'have revival in his suitcase' – he cannot reap where the local Christians have not sown.

Normally the BGEA run a crusade in conjunction with locally recruited staff. In this case, BGEA staff such as Williams worked alongside Mission England people, in Williams's case with Gavin Reid, Mission England's director and one of the men whose idea the whole enterprise was in the first place. Williams arrived from Amsterdam in September 1983 and began to set up the advisory structure to work in parallel with the already existing Mission England organisation. He has under him BGEA co-ordinators, who work in the regional offices along with the local directors and committees. (This part of the structure will be explained later.)

As Henry Holley, one of the key members of the Graham team has explained, the BGEA leans over backwards to be sensitive to local feelings. So when Williams and his staff came over, they emphasised that they had not arrived with set formulae but with advice based on long years of experience, all of which was adaptable to local needs. Each co-ordinator was not the boss, but the 'coach' to the local director and his committee. All was done after close consultation between Mission England and BGEA staffs, with Williams explaining that when a problem arose his motto was 'let's pick the best methods for here'. As he said, 'my job is to work myself out of a job' – his aim was to find the key people who shared his vision for reaching the lost, put them in place, and then leave. Much of the success of Graham's crusades has been due to this attitude.

To Williams, one of the most important distinctives of

Mission England was the emphasis they put on nurturing converts. (A leading British member of Mission England mischievously suggested that this aspect of the operation gave it the edge over anything with which Billy Graham had been involved before in terms of follow-up.) All those at the meetings enquiring about the faith were to be placed into small nurture groups attached to participating churches. Statistics had shown that over 71 per cent of those who became closely involved in such groups were still actively involved in Christian things a year later – by contrast, of those not joining a nurture group, 80 per cent had nothing to do with the Church a year after going forward at a crusade. Mission England was therefore determined to ensure that everyone going forward was followed up effectively.

Furthermore, the nurture group system was aimed at showing new Christians how to study the Bible. Often older Christians forgot to show them how – they would tell them to read it and be guided by it, and leave the new convert bogged down in the genealogical passages of Scripture, keen to learn but perplexed as to how to apply what was on the page to daily life. The small nurture groups, Williams explained, were designed to get round the problem and help the young Christians effectively to grow in the faith. Often new converts, now that they had been born again, were left entirely to their own devices, and Williams's 'biggest frustration' about evangelism was the utter lack of personal attention to new believers provided by those already in the Church.

At evangelism school

As seen earlier, in the USA and other countries where the BGEA run the crusade, the meetings are often accompanied by a school of evangelism for local workers. In the part of Mission England that could be covered by this book – the meetings in Bristol – no such event took place. But it is important, as this is a chapter on Billy Graham as opposed to an account of Mission England, to examine the way in which Graham and his team are thinking, because the attitude with which they came to England was no different from that with which they come to any other crusade or mission, whether they control it or not. Much of the information in this chapter came from the fortnight I spent with members of the team in a crusade in Orlando, Florida in 1983, during the course of which I attended some sessions of the school of evangelism.

Graham's opening address to the assembled ministers and their wives set the tone. Preaching, he reminded them, was at the centre of God's message for today, something too often forgotten. 'God's organisation on earth,' he told them, 'is the church', and, he added significantly, 'if the churches are doing the work of evangelism' then parachurch organisations such as his own may not be needed in future generations. Furthermore, 'God only uses those who have experience with Him.' God judged nations, and as Graham could hear the hoofbeats of the Four Horsemen of the Apocalypse coming ever closer, maybe only a real revival could prevent them from coming.

Many of the speakers at the School had flow charts and diagrams. At least two did not. The first, Joseph Aldrich, the successful North American minister and writer, told the ministers about 'life style evangelism' and how he had had to learn it the hard way in one of the toughest parts of urban USA. There were no altar calls, he reminded them, just living the Gospel and being a witness to the risen Saviour in one's neighbourhood.

But by far the most impressive speaker was Professor Lewis Drummond, who has studied in England and now teaches at Southern Baptist Seminary in Kentucky.

Drummond based his lecture not on diagrams but firmly on the book of Acts, and delivered it in a lively style that got every minister listening eagerly.

Instant evangelism, he reminded them, simply did not exist. Gimmicks fizzled out while solid, continuous evangelism bore fruit under God. The 'get 'em down the aisles evangelism' adopted by many churches was the opposite of the Biblical pattern. Five things were needed for genuine, lasting, in-depth church growth.

The first was 'an exalting into prominence of the Word of God'. Ministers should 'get people into the Book' – having first got into it themselves. What was needed was solid, expository preaching, not the 'topical', syrupy stuff of today. Like John Stott and Martyn Lloyd-Jones, Drummond believed that too often congregations were only feeble beause of the feebleness of the preaching which they received.

Second, Acts 4 showed that prayer to the 'Sovereign Lord' was essential. 'It's the churches that have the great prayer ministries,' he told them, 'that go [and] reach people. If you do anything under God, get those people on their knees.' Ministers often complained that they couldn't attract non-believers into church. 'When God comes,' Drummond reminded them, 'you can't beat people away with a club.' When the Holy Spirit fills a church, and gives God's people boldness, then things will happen. Even two faithful Christians praying will be enough.

Third, Acts 8 showed that pastors had to 'teach people how to witness'. This was not the preachers' power getting the unconverted in, but the sharing of the Gospel by ordinary lay men and women in the church. This was 'nothing instant, nothing flashy, just doing the job'.

Fourth, Acts 2 showed that the aim of evangelism is not to 'grab converts' but to make disciples. The 'easy believism' mentality had to be scrapped – what the Bible wanted was 'genuine conversions'. This took time and a lot of effort but real growth, not instant splash, should be what the churches want.

Last, pastors should be 'employing the principle of church growth that works where you are' – i.e. what worked well in one place was not always sure to succeed elsewhere. There had to be a 'right theology' – of ministry, of growth ('we do as we believe'), a 'right understanding of the community . . . right goal setting' and realistic targets. Above all, Drummond reminded them, 'we've just got to have the Holy Spirit among us'. Without Him, nothing is possible.

It is significant that working through the local churches has been a hallmark of Graham's ministry. Often, if an area is full of thriving churches, he will refuse to go there and will concentrate instead on those which have struggling churches and where the needs are great. In the USA, the team have often found that the response has been far better in areas with few churches, and where the task of the local Christians is harder, than those where church attendance – and complacency – is high. Bob Williams often worries if things go too well at the beginning, as people then often pray less. Problems can often create the kind of 'pleading, dependent prayer' which God uses to do His work.

Bristol

Around the time that Graham was being asked by Gavin Reid and others to come again to Britain, a group of Christians in the South-West were thinking along the same lines, but on an altogether less ambitious scale. One of them was a local farmer, Anthony Bush, whose wife had been converted as a result of Graham's ministry. He found that despite the local evangelists who had been active in the area, the city 'hadn't meaningfully been covered' in the way he and other Christians had hoped. 'There was undoubted blessing' in all these activities, he recalls, 'but never more than 80 churches got involved.' Bush felt that a visit by Billy Graham would reach the whole city and persuade far more churches to collaborate corporately in evangelism.

So, on his personal initiative, Bush wrote in early 1981 to all the local denominational leaders and evangelists, and most of them replied by saying that they would be happy to participate in a Graham visit. (One of the few that didn't went ahead and organised an evangelistic outreach of his own!) Once Bush heard that Graham was coming to Britain after all, he decided that the time for his 'Evangelical initiative' had come. So, he recalls, 'we got a strong Evangelical group – it is with the Evangelical that truth lies' – and committees to organise the meetings in the Bristol area were established in spring 1982, under Bush's directorship. An office opened in August 1982, and local ministers were sent the details of all the preparatory courses mentioned earlier.

The leading members of each committee – church life, youth, follow-up and counselling, prayer, women, etc – were all Evangelical, but in accord with their view that non-Evangelical ministers could be influenced if they became involved, information was sent to a wide body of local ministers. (As will be seen, not all local Evangelicals were entirely happy about this.)

The first phase was prayer, training and local evangelism, and this has been explained by popular local evangelist, Graham Loader of the Pocket Testament League. Some four years earlier he himself had set up a monthly prayer meeting of concerned Christians to pray for the needs of the area, so he was the natural choice as prayer co-ordinator for the South-West when Mission England got going in Bristol. He established a prayer task group and contacted local churches, asking them to set up 'prayer triplets'. These were groups, of three Christians each, committed to meeting regularly for fifteen minutes at a time, with each person praying for three non-Christians. Soon there were thousands of such groups – one woman in Bath organised additional days and special months of prayer, and many churches found their prayer lives completely altered for the better.

The effect of all this prayer rapidly became apparent. By January 1984, five months before Billy Graham was due to arrive in Bristol, over 3,000 people had professed conversion – many of the prayer triplets were soon made up of those who had become Christians through people in the original triplets. The same was true of the Christian life and witness classes. These were seminars, five per session of eighty minutes each, designed to recruit counsellors whose job it was to talk to the people going forward at the Billy Graham meetings – the enquirers. But many of those attending discovered that they needed to be born again themselves – in one class in Bath, for example, seventeen people were converted as a result of attending.

So while many of the activities were aimed at being preparatory to phase 2 – the stadium meetings – such was the spiritually rejuvenating effect of the early activity – the increase in prayer, and lay evangelism by ordinary

Christians – that thousands of lives were changed even before Graham arrived. As Anthony Bush said, the whole enterprise would thus still have been worth while even if Graham had cancelled his visit. The Holy Spirit was at work in the local churches, and people were coming to Christ, one might add, in the New Testament way, through prayer and faithful witness on a small but very effective scale.

Different churches were changed in diverse but none the less very substantial ways. Typical of one of the larger Evangelical churches in the area is Christ Church, Clifton, with up to 1,000 or more attending its Sunday services. It is, according to the vicar, Canon Paul Berg, essentially a middle-class church with many families in the congregation moving upward socially – over 70 per cent are under 35 – and with a student population of 30 per cent of its total. (It is near Trinity College, where Jim Packer was vice-principal.)

The church was already very active evangelistically. It had a mission of its own, led by Eric Delve, ran a series of courses on Christian basics and had, in addition, forty housegroups, each of which could provide effective nurture for the new Christian. So the church was initially inclined not to participate in Mission England. They had also found that many of their own numbers had been converted through friends, and not through meetings. As Paul Berg pointed out, the 'big mission isn't the predominant thing that brings people to faith in Christ'. When the church was polled, of the 1,058 that replied, almost twice as many (39.5 per cent) said they had been converted through a non-Christian friend, as had been the result of an evangelistic meeting (20.1 per cent).

But in the end, they changed their minds. Billy Graham's visit would, they decided, be a 'very useful tool' in their own activities – as Paul Berg explained, being involved 'was a natural thing to do – it doesn't take the place of our own evangelistic activities'. So Christ Church became deeply involved – Paul Berg was made chairman of the church life task group, and the church provided about 140 choir singers, approximately 80 counsellors, 100 nurture group trainees, as well as stewards and follow-up staff. Members of the congregation bought over 4,000 tickets to take non-Christian friends to the stadium meetings; and on the Sunday of the Mission, Dr John Wesley White, one of Billy Graham's most eminent associate evangelists (he has an Oxford D.Phil and has preached in countless universities in many lands), gave the evening address.

Not all the churches in the South-West have anything like the resources of Christ Church, and a typical example is Mount of Olives, in Redland, 'the other side of the tracks' in social composition. 'Pentecostal people,' its minister, Warwick Shenton explained, 'are naturally enthusiastic about evangelism', and the church already had regular evangelistic outreaches on Sundays.

But the advent of the Mission spurred on a greater interest, especially in neighbourhood door-to-door evangelism. In addition, the church decided to hold a special 'highlight service' of outreach once a month.

One of the best results, Shenton felt, was that his congregation saw the life that existed in other Evangelical churches outside their own denomination. Mount of Olives was a natural venue for the area Christian life and witness classes, and the 'tremendous sense of oneness' that developed with his church and other local Evangelicals greatly enhanced their vision. Everything that was being organised was so big that 'unless the Holy Spirit is in it it will explode'. As he added, the battle for the souls of the unconverted 'was won before Billy got on his feet' – in the prayers of the local Christians. The whole enterprise was a 'super example of God's sovereignty'.

Also attached to the Mount of Olives was Peter Kay, now a missionary in Kenya, but chairman of the inner city and housing estates task group for phase 1. It is often in such areas that the main effect of Graham crusades can be seen, as the Rio de Janeiro crusade in Brazil so graphically showed. Such churches, and those in Bristol are no exception, are usually small and struggling, and exist in areas seen as impervious to the Gospel. Kay and the Group were very sensitive to the feelings of such people, who suspect anything on a large scale, and whose ministers are often working men who preach part-time.

So instead of the inner city ministers being asked to large, anonymous, 'out there' Mission England meetings, seminars were held in their own areas, designed to find out from them which aspects of the Mission would best help their local needs. Ten full-time evangelists were already working in the area, seven of them in the hardest to reach with the Gospel. Arthur Blessit, with his own special style, had made a big impact in the docks. The fact that he had visited them 'gave a sense of worth' to local people, and heart to the little churches. Blessit, the dockers saw, was 'a real man', not just a preacher for women and children.

All this meant that the local churches on the housing estates 'caught the vision' and 'invited their friends'. On one estate, after the Mission began, a whole double-decker busload attended, half of whom were unchurched invited guests. The little churches, many of whom had congregations of under fifty, were greatly helped by the fellowship with one another that arose out of all the activity, and a 'real plus' was the fact that the black churches in the St Paul's area felt able to collaborate with the near-by white Evangelical churches in Gospel unity. In addition, a video entitled *Ordinary People*, giving the testimony of three people from very ordinary backgrounds, was prepared for showing on the housing estates in church members' homes.

Not every minister in the South-West felt able to collaborate. Many non-participants were Evangelicals who fully agreed with Graham's message, but felt unable to take part for the reasons given below. One of these, the minister of a thriving church in Bristol (and who asked to remain anonymous as some of his congregation were privately involved), gave four reasons. First, he explained, he could 'no longer accept "decisionism" '. While he prayed that many who went forward would genuinely be saved – and was sure that many were – he felt that people who went forward could often think that it was that act that had saved them, something which could cause them great problems in future years. There were too many around who felt that they had tried

Evangelical Christianity as the result of going forward, and who now thought that it had failed them, so were consequently against it. The minister was especially disturbed when, on family night, Billy Graham asked whole families to go forward.

The entertainment side of evangelism also worried him – he, like many others, had disliked all the razzmatazz of the 'Prepare the Way' side of phase 1. Furthermore, he was most unhappy at the way in which non-Evangelical churches, including Roman Catholics, were taking part. He saw Graham's poster 'outside scores of churches where the Gospel is never preached'. Bush explained that this was to ensure that non-Evangelical churches get to hear the Gospel – which was why Mission England did not have a very definite basis of faith such as the Lausanne covenant.

But non-participating churches feel that liberals will probably come out of curiosity anyway, and that to ask them to collaborate only sows confusion in the eyes of non-Christians, who are made to feel that there is no difference between the two positions. God had undoubtedly blessed Graham's preaching of the Gospel – had he insisted on a firmly Evangelical base, the minister had no doubt that the crusade would have been even more blessed.

Last, all the planning seemed to this minister to be 'engineered'. When God sent true revival, it was not as the result of a rush of human activity, because revival, by its very nature, 'must be sent down' from God above. Graham's appeal seemed to him too anxious to get people to go forward for all sorts of reasons – if God was really working in someone's heart, that person could be saved hours, days or even longer after the meeting, and be no less converted as a result, even though he or she had not gone forward. The 30,000 people who came to the Mission meetings represented the whole South-West of England – if real revival came, as it had done in Whitefield's time, there would have been many, many more.

Graham comes to Ashton Gate

May came at last, and Billy Graham and his team (including British staff such as Maurice Rowlandson) arrived in Bristol. Many of the old team are well known and deservedly much-loved favourites such as Cliff Barrows, who masterminds the stadium events, and the singer, George Beverley Shea. Both of these, along with Graham's childhood friend and now principal aide, T. W. Wilson, have been with Graham for over forty years. In human terms, it is their faithfulness and commitment that has brought about much of Graham's success. Graham once said of Barrows that he had never seen him lose his temper even so much as once in forty years and one could well believe it. (When I spent two weeks with the team on a mission in the USA I found this to be very true of all the senior members of the Graham team.) People such as Barrows, Shea and Wilson liaise closely with local Christians in whatever country Graham visits, and their natural warmth and humour, as well as their Godliness, explain much of the affection in which Graham and his team are held.

Two of the publicly less-known members of the regular team deserve special mention, as much of what they do is behind the scenes. These are Russ Busby, Graham's personal photographer, and Roger Palms, the editor of *Decision* magazine. Busby's immense sense of fun is appreciated throughout the world (he also travels with Franklin Graham on relief projects), especially among young people, who enjoy his easy-going, unfussed style. His main job, he says, is to keep the other members of the team humble, which he does through a lively sense of humour that often hits straight on target. When people try to impress the team, he swiftly sees through the façade to the real lack of humility underneath. Palms is a kind of resident intellectual, a thoughtful, Godly man, reminding everyone of the deeper spiritual issues in a sensitive way. After an appeal is over, he will walk quietly over to the counsellors and find the human stories of ordinary people whose lives have been changed by the crusade. It is all too easy to forget, amid all the hoopla, that each crusade is about individuals, not anonymous masses, coming to

Christ, and Palms's reports aim to redress the balance and remind everyone what it is all about.

The first night

The opening night, Saturday, May 12th, 1984, was also the start of Graham's visit as a whole, so the preliminaries were unusually long. The meeting began at 3 p.m. after an introduction with his usual gusto by Cliff Barrows, with songs from Graham Kendrick. Then Anthony Bush spoke, after which Barrows introduced Paul Berg, who prayed for the occasion. Tony Dann, the South-West chairman, who was at Oxford with Martyn Lloyd-Jones's daughter Elizabeth, formally announced the start of phase 2 of Mission England. Gavin Reid, the Mission England director, then told the 30,000-strong congregation that Graham's arrival was, for him, the fulfilment of a nine-year dream. He read a message of support from the Archbishop of Canterbury which, he proclaimed, 'says it for thousands of us'.

Graham himself then appeared, to loud applause. (Roger Palms asked not long before, 'Whatever happened to the traditional British reserve?') Graham told everyone that he had been in Bristol thirty-eight years before and was glad to be back. After a few self-deprecating jokes, he reminded the audience that in Whitefield's day, Bristol had been the start of great things and, as many in the stadium were from South Wales (made part of England for Mission purposes), he related the story of the 1904 revival.

People were, he said, 'once again experiencing spiritual renewal and revival'. It might well be, he felt, that Bristol could be the beginning of a 'twentieth-century revival . . . the only hope for our world at this hour'. The church today, he proclaimed, 'needs to recapture this vision . . . proclaiming God's message'. No Gospel and no evangelism meant no church. Conversion was 'coming alive through Jesus Christ' and people needed to be saved today as much as ever. God 'gave us His son to die on the Cross' – Jesus rose again and is coming back. 'We must,' declared Graham, 'respond to God's offer.' Christians around the world were praying for Mission England – the BGEA had sent out 100,000 prayer telegrams and, Graham proclaimed, 'God is going to answer their prayers'.

Cliff Barrows then introduced the country and western singer, George Hamilton IV who, like Graham, comes from rural North Carolina. Hamilton, in folksy language, gave his testimony then sang a few Gospel songs. (Cliff Richard sang on the third night, to over 32,000 people, and received rapturous applause.)

After some more songs from Kendrick, and from George Beverley Shea, whose voice was as magnificent as ever, Graham finally rose to give his address. He asked everyone to pray. 'Some of you,' he told the audience, 'are here out of curiosity' – that was fine. Others were there because a friend had brought them – that, too, was all right. But for whatever reason they had come, they all had two types of ear: the physical and the spiritual. God's voice, he said, was 'whispering to you . . . His willingness to give you eternal life – today'. Everyone was at the crossroads – and 'you must make the choice' that day. 'Jesus,' he explained, 'never allowed neutrality.' He would preach today's sermon as if it was the last sermon he would ever preach, and the last his audience would ever hear.

'Something like this might never come again' to the South-West, Graham reminded his listeners (his introduction was much the same every night). This was 'a moment in history' – never again would so many be praying for those in the audience as were doing so for this Mission. He then told them that when in Sydney, Australia, in 1979, the Archbishop had told him to preach on John 3: 16 – the 'Gospel in a nutshell'. In Bristol Graham preached on this twice – on the first and fifth nights.

On the fifth night it was pouring with rain and rather cold. Yet the crowds came in strength as on all previous occasions. I had come most nights on a church bus – with eager counsellors such as 18-year-old Nick Perham, local solicitor Christopher Berkeley, or 85-year-old Dick Knight, all of whom had stories to tell of the people who had come forward. Non-Christians also came, not sure what they would hear. On the fifth night, I travelled in with a coach of students from an education college near Bath. Some students had already been converted and Karen, the college missionary secretary, was hoping that more would respond that night.

Graham opened with some jokes about the downpour, gave some news of his wife who was in hospital back in the USA, and then began on his text. 'Jesus,' he declared, 'said you can be born again.' The pressure of the arms race was now greater than ever before – unless there was spiritual rebirth, there could be war. But Graham then reverted to his main theme and told of a Roman Catholic professor from Poland who realised, on meeting a black lady on a bus, that despite his position, he too needed to be born again. Life was becoming more and more uncertain. People either went up – or down. Down was drugs, depression and despair – up was to God. 'I'm asking you,' said Graham, 'to head up.' Often we looked in the wrong place for the answer to our questions – 'Come,' he told them, 'to the word of God.'

Bad people, Graham felt, could see the need to be born again, but Nicodemus was a 'religious ruler . . . seeking for fulfilment that he hadn't found'. Jesus knew that his façade was 'not enough' – He knew that it was 'what was *in* man' that really counted. 'We're all born wrong . . . we've all sinned against God', and 'something needs to be done with the heart' where sins originate. The Bible gave two words for sin: the first was 'transgression' (1 John 3: 4), the second was 'iniquity'. When he was young, he said, he didn't like going to church – his father made him go. But just before he was going to leave for good, he was 'born again'. Suddenly he enjoyed church as never before.

There was much about the new birth that we couldn't understand – Graham himself couldn't understand computers, for example. But how could one quantify a mother's love in a laboratory? Jesus talked of being 'born into the family of God', and those listening could be spiritually born again 'right now'. Graham reminded them, 'You can't inherit the new birth, you cannot get it by works . . . you can't buy it . . . all our righteousness is as filthy rags.' Nor could the new birth be imitated artificially. No, as Paul explained in Corinthians, becoming a Christian was 'passing from death into life'. The new birth 'brings about a change of heart . . . it determines our destiny'.

How is this done? Firstly, people have to receive the Word of God, in this case through the 'foolishness of preaching'. Then the Holy Spirit must convict the sinner of sin. 'There's no way I can lead the Christian life', Graham pointed out, but the 'Holy Spirit comes to live within' the believer, who ever comes to faith in God through Jesus Christ on the Cross. He died, Graham reminded them, 'on the Cross for you'. Those listening needed to repent of their sins, receive Christ by faith, and be willing to serve and follow Him, even if it was costly.

On all nights, the appeal was much the same, opening with his famous phrase, 'I'm going to ask you to get up out of your seats' to let Christ come into their hearts that day. 'Get up and come right now . . . You may be the only one in your area – but you come', he said one evening. After a pause of a few minutes, he added, 'you can bring a friend with you to Christ today'. It was important to go forward. Then after a while, he declared, 'You haven't come yet, and God is speaking to you.' Graham then told of how he himself, when he went forward in Ham's crusade, had done so in the last verse of the last hymn – he often wondered what would have happened if they hadn't sung that last hymn.

Eventually, several thousand came forward every night. They all did so in silence. One of Graham's best features being his cultural sensitivity, he will adjust according to what a country feels is appropriate. In America, the choir sings 'Just As I Am' at full volume during the altar call. In Britain, this is regarded as emotionally manipulative, so Graham is anxious to leave it out. While his message never changes, his methods do, and there is something very special about the people coming forward, not against a barrage of noise but in contemplative silence.

Graham always prays a committal prayer before going on to tell those who have gone forward of the change in life style that their decision will cause. He tells them to read their Bible, join a Bible-believing church, and reach out to their friends with the Gospel. The enquirers are then contacted by counsellors – either general or specialist, as required – for children, for those with particular problems such as drugs, marriage difficulties, or those from Islamic or other backgrounds.

The counsellors write down the names and addresses of the enquirers, after explaining their decision to them. Four kinds of response are listed: Salvation, assurance, rededication, or 'other'. The counsellor keeps the top copy (to keep in touch with the enquirer), while the lower sheet is taken round to the follow-up room, managed in Bristol by well-known local evangelist Roger Chilvers. Those enquirers who name a particular church are referred automatically to it, and the minister is informed, by first post the next day. Similarly, those requesting a denominational church are sent to one of their choice (this, controversially, includes Roman Catholics, whose names, in Bristol, are given to a sympathetic Catholic bishop, to place in special nurture groups.)

But, as Chilvers has pointed out, the follow-up in Mission England is carried out on a 'more comprehensive' scale 'than is normally done' in Graham crusades. As seen earlier, the special feature is the nurture group. Ministers have not always followed up enquirers as effectively as they should, so Mission England has decided to use a dual referral system. All enquirers are sent to church-based nurture groups, each of which has a trained leader, and all the names are sent to nurture group co-ordinators as well as to ministers.

Enquirers not specifying a church have their names sent to the designating committee of local ministers (Pastor Shenton of Mount of Olives served on the committee in Bristol). All enquirers are sorted the previous night by address or postcode, and participating churches in that postcode are recommended to the designating committee. They choose the appropriate church for the enquirer – suitability not denominational balance is the key – and ministers can overrule the postcode system if they know of a better church for a particular individual in a neighbouring district or postal area.

The response in Bristol was overwhelming. Enquirers, according to Roger Palms (and my own random survey) came from a wide variety of backgrounds. One was a 20-year-old Oxford student, who had studied the Bible in school, but only on hearing Billy Graham did he realise 'that there was anything personal behind it'. An 80-year-old man, who had attended church for sixty years, realised at the meeting 'what Jesus did for me on the Cross. I'm free now', he added, 'I know I am going to heaven.' Two of the college students brought by Karen, Nick and Kerry, discovered the Saviour for whom they had been seeking for some time. Like many who go forward, theirs was no sudden decision, but the culmination of a process, of contact over a long period of time by Christian friends who had been praying for them.

On average, 4 per cent of Graham's audiences go forward at a meeting – at Bristol the average was well over 8 per cent. If one takes the night Cliff Richard came, May 14th, 2,642 came forward. But this does not mean, as many suppose, that this was the number converted that day, as the Graham team analysis makes clear. Of the enquirers, 55 per cent were professing salvation – 956 females and 488 males. Of the rest, 15 per cent sought assurance, 17 per cent wished to rededicate their lives, and 13 per cent gave 'other' as the reason they went to the front. Two-thirds of the overall total were female, and by far the largest category of those going forward were under 25. Of the grand total of 2,642, 331 were under 12 years old, 1,108 were aged 12–18, and 304 were of student age (19–25).

Not all the younger enquirers I spoke to seemed exactly sure of what they had done, and only when the nurture groups are firmly established will the true impact of Ashton Gate be fully seen. Furthermore, BGEA statistics overwhelmingly demonstrate that it is the enquirers brought along by ordinary Christians from local churches that truly last. People who have been nurtured and prayed for, just as in New Testament times, by faithful Christians in their own area or workplace, are the statistics that really count. Many of these are often not converted at the stadium, but in the homes of their Christian friends, hours, days or even weeks later. Their names may never appear on counsellor cards or computer indices – but they are eternally written in the Lamb's Book of Life.

The Man and the Method

Even though Graham has made mass crusade evangelism something which Christians need no longer be ashamed of, is it none the less a Biblical method, or merely a human one given a clean bill of health by Graham's honesty and straightforwardness?

Those against mass evangelism point out that it is clear from Scripture that there was no evangelism conducted in New Testament times apart from the local church. Evangelism was carried on by local Christians sharing the Good News of Jesus Christ with the people with whom they were in regular, daily, contact. Not only was evangelism local, it was built into the everyday life style of each individual Christian. The idea of meeting evangelism – the notion that non-Christians hear the Gospel primarily through listening to it at specially called meetings – is also foreign to the New Testament pattern.

On this score, they argue, the very idea of mass evangelism is entirely wrong. Anything that is not in the Bible must be rejected if the Church is to be truly loyal to Scripture. The missionary journeys of the Apostle Paul, they add, were also church based. He was always commissioned by a local church, and spent his time setting up local churches wherever he went. Far from hurtling into a place for only a week, he would often remain in a city for months or even years, and keep in close personal contact thereafter.

Certainly, crusade evangelism does not appear anywhere in Scripture. But arguments from silence are always dangerous. Because a method is absent, it does not follow that it is necessarily *wrong*. (Nor, however, can it therefore be claimed by its supporters that it is the best – if it were the *best* way of doing things, surely God would have included it in the Bible.) Many of the churches that oppose Graham use organs for singing and one of their criticisms of the crusades is that they use modern musical instruments such as guitars. Organs appear nowhere in Scripture. Does this mean, therefore, that organs are unbiblical, and actually wrong? Silence can be interpreted either way.

The defence of Graham's method of mass evangelism (as opposed to mass evangelism in general, which can often be quite different) is precisely that he bases it around local churches. The revolution that he created in crusade evangelism is not simply that he cleaned its image up, important though that was. It is that he entirely altered its nature. Till Graham, as seen earlier, itinerant evangelists often used to attack local ministers. Graham, by contrast, always insisted on working through them and would not come to their area unless they invited him to do so.

Crusade evangelism as redefined by Graham is therefore a parachurch organisation run closely with local churches, and not a rival to replace them or supplant their God-created role. As he himself said in Orlando, one of the reasons that mass evangelism came into being was that the churches were failing to fulfil their clear Biblical duty to proclaim the Gospel. It was only natural that Christians who had a burden for the lost should seek to do something about the sad state of affairs. But, as Graham also pointed out, should the churches once start to carry out their duty and be effective ambassadors for Christ, then parachurch organisations such as his own will cease to be necessary.

Crusades can show local churches what can be done – the example quoted earlier in this chapter of Mount of Olives church is a good one because that church is typical of many. A large proportion of the ministers at the school of evangelism were from similarly sized churches. The clear message they received, from Graham himself, from Lewis Drummond, and from the well-known preacher and speaker Joseph Aldrich, on life-style evangelism, was geared to show them that God could work through them too, and that their churches had an explicit Divine Commission to carry out, from the minister through to the humblest member of the congregation. The local church is as much the centre of God's strategy as it has ever been – and it has often taken mass evangelist Billy Graham to say so.

Graham's Biblical emphasis on the local church has, unfortunately, led him into an area which prevents many Bible-believing churches, that fully share his zeal for evangelism and his Christ-centred message, from co-operating with him. This is his policy of inviting all the local Protestant churches – and Roman Catholic in some countries – to participate in the crusade in their particular city or region. In the past, this has meant that many liberal churches have taken part. Often, eminent clergy whose views are far from Evangelical, and whose Gospel is very different from the one which Graham proclaims, find themselves as honoured guests on his platforms, to the consternation of many local Christians, who have frequently had a terrible time with these very people. This problem has grown the more famous Graham has become – appearance on his platform confers a considerable degree of respectability to those concerned.

To the Graham team, the fact that a liberal church wishes to participate means that it can be influenced for the Gospel. Similarly, if an eminent liberal theologian lives in the area, it is only courteous to ask him. Furthermore, by his presence on the platform, he is hearing the truth, and can be gained for Jesus Christ thereby. These views, while well motivated, unfortunately miss the point. To have liberals involved, many Evangelicals feel, only creates confusion.

The essence of the Evangelical message, the one that Graham himself preaches, is that it is the only truth, the only truly *Biblical* message for today. Evangelicals therefore have to take good care to differentiate themselves locally from those who proclaim a compromised, watered-down version of the Gospel. Then, along comes the crusade, and local non-Christians, whose conversion is the whole purpose of the crusade, see Evangelicals and liberals working together, side by side, as if there was no difference in the doctrine of salvation proclaimed by the two. Then, in the crusade meeting, the non-Christian sees Evangelical leaders sitting alongside well known theological liberals, who, as in the case of the Harringay crusade of 1954, are sometimes known to be opposed to the Evangelical position.

The Graham team argue that it is the liberals who are compromised – by publicly appearing with Evangelicals. But others feel that for liberals and Evangelicals publicly to co-operate only creates confusion in the minds of non-Christians and new converts, and is therefore best avoided. This is not to say that liberals should be ostracised, rather to say that Evangelicals should collaborate only with those who preach the Biblical Gospel. Unfortunately, many liberals, unable to fill their own churches because of the way in which they have diluted the message, take part in crusades in order to gain the converts they are in no position to garner themselves.

Graham always emphasises that new converts should go to Bible-believing churches – and he is right to do so. Many Evangelicals who love him and his message wish that he could apply the same rule for those who take part in his crusade. Many more Evangelical churches would do so were he to make this simple move. As it is, he only gives ammunition to his enemies, who frequently lack his charitable spirit. They are able, unfairly, to claim that he himself is a compromiser because he associates with liberals. A change of policy by Graham would swiftly rebut this allegation, and be greeted with pleasure by many who share his Gospel.

'Going for decision'

In his crusades Graham, according to John Pollock, is out to get decisions. The words he uses are much the same from year to year, and can be seen earlier in this chapter. Many of Graham's fellow Evangelicals feel that the method he uses, coupled as it is with choirs singing, music and other well-known formulae, is putting too much pressure on the human will, and relying on man-made methods instead of on the almighty power of the Holy Spirit. The altar call, they argue, is a nineteenth-century invention (made famous by the evangelist Finney) and is unknown to the New Testament.

Others, more sympathetic to Graham, have another objection. Billy Graham is, they point out, undoubtedly anointed by God for the task he has carried out over the years – there is no human explanation for the success that Graham has had. They note too that Graham has consistently claimed that it is the power of the Holy Spirit at work that is the key to the whole enterprise – unless He is present, then no amount of human organisation will make the slightest difference. God has ordained Graham to preach the Gospel, and this he has done, without compromise.

If this is so, they feel, and as Graham has the view of the Holy Spirit that he has, together with a total reliance on God and upon the power of answered prayer, then why has he used methods that, to them, smack so much of strong human pressure? Since over 80 per cent of converts came as a result of being brought by Christian friends, this means that human methods to entice people to come – rock groups, superstar testimonies, and so on, are surely not needed. In addition, since the Christians will have been praying for their unconverted friends for some time (especially if they have been active in one of the 'Operation Andrew' clubs), it does not matter so much if the non-Christian does not go forward *that* night – his or her Christian friends will not only continue to pray but also make sure that Graham's clear Gospel message is not forgotten.

Graham team members such as Roger Palms point out that it helps many people to have had a specific moment when they became a Christian. This is undoubtedly true. But if Graham is truly anointed by God, which his career would seem to indicate that he is, then two interesting queries arise. First, it is the preaching of the message that people have really come to hear, and through which, in God's power, they are saved. In some countries, Graham has had to dispense with the long preliminaries, and even with the altar call. Yet the response has been none the less for lack of those two items. In other words, if Graham simply preached his message, without the preliminaries, the same number of people would attend, and the same amount of people go forward – because God would bless the faithful proclamation of His Word.

Argument from silence is dangerous – and the fact that music, testimony and so on were entirely absent from the methods used by the early Church is no reason for saying that such modern methods are wrong. Yet, many people feel, the simple reliance on the preaching of the message, the witness of obedient Christians, and total dependence on the Holy Spirit – the methods of the New Testament – is still valid today, and if a mass evangelist were to rely on them alone, the God who so singularly blessed them in the days of the Apostles would do so again in our day.

Perhaps the best example is set by Martyn Lloyd-Jones during the Harringay crusade. He was profoundly unhappy at many of Graham's methods (which he felt placed too much pressure on the will) and at the fact that many liberal clergy appeared on the platform. Yet he prayed regularly every Sunday that many would be born again through Graham's faithful proclamation of the Gospel, and welcomed all the converts coming to his church. While not participating himself, he was very happy talking with Graham privately in the study at Westminster Chapel, and when Graham fell ill took him to see a doctor friend.

Above all, he himself preached the Gospel to unbelievers every Sunday evening and, although he never had any altar calls, saw conversions every week. He showed that the only people who have the real right to criticise are those who share Graham's zeal for the lost and his desire to see God's Kingdom grow. Graham today speaks very warmly of Dr Lloyd-Jones, despite their differences, and it is a shame that Graham's critics have often let a good case go by default because of the stridency and unbiblical lack of love with which they have attacked him.

Moscow . . . or how far should one go?

The main difference that many Christians have with Graham is not so much with his method, or with what he preaches, but with his underlying theology of salvation. A vivid illustration of this was Graham's trip to Moscow, described earlier in this chapter. The question amounts to this: people come to hear Billy Graham because he is a world-famous evangelist. They are born again at one of his meetings. Suppose, instead, that Graham had not been able to come to the meeting that night – say, he had a cold, or had been prevented by the authorities from coming. Would those people who were saved in the first instance not have been in the second? Suppose the crusade had been cancelled – what difference would this make to the eternal destinies of those who would have been saved at the crusade had the cancellation not have taken place?

Graham, as quoted at the beginning of this chapter, said of his own success in 1951,

> The glory, and the praise and the credit must go to God the Holy Spirit. It is the Holy Spirit that convicts, the Holy Spirit that regenerates, and it is the Holy Spirit that carries on the work after we've gone. It is actually all a supernatural performance and a supernatural process. All we are is witnesses to the saving grace and power of the Lord Jesus Christ.

Thirteen years later, he told students at Harvard Divinity School (quoted by Pollock),

> I used to think that in evangelism I had to do it all, but now I approach evangelism with a totally different attitude. I approach it with complete relaxation. First of all, I don't believe that any man can come to Christ unless the Holy Spirit has prepared his heart. Secondly, I don't believe any man can come to Christ unless God draws him. My job is to proclaim the message. It's the Holy Spirit's job to do the work.

When, in 1982, he was asked to go to Moscow, his reaction was that 'it was a God-given opportunity to proclaim the Gospel in a country where I have not had this privilege before'. As the article in *Christianity Today* of June 25th,

1982 noted, he 'hoped to be permitted eventually to hold preaching missions in large cities throughout the Soviet Union', though 'this goal did not loom as large for Graham as it did in the public news media'. He wished to plead the case of persecuted Christians with the authorities (Henry Kissinger, the Pope, and many leading Evangelicals advised him on this), and to put his case at the conference for nuclear disarmament and an end to the arms race. As the article states, 'Certainly these are worthy goals. No fair-minded person – let alone any Evangelical Christian – could object to them.'

The issue is whether Graham paid too high a price to achieve these goals, and thereby tragically discredited the cause of the Gospel he was so anxious to proclaim.

The secular press was unremittingly hostile. *Newsweek* felt that he was being totally naive. He was, it commented, 'manipulated by practised Soviet hands' from the moment he stepped off the plane. Its reporter, Andrew Nagorski (who was later expelled by the Soviet authorities for his rather too accurate portrayal of the truth about life in Russia), felt that 'throughout his six-day visit, Graham gave no hint just how limited a view of Soviet life his hosts were permitting him'. News of his activities was censored but, Nagorski wrote, 'Graham proved to be his own most effective censor.'

At the Baptist church, admission was by invitation only – most of the people hearing him were either Christians already, or KGB. (Roger Palms has pointed out that the KGB need to hear the Gospel too.) Throughout the nuclear conference, although Graham implicitly attacked the Soviet handling of freedom and justice, he did not take part in activities which attacked the government's handling of human rights. *The Times* correspondent thought that Graham 'felt obliged to go out of his way not to offend his hosts by speaking out against religious repression'.

According to *Christianity Today* Graham regrets that he did not put some things more clearly, in a way that could not be mishandled by an unsympathetic press. It points out that he is an evangelist, not a diplomat, and that much of what he said was quoted out of context. Much of the secular press coverage was unfair, written as it was by people who did not share Graham's love of the Gospel, and therefore could not understand his motives in visiting the USSR. So it is worth looking at what authoritative Christians have to say on the matter.

The best informed source for Christianity in Communist countries is Keston College in London, who have countless sources among Christian believers behind the Iron Curtain, and whose knowledge of persecution there is unsurpassed. They felt that the 'Soviet authorities were obviously very anxious that Dr Graham should attend the peace conference; he was therefore in a very strong bargaining position. He could have made one of the specific conditions of his attendance the release . . . of the Siberian Seven.' He could also, in asking governments to abide by agreements on religious freedom, have requested the Soviets to 'comply with these agreements in the form of one specific gesture'. As the propaganda value of his attendance was very high, he could probably have achieved these things – yet he did not ask for them.

Graham is one of the people who can claim credit for the release of the Siberian Christians. Yet one of them, Liuba Vaschenko, told a Keston College source, of Graham's visit to them, this 'could have been any man of God visiting us. If we had some hopes of Mr Graham's chances of helping us, all has turned to disillusionment.' Indeed, Keston College noted in its bulletin, the reactions of most of the Russian believers whose views reached them 'have, to date, been unfavourable. Believers express no animosity to Dr Graham personally but feel he was used by the Soviet authorities.' A Baptist elder wrote, 'We understand Billy Graham has been deceived. We pray for him, and hope that he will allow God to open his eyes to the truth.' This is from those who share Graham's love of the Gospel.

According to *Christianity Today*, the 'question of whether Graham did the right thing in going to Moscow depends on how highly a person values the proclamation and power of the Gospel. Only time and eternity' they feel, 'will reveal the full answer. But at this point we are not prepared to condemn him.' Certainly Christians should be very careful before they do so – how many of the critics have the concern for the unsaved, in Russia and elsewhere, that Graham has?

But the real issue was revealed in the article's subheading: 'Billy Graham presented the claims of Christ to many who had never heard before *and might never hear again*' (author's italics). This is the nub of the issue. Suppose Graham had refused to come or, say, made the preconditions Keston College thought that he ought to have laid down, and had been rejected as a result? What if he had succumbed to a severe cold and been forced to cancel the trip? Would those people who heard the Gospel clearly spelled out by him in Moscow then never have heard it?

Or, as many feel, would the loving, Sovereign Lord who wished to see them come to true salvation through His Son have sent them another messenger, one who would not have been so controversial, and one who would not have had to make the compromises that Graham undoubtedly thought right to make for the sake of the Gospel?

If the people who heard the Gospel in Moscow would otherwise *never* have heard again – and suffered eternal perdition as a result – then one can easily argue that Graham was right to go. Embarrassment and misunderstanding from the secular press are a small price to pay for saved souls. But as a secular journalist, William Safire of the *New York Times*, pointed out, the Gospel is today being proclaimed all over the Soviet Union, often at great personal risk and sacrifice, by Russian Christians.

Surely, some of Graham's fellow Evangelicals feel, God can raise up His messengers in the USSR today and indeed is doing so with much power. It is not, therefore, a question of whether one believes in the proclamation and impact of the Gospel or not, but how people will hear it and through whom. Surely, they argue, if Graham had not gone, God would have ensured that those who missed him would still have heard the Good News of Jesus Christ.

Graham has rightly stated that we live in one of the most significant moments in history – one in which the Gospel has been preached as never before in countries that have lain in spiritual darkness. One of God's greatest instruments in this has been Graham himself. The crusades in India, Korea, South America and other places show beyond doubt the role under God that he has played. On the other hand, there have been mighty revivals in recent years in countries to which Graham has never been.

A good example is China. In 1951 all foreign missionaries were expelled. In the years 1966–76 the Church underwent the most savage persecution, in which many were martyred. But the local Christians went on evangelising, quietly but faithfully. The Church, estimated at two million in 1951, now numbers at least fifteen million (or, according to the Chinese Church Research Centre in Hong Kong, fifty million). This growth is almost unprecedented in the history of the Christian Church. Yet since 1951 there have been no crusades, no mass evangelism, no visits by Billy Graham. The same is true, on a smaller scale, of a country such as Romania – Hungarian Christians reckon there are more Christians in the Hungarian minority in Romania than in Hungary itself, a land which Graham has visited.

Graham has summed it up correctly, and in its true perspective, in a statement appearing in Pollock's book, *Billy Graham: Evangelist to the World*. He feels that

> with all my heart as I look back on my life, that I was chosen to do this particular work of evangelist as a man might have been chosen to go into East Harlem and work there, or to the slums of London like General Booth was. I believe that God in His sovereignty – I have no other answer for this – sheer sovereignty, chose me to do this work and prepared me in His own way.

This is surely the Biblical way of looking at things. If Graham had not gone to Moscow, God would still have been glorified in the Soviet Union, and other messengers found. But in other places, Billy Graham was without doubt the right man to be there, bringing the Good News to those who will be saved. Graham has said, 'I have that confidence every time I preach', that the Holy Spirit will convict and save the lost.

God can bring revival without Billy Graham or through a Graham crusade. Either way, God is glorified, and His Kingdom increased, something at which all Christians, whichever interpretation of Paul in Romans and Ephesians they take, can rejoice.

A call for peace

One of the issues in which Graham has become involved is the debate on nuclear weapons. There has been, he has said, a 'quantum leap in technology' resulting in a 'quantum leap in our ability to destroy our entire planet', with the end of human life. 'The whole human race,' he told the Moscow peace conference, 'sits under a nuclear sword of Damocles.' While many political issues are involved, the 'nuclear arms race is primarily a moral and spiritual issue that must concern us all'. Man has new technology, but is morally unchanged. It is here, Graham feels, that the real change must come.

Life, he points out, is sacred. But man has rebelled against God, and has created a world of sin. Therefore, the 'problem is in the human heart, which God alone can change'. The hatred that could propel humanity into nuclear war is a direct result of sin. Graham is 'not a pacifist' nor a supporter of unilateral disarmament – he agrees with legitimate defence in a fallen world. But the 'unchecked production of weapons of mass destruction' threatens, he feels, to 'destroy the sacred gift of life'. The nuclear arms race, therefore, 'is not God's will'.

To him, there are three kinds of peace – spiritual, between man and God; personal, within a human being; and relational, between man and man. Christians should be for peace in all areas, made possible by Jesus Christ at Calvary. The question arises – what can Christians do for peace on earth? To Graham – 'We must be realists, but we must also be optimists' – God is Sovereign, in history. 'We do not live in a world of blind chance . . . God will accomplish His will for the world which He created.' Christians should be at the forefront of the movement for peace.

Graham, in his address in Moscow, outlined various practical suggestions. He made clear that he was not being political or nationalistic in his views. Christians should 'call the nations and leaders of our world to repentance'. No nation was exempt from blame. Then, they should 'call the nations' and leaders 'to a new and determined commitment to peace and justice' – a 'disarmament race' that would be 'equal on both sides, verifiable, and lead to at least a few generations of peace'. While true peace would not come till God's Kingdom prevailed, over 95 per cent of people would, Graham feels, vote for peace.

Graham would urge deeds, not words. But he would ask all leaders to start the disarmament process by a 'moratorium on hostile rhetoric', to lessen tensions. Positive steps to increasing trust, such as international exchange between peoples, would help, as would a recognition by all governments 'to respect the rights of religious believers as outlined in the United Nations Declaration of Human Rights'. (*Christianity Today* noted that the Soviet bloc delegation listened to this part of his speech in stony silence.) Similarly, world leaders should get to know each other 'simply . . . as human beings'.

World leaders should, he stated, take steps to begin real talks aimed at 'major arms reductions', with the 'ultimate goal of eliminating all nuclear and biochemical weapons of mass destruction' – what Graham has called 'SALT 10'. This may, he admits, 'be impossible to achieve, but it can be our ultimate goal'.

All Christians should pray for peace and dedicate themselves to the task of being peacemakers on earth. Both the superpowers faced a 'common enemy' – the 'threat of impending nuclear catastrophe'.

These views have proved highly controversial. No one could actually be against peace and for nuclear war. But some have wondered whether Graham, in his legitimate desire for world peace, is being sadly rather naive. The reality of the situation, they feel, is that the West is faced by a power of total hostility to justice, liberty and human rights, and that the existence of nuclear weapons has proved an effective guarantor against takeover by the Soviets of the free West. Graham, they think, has failed to take the inherent evil of the Soviet regime into account. Pleas by him will fall on stony ground, however well intentioned.

Others have also come out against the use of nuclear weapons on moral grounds, while emphatically rejecting the total pacifist option. Certainly this is an issue on which Christians profoundly disagree in practice while they are united in principle. It may be that Graham is overoptimistic in his views on the chances of the Soviet Union consenting to eventual total nuclear disarmament, and has not been as outspoken as he should have been against the violation of human rights in the Soviet bloc. (Christians in the Philippines have said the same about his silence over the abuse of liberties by the right-wing government during his crusade there.) But he has shown that Christians are capable of serious thought on the major issues of the day, and that they are aware of the world in which God has placed them. Even if one disagrees with his 'SALT 10' idea, he has at least caused Christians to consider the most serious secular issues of our day.

Above all, in an age where many people fear the future, and for the very survival of the human race, he has made clear his belief in the almighty Sovereign Lord. Even as God destroyed the armies of the Assyrians before Jerusalem (as recorded in 2 Kings 19), so He is still powerful to act today. Furthermore, the nuclear issue has concentrated the minds of many to thinking towards eternity.

Graham has been the evangelist to the world in the Age of the Bomb, and the sober effect that the threat of nuclear holocaust has created has helped many to listen to him with a renewed sense of seriousness. It may well be that God has allowed the threat of nuclear conflict to hang over the West to bring them to their senses, even though He does not intend to allow such a final catastrophe to happen. Billy Graham has played his part in reminding the world of their fallenness and need of a Saviour, and the possibility of mutual annihilation of the human race is a vivid illustration of the Biblical picture of the true nature of sinful Man.

Billy Graham – God's ambassador

Much has been made in the official Graham literature of the awards and distinctions that have been bestowed upon him, of his consistently high ratings in the opinion polls, and of the contacts he has made with the great and famous. In many ways, this is right. Graham has given a respectability to the Christian faith that has helped to spread it. It is good that an Evangelical Christian has been able to share the Gospel with people at the top of society, with the decision makers who determine how ordinary men and women live. It is often forgotten today that such rulers need the Gospel too – the Bible enjoins Christians to pray for them, and Graham's status has given him a unique degree of access to them. Similarly Graham has been seen by millions on television, news bulletins and popular talk shows, and he has taken full use of the opportunities thus given him to proclaim the Gospel to those watching.

But John Gholdston's observation, that Billy Graham has remained 'folks' is often overlooked. The Graham team, reacting quite rightly against snobbish dismissals of Graham as a simple country hick, have perhaps, in emphasising his secular honours such as tea with the Queen, failed to see that Graham's North Carolina background is, in human terms, by far one of his greatest strengths.

Graham has made the Gospel credible, and in an age of doubt this is far more important than respectability gained by chats in the White House, vital though they are in giving him a unique platform from which to proclaim the Good News of Jesus Christ. His transparent sincerity has convinced thousands that Christianity is no longer something that they can afford to reject. The straightforward, uncomplicated style of his preaching makes it understandable by people of all kinds of ability and background – from professors to simpletons and from royalty to peasantry.

Much of this can be attributed to the decent, honest, natural virtues that are the hallmark of the part of the USA from which Graham comes. Such characteristics may have been rejected in a so-called sophisticated urban age, but to the majority of those who have heard Graham around the world, they are traits with which his listeners will readily identify. The same refreshing innocence (which is a marked feature of many major American stories set in rural USA, such as *The Waltons*) that led Graham to be duped by Nixon has been one of his greatest strengths in reaching out to the millions of the Third World.

For, as noted earlier in this chapter, perhaps the most re-markable feature of Graham's ministry has been the fact that in the post-imperial age, one which has often been marked by strident anti-US feeling, he, Billy Graham, has been the most successful mass evangelist to the world this century. Many Americans have succeeded in their home territory, only to fail miserably abroad. Graham, on the other hand, is now almost more successful in other countries than in his own, and some of his greatest results have come in nations whose culture and thought patterns are about as far removed from those of the USA as it is possible to imagine.

It is perhaps no coincidence that the moment he ceased to think of himself primarily as an American, but as an evangelist to the World, that his most significant ministry began. He has had the wisdom to do what many have failed to do: to keep the message, of the Good News of Jesus Christ, totally unaltered and uncompromised, while at the same time adapting to different cultures and situations in his travels round the World. He has also found an utterly dedicated team of Godly men, and stuck by them, thus giving himself a valuable degree of continuity.

Above all, Graham has been faithful to the Gospel – and it is surely this that God has used and blessed. People inviting Graham know that they can trust him fearlessly to proclaim the truth. His career, as T. W. Wilson has so rightly said, is proof of the Sovereignty of God to save the lost. The Church of Jesus Christ has seen an unprecedented growth in the last forty years, especially in countries where the Gospel was either unknown or believed only by a tiny handful. In such an age, one in which God has been seen to be alive as never before, Billy Graham has been God's ambassador to the nations. Surely no higher tribute could be paid to a man than that.